RADICAL
INNOVATION

RADICAL INNOVATION

HOW MATURE COMPANIES CAN OUTSMART UPSTARTS

RICHARD LEIFER

CHRISTOPHER M. McDERMOTT

GINA COLARELLI O'CONNOR

LOIS S. PETERS

MARK P. RICE

ROBERT W. VERYZER

HARVARD BUSINESS SCHOOL PRESS

BOSTON, MASSACHUSETTS

Library of Congress Cataloging-in-Publication Data
Radical innovation : how mature companies can outsmart upstarts / Richard Leifer . . . [et al.].
   p. cm.
   Results of the long-term Rensselaer Radical Innovation Research Project, which began
in 1994.
   Includes bibliographical references and index.
   ISBN 1-57851-903-2
     1. Reengineering (Management) 2. Technological innovations—Management. 3.
Research, Industrial—Management. 4. Competition. I. Leifer, Richard, 1942–

HD58.87 .R33 2000
658.4'063--dc21

                                                                    00-033597

The paper used in this publication meets the requirements of the American
National Standard for Permanence of Paper for Publications and Documents
in Libraries and Archives Z39.48-1992.

CONTENTS

PREFACE

This book is written for men and women in established companies who are working to conceive of breakthroughs and bring them to the marketplace. The information and insights we present are derived from our five years' experience observing and sharing in the struggles, failures, and successes of people confronting the challenges of radical innovation. Though we offer a variety of recommendations for dealing with these challenges, in the end, radical innovators must be prepared to try one approach and then another—until they find one that works in their own particular environment.

The Rensselaer Radical Innovation Research Project began in 1994, as the result of a series of intense discussions by a number of our faculty around two emerging trends. First, new technologies and the radical innovations that came from them were driving a transformation in all sectors of our economy at a phenomenal rate. The second trend we saw was the increased rate at which relatively small, new entrepreneurial firms were generating radical innovations and taking them to market. At the same time, mature, manufacturing-based industrial companies found themselves with a reduced capacity for radical innovation because of the emphasis in the 1980s on restructuring and quality management. To regain competitiveness in the world marketplace, they had focused on taking costs out of current operations and maximizing the yield from their portfolio of products through incremental innovations. In the 1990s they found themselves under tremendous pressure from stakeholders to sustain their stock prices. The race to regain the capacity to discover, develop, and commercialize radical innovations was on. We saw an opportunity to follow, in real time, the efforts of established firms as they tried different ways to develop this capacity. Our goal was to contribute to the knowledge base about radical innovation and to provide insights that could advance the state of practice.

In order to undertake a project of this magnitude, we submitted proposals for collaboration with two world-class partners—the Sloan Foundation and the Industrial Research Institute (a professional association of the technology leaders of Fortune 1000 companies). Both proposals were enthusiastically received. The Industrial Research Institute formed a subcommittee dedicated to our project, and the Sloan Foundation provided a major, multiyear grant. In early 1995 we were off and running.

With the help of our industry partners, we developed a definition of radical innovation (presented in chapter 1) that we could use to "qualify" projects for inclusion in the study. IRI member companies that volunteered to participate (Air Products and Chemicals, Analog Devices, DuPont, General Electric, General Motors, IBM, Nortel Networks, Polaroid, Texas Instruments, and United Technologies's Otis Elevator Division) each nominated one or more radical innovation projects. Ultimately, twelve projects in these ten firms became the focus of our study. In each case the research team made an initial site visit for three purposes: first, to determine which projects best met the criteria; second, to set expectations for those who would be interviewed; and, third, to collect background information to help prepare the members of our research team for data collection. In the fall of 1995 we began the site visits.

How We Learned about Radical Innovation

Our understanding of radical innovation and how it can be managed comes primarily from in-depth analyses of our twelve radical innovation projects. Our research effort utilized case study research methodology, which asks "how" and "why" questions to explore a complex phenomenon about which there is little or no theory. The questions are designed to push the envelope of thinking of practitioners and academics about a very difficult subject and do not provide singular solutions to the challenges we have identified.

During our field research, we conducted interviews with key individuals—both within project teams and within the rest of the organization—over a period of five years. The interviewees included project members, project managers, researchers, business unit managers, personnel in business development organizations, and senior corporate managers in each of the ten companies. Typically, a subset of the members of our multifunctional team traveled to each company for a full day of intense, in-depth interviews. The Rensselaer visiting team worked from a standard set of interview questions covering all aspects of radical innovation project management. Sub teams of our researchers interviewed each company representative, and each representative was interviewed by more than one subteam. Using this data-gathering approach, we were able to engage a variety of perspectives in asking key questions and in filtering the responses. Each interview was recorded and later transcribed. In subsequent years, we repeated the process via teleconferencing. The mass of interview data composed the information database from which we derived our findings.

To test our findings and extend our thinking, we held a series of conferences, workshops, and seminars with project, mid-level, and senior managers from a number of other companies, in addition to those in our research sample. These included 3M, AT&T, Alcoa, Arch Chemicals, Armstrong, Ford, Hewlett-Packard, Kodak, Lucent, Mitsubishi, NCR, Procter & Gamble, and Westvaco.

FUNDAMENTAL QUESTIONS

The managers of the firms that provided projects for our study and those who participated in our workshops and seminars acknowledged that radical innovation was difficult for them. For example, the manager of TI's Digital Light Processor project embarked on a benchmarking study of other mature companies to identify best practices in managing radical innovation. At the end of this exercise, he concluded that none of the companies he had studied were satisfied with the way they were managing radical innovation, nor were they particularly good at it. The participants in our study were all intensely interested in finding ways to implement radical innovation more effectively. They were committed to building a more systematic approach and a managerial discipline for radical innovation in their companies. To help them achieve these goals, we addressed the following fundamental questions:

- What are the characteristics of the radical innovation life cycle that require different managerial approaches from those that are effective in incremental innovation?

- How can firms deal with the fundamental conflict between mainstream operating units (with their emphasis on incremental innovation projects and short-term results) and the parts of the firm engaged in radical innovation?

- What are the most difficult challenges that companies must deal with effectively if radical innovation is to succeed, and what competencies, resources, and managerial/organizational approaches can be deployed to overcome these challenges?

- How can firms build and sustain a competency for managing radical innovation projects over time in order to support continued growth?

Our goal, from the beginning, was to help mature, established companies improve their performance in initiating and developing radical innovations and in developing the business models and organizations to bring them successfully to the marketplace. We hope this book will contribute to the achievement of this objective.

CHAPTER 1

THE RADICAL
INNOVATION
IMPERATIVE

You have heard it a thousand times before: "Small entrepreneurial firms are the source of most radical innovations. Large companies have a tough time getting it done."[1] This widely held belief is supported by the success of entrepreneurial ventures in Silicon Valley, along Boston's Route 128, and wherever else new companies with radical innovations sprout and take root. Think of the upstart firms that have pioneered the technologies and business models that now dominate the Internet and e-commerce (America Online, Amazon.com, Yahoo!); personal computing (Intel, Microsoft, Dell); and biotechnology (Genentech, Biogen). The failure to develop and introduce breakthrough innovations puts established firms at risk of being knocked out of the game by the entrepreneurial newcomers. What if mature firms could figure out how to outsmart upstarts?

Leaders of established companies acknowledge that radical innovation is critical to their long-term growth and renewal.[2] Indeed, the relationship between business growth and innovation is widely understood by executives today, thanks in part to the writing of a number of consultants and business scholars.[3] The general understanding to be gained from these works is that becoming lean and mean can make you competitive, and incremental innovation can keep you competitive with current product platforms. But only radical innovation can change the game.

Radical innovation transforms the relationship between customers and suppliers, restructures marketplace economics, displaces current products, and often creates entirely new product categories. Radical innovation provides a platform for the long-term growth that corporate leaders desperately seek. Unfortunately, recognizing the importance of radical innovations and successfully developing and commercializing them are two different things.[4]

Incremental innovation is not as great a problem for established companies as radical innovation. During the 1980s, U.S. and European firms were competitively challenged in many industries by Asian firms. They took a beating in memory chips, office and factory automation, consumer electronics, and automaking.[5] These behemoths were routinely outmaneuvered by new competitors. Kodak watched as videotape camcorders reduced its home movie business to cinders. Xerox's lock on the photocopier business was broken by Canon, Sharp, and others. Consumer electronics products made by Motorola, Zenith, and RCA were largely displaced by new ones introduced by Sony, Panasonic, and Toshiba. On the automotive front, Toyota, Honda, and Nissan expanded their inroads into the North American market, winning universal kudos for quality and reliability. Effective incremental innovation and dramatic improvements in operating efficiency were the two keys to the success of these Asian firms.

In response, U.S. firms increased their competencies in managing the development of incremental innovation in existing products and processes, with an emphasis on cost competitiveness and quality improvements.[6] Extensive study of incremental innovation by both business managers and academics led to a variety of prescriptions: six sigma quality in manufacturing, concurrent engineering, reduced cycle time, just-in-time inventory management, and phase-gate product-development systems, to name just a few. These prescriptions were widely adopted and helped many American companies regain their competitive positions in the world marketplace.

The attention of managers to incremental innovation, however, came at a price. It diminished the focus and capacity of America's largest companies to engage in truly breakthrough innovation. Central R&D labs, traditionally the source of radical innovation ideas, were redirected to serve the immediate needs of corporate operating units. Those units, always under pressure to maximize short-term financial performance, were reluctant to invest in high-risk, long-term projects. Instead, they sought incremental improvements to existing products and technologies.

The negative consequences of too much attention to incremental innovation have been recognized by many business scholars. James Utterback and Clayton Christensen, among others, have noted how firms that dominate one generation of technology often fail to maintain leadership in the next.[7] Either through hubris or a lack of inspiration or capability, industry leaders continue investing in the technologies that made them successful, even when more effective technologies—"disruptive technologies," as Christensen calls them—appear on the horizon. The big steel producers in the United States learned this painful lesson when Nucor operationalized continuous casting of rolled steel, a radical innovation that Big Steel had known about but had failed to take seriously. Kodak, which has dominated film-based photography since its creation by founder George Eastman, now finds itself in a race with many contenders for the next generation of picture taking, one that has eliminated film in favor of digital imaging. In each of these cases, and hundreds like them, products based on one technology were undermined by radically new ones—and incremental improvement to the old technology has done little more than delay the eventual rout.

Both business history and our own observations of the progress and failure of contemporary enterprises point to certain truths about incremental innovation. It allows firms to address the ever-changing needs of current customers and keeps cash flows healthy, but it must be supplemented by periodic infusions of *radical* innovation.

Of course, not every organization feels compelled to pursue new markets and customers through radical innovation. Doing so, some will tell you, is risky and cannot be relied on to produce results. They are right on both counts. Attempts at radical innovation produce more failures than successes, and the magnitude and timing of results are highly unpredictable. Faced with these double-barreled negatives, it is not surprising that executives feel more comfortable in other approaches to future growth: sticking to their knitting; gaining access to innovative technologies through acquisitions; or being a "fast follower" as new concepts enter the competitive arena. Each of these strategies has merit, but few great enterprises of the past half-century have relied on them as substitutes for real innovation. Companies that have succeeded over the long haul—such as Corning, GE Medical Systems, Hewlett-Packard, Motorola, and 3M—punctuate ongoing incremental innovation with radical innovation.[8]

The difficult and unresolved problem of radical innovation for large, established enterprises is what concerns us in this book—a concern shared by many executives and R&D personnel. Though thoughtful executives recognize the importance of radical innovation, few are familiar with the process through which it emerges. The result is that when radical innovation happens, it often occurs in ways that few—inside and outside R&D—really understand. Logically, what is not understood cannot be managed effectively.

For five years, from 1995 to 2000, our team of researchers followed the development and commercialization activities of twelve radical innovation projects in ten large, established firms: Air Products and Chemicals, Analog Devices, DuPont, General Electric, General Motors, IBM, Nortel Networks, Polaroid, Texas Instruments, and United Technologies Corporation (Otis Elevator Division). Our intention in this book is to help senior executives, R&D managers, new business development managers, radical innovation project leaders, and others involved in innovation activities recognize the patterns in which radical innovation occurs and identify the managerial competencies needed to make the normally long and bumpy course of innovation shorter and more productive.

WHAT IS RADICAL INNOVATION?

Scholars have long distinguished between what we call *radical* and *incremental* innovations, although not always in those words. For example, James March made a distinction between *exploitation* of existing technology and *exploration* of new technology.[9] Exploitation has to do with refining or expanding existing products or processes, whereas exploration involves something fundamentally new, including new products, processes, or combinations of the two.[10]

In our view, incremental innovation usually emphasizes cost or feature improvements in existing products or services and is dependent on *exploitation* competencies. In contrast, radical innovation concerns the development of new businesses or product lines— based on new ideas or technologies or substantial cost reductions— that transform the economics of a business[11] and therefore require *exploration* competencies.[12] This way of differentiating between radical and incremental innovation is echoed in the terminology used by a number of other researchers.[13]

Although the theoretical work of others is useful in defining a continuum of innovation types, our search for a more practical definition led us to seek the input of practicing technologists. We engaged industry representatives from the Industrial Research Institute (IRI) in the development of a pragmatic definition of radical innovation—one that captured the key aspects of projects that our industry partners considered "radical." We started with the requirement that any radical project effort should be targeted at commercialization (that is, it could not be simply an exploratory research project). Thus, we agreed that we would consider only formally established projects with explicit budgets and organizational identities. In the end we arrived at the following definition:

> A radical innovation project is one with the potential to produce one or more of the following:
>
> • an entirely new set of performance features;
>
> • improvements in known performance features of five times or greater; or
>
> • a significant (30 percent or greater) reduction in cost.

Thus, a radical innovation is a product, process, or service with either unprecedented performance features or familiar features that offer potential for significant improvements in performance or cost. In our view, radical innovations create such a dramatic change in products, processes, or services that they transform existing markets or industries, or create new ones. By this definition, examples of radical innovation include computerized tomography (CT) and magnetic resonance imaging (MRI) in the field of diagnostic imaging; the personal computer in computing; and pagers and cellular telephones in mobile communications. The subsequent incremental and generational improvements in these technologies were not radical innovations as we define them. Our definition is driven by new value added to the marketplace rather than by technical novelty or newness to the firm.

We further distinguish types of radical innovation with respect to alignment with the firm's established lines of business. When we looked closely at the variability of radical innovation projects, we identified three types:[14]

> **INNOVATION WITHIN THE TECHNOLOGY/MARKET DOMAINS OF EXISTING BUSINESS UNITS.** These kinds of projects aim to replace existing technologies for essentially the same customers and markets. For example, GE's development and commercialization of magnetic resonance imaging technology was a radical innovation, but the application space was already served by GE's Medical Systems business unit. This type of radical innovation strengthens a firm's position with familiar markets. A project idea that aims to serve current customers has an obvious home when it matures and is ready for commercialization. Thus, a constructive relationship between the business unit and the project can be established as it evolves, and organizational uncertainty is reduced. The infrastructure for contacting customers, understanding markets, and delivering the innovation are assumed to be well understood. Critical management issues involve cannibalization of current lines of business, and technological uncertainty in both development and production.

> **INNOVATION IN THE "WHITE SPACES" BETWEEN A FIRM'S EXISTING BUSINESSES.** Radical new products that fall into the white spaces between existing businesses end up in either a new business unit or an existing one that is prepared to expand its scope. Though the markets served by these innovations are new for the firm, they are within the firm's current strategic context. The IBM PC, for example, fell within IBM's strategic context of computing but served new customers in new ways.

INNOVATION OUTSIDE A FIRM'S CURRENT STRATEGIC CONTEXT.
Innovations in this category open new and entirely unfamiliar
markets. For example, Analog Device's accelerometer chip ultimately found its application in the auto industry—outside the
company's strategic context. The auto industry and the technical applications were entirely new to Analog Devices. This third
category embodies the highest organizational uncertainty.
When it occurs, either the strategic context of the organization
must be reset[15] or the innovation must be "spun out" as a separate venture.

THE MANAGEMENT CHALLENGE

Given our definition of radical innovation, every corporate
leader should be pounding the drum for projects aimed at producing breakthrough innovations. After all, if R&D labs could consis-
tently churn out products with five times or better performance
features, or entirely new product categories with new features, or
new ways of slashing cost on existing products or processes by 30
percent or more, concerns about growth and corporate survival
would be put to rest. But as most people know, and as our industry partners have confirmed, radical innovations are extraordinarily
difficult to manage. We identified seven important challenges, listed
in table 1-1, that confront mature firms seeking to create and sustain a capacity for radical innovation. Each challenge requires the
development of specific competencies.

This book discusses each of these seven managerial challenges
and offers practical advice for developing the competencies needed
to overcome them. Chapter 2 explains the nature of the radical innovation phenomena and identifies four types of uncertainty that need
to be reduced for radical innovation projects to be successful. Chapters 3 through 9 focus on the seven challenges defined in table 1-1
and provide keys for effectively dealing with each of these challenges.
Finally, chapter 10 summarizes our findings and provides a vision
of how mature firms can foster and sustain radical innovation.

As mentioned earlier, the material in these chapters is based on
a five-year effort conducted in collaboration with the Industrial

TABLE 1-1

Seven Challenges in Managing Radical Innovation

Managerial Challenge	Competencies Required to Address the Challenge
Capturing radical ideas in the "fuzzy front end"	Generation of good ideas Recognition of opportunities enabled by breakthroughs Development and implementation of an effective approach to initial evaluation
Managing radical innovation projects	Articulation of a vision Uncertainty-mapping capability Development of and ability to follow a learning plan Recruitment of champions Effective management of organizational interfaces
Learning about markets for radical innovations	Commitment to asking different market research questions Willingness to conduct market research in new ways
Resolving uncertainty in the business model	Understanding of what the firm should outsource and what new competencies it should develop Adaptation of the business model in response to learning
Bridging resource and competency gaps	Resource acquisition Establishment and management of internal and external partnerships
Accelerating the transition from radical innovation projects to operating status	Accurate assessment of the transition readiness of the project and the receiving unit Development of people, practices, and structures for successful transitions Ability to build bridges between organizational units
Engaging individual initiative	Ability to effectively define the roles of senior management, key individuals, and the project team Building of appropriate reward systems and career paths Promotion of informal networks

Research Institute and sponsored by the Sloan Foundation. The companies and projects we studied are as follows:

AIR PRODUCTS AND CHEMICALS CORPORATION developed an ionic transport membrane (ITM) for separating oxygen from air and was working on systems to meet the needs of three different application domains. The business model developed by Air Products projects a 30 percent cost savings for its industrial customers.

ANALOG DEVICES, INC., developed a micro-electromechanical system (MEMS) accelerometer, a small microchip capable of detecting changes in speed. In the initial application, the accelerometer would displace an electromechanical automobile air bag actuator at an order-of-magnitude lower cost.

DUPONT was home to two of our projects. The first developed an electron emitting material with properties that made it attractive in electronic display applications. The second project developed an environmentally friendly polyester film that could be recycled or decomposed.

GENERAL ELECTRIC developed a digital X-ray imaging system to compete with existing film-based X-ray systems, including its own. A digital system would eliminate the need for film development and would make it possible to send images as data to remote diagnostic specialists. It would open up a wide range of additional applications.

GENERAL MOTORS, like several of its major rivals, was pursuing the development of a hybrid vehicle capable of drawing power from both electrical and conventional engines. It hoped that hybrid power technologies, combined with others, would produce exceptional mileage performance (50 to 80 miles per gallon) and exceedingly low pollutant emissions.

IBM was the second company with two projects in our study. The first developed a new generation of communication chips using silicon germanium (SiGe). This innovation aimed to increase switching speeds and greatly reduce power requirements. The second IBM project pursued development and integration of display, memory, and battery technologies to enable the creation of an "electronic book."

NORTEL NETWORKS (and its spinoff, NetActive) developed novel products and services that allow digital content to be activated over an Internet link between the consumer and a NetActive server.

POLAROID applied highly innovative manufacturing technologies from its traditional product arena to the creation of low-cost, high-capacity computer memory storage devices.

TEXAS INSTRUMENTS developed a Digital Micromirror Device (DMD)[16] component capable of creating a screen image by bouncing light off up to 1.3 million microscopic bidirectional mirrors squeezed onto a one-square-inch chip. Potential applications were sought in the hard copy, home video projection systems, business conference projection systems, and large screen movie theater markets.

OTIS ELEVATOR DIVISION OF UNITED TECHNOLOGIES aimed to develop a bidirectional elevator to solve the problem of moving people within extremely tall buildings and to minimize the consumption of valuable real estate by elevator shafts.

To provide a context for our discussion of the management challenges associated with the commercialization of radical innovations—and leading-edge practices targeted at resolving them—we offer an in-depth examination of the radical innovation life cycle in the next chapter.

CHAPTER 2

THE COURSE OF RADICAL INNOVATION

THIS CHAPTER EXAMINES THE RADICAL INNOVATION LIFE CYCLE and the uncertainties that must be overcome. Though no two radical projects in our study were the same, we observed patterns in their long journey to the marketplace—patterns unlike those in incremental innovation projects. There is practical value in understanding the patterns in and the differences between the more common incremental innovation projects and the less common radical innovation projects. This understanding is the starting point for identifying management practices that can make the course of radical innovation shorter, less circuitous, less expensive, and more certain.

Uncertainty plagues radical projects and puts its mark on their course of development. There are technical uncertainties such as, Can we make this work? and market uncertainties such as, Who will buy it? What are the useful applications? But even more vexing are the organizational and resource uncertainties: How can we defuse organizational resistance? What strategies can we use to overcome a lack of continuity in support and resources? How can we get the organization to hold appropriate expectations and adopt appropriate metrics? What can we do to protect the project from changes in strategic commitment? These uncertainties underscore conflicts between the mainstream organization and the unit engaged in radical innovation.

The radical project life cycle is also marked by discontinuities, gaps, critical transitions, and leverage points. Once these are understood, we can identify the management practices, organizational approaches, competencies, and resources needed to make projects more successful.

The story of Biomax,[1] a hydro-biodegradable polyester material developed by DuPont, illustrates the typical life cycle of a radical innovation project. Its development followed a long and difficult route from initial idea to the marketplace. Like all radical innovation projects, the future of the Biomax project depended on the resolution of many uncertainties. Though every innovation project is unique in the details, the Biomax story reveals the typical patterns in the activities and transitions experienced in radical innovation projects.

DuPont's Biomax:
The Push for Commercial Applications

Biomax, a polyester material that can be recycled or decomposed, holds up under normal commercial conditions for a time period established in the product specifications. The material itself can be made into fibers, films, or resins and is suitable for countless agricultural, industrial, and consumer products: mulch containers, mulching film, seed mats, plant pots, disposable eating utensils, blister packs, yard waste bags, parts of disposable diapers, blown bottles, injection-molded products, coated-paper products, and many, many others. In the United States alone, where the average household creates more than three tons of disposable waste each year, the number of potential applications for Biomax is immense. Its development represents a potentially huge business for DuPont and an important solution to the mounting problem of solid waste in developed countries.

In 1989, at the inception of the project, DuPont executives were pressing research units to find new products with commercial applications. In effect, these units were told to "invent their way out" of the company's financial malaise. One of these research units had developed a new "melt-spun" elastomeric material and was seeking commercial applications through the $uccess Group, its business development unit. The initial target application was as a substitute for the tapes then used on disposable baby diapers, which at that time were made of the more expensive DuPont Lycra[2], an elastane fiber. Rather than lose that business, however, the division dropped the price of Lycra. The project had reached its first dead end.

A senior research associate of the $uccess Group, Ray Tietz, had noted the degradable characteristics of this new material. "One of the problems they had with the fibers we made with this material was that it would disintegrate if you boiled it in water. This was because of the sulphonate in it. I knew that if I made a polyester with this stuff in it, it would probably hydrolyze quickly—it might even be biodegradable."[3] The project team initiated a search to find a customer for whom degradability would be an important benefit. A logical target was Procter & Gamble, a major vendor of disposable diapers.

Procter & Gamble first introduced the disposable diaper in 1961 and by 1989 had built it into a huge business. Its success, however, coincided with a period of growing environmental awareness. P&G was concerned that government regulation might be imposed that would either ban or significantly restrict the use of this class of products, and hence was responsive to the proposal from the $uccess Group. P&G defined additional design challenges beyond biodegradability and encouraged the Biomax team to undertake development of the new material.

The project team accepted the challenge and went to work to create a material that would address P&G's design objectives. "We spent a lot of research effort trying to make a degradable polymer that would be tough enough for the job," Teitz later recalled. Months of effort produced a new laminated material that Teitz and others in the $uccess Group thought would meet P&G's needs. Time and events, however, combined to work against them. Recognizing that political pressure for restrictive regulation was on the wane and that cost-conscious customers would not pay a premium for biodegradable materials, Procter & Gamble discontinued interest in the material under development.

The project team had reached its second dead end. Furthermore, the standards for environmental acceptability were becoming more stringent. Being degradable (i.e., a substance that would disintegrate) had become passé; the new standard was *bio*degradability. Further, anything that tried to pass itself off as biodegradable had to disappear in a reasonable period of time. As of 1991, two years into the project, no one knew for sure whether DuPont's new material would qualify as biodegradable. At this point, the original project manager was replaced.

Credibility on the issue of biodegradability would be a necessity for market acceptance. To test the material, which by this time had been registered as Biomax, and to assure the credibility of its data, the project recruited a highly respected company scientist on a part-time basis. Henn Kilkson was a DuPont Fellow with experience in biodegradation. His job was to design and implement a system for evaluating the biodegradation of the new material. The initial trials in Europe and the United States determined the rate of disintegration, but failed to definitively establish biodegradability. A third test conducted with a municipal composting facility in the United States finally produced positive results. Not only did the mesh bags used to enclose the waste decompose quickly, but they also degraded biologically as well. Unfortunately, real customers willing to write out real purchase orders were still illusory.

By 1992, the $uccess Group had been disbanded, and Biomax seemed destined to sit on the shelf—one of many good ideas developed by DuPont scientists for which no market application could be found. However, the material caught the eye of Terry Fadem, the head of the corporate new business development organization, who thought that Biomax was worth another try. Even though a real customer had not yet signed on, the new polymer had two important features: first, no major capital investment would be needed to produce it in commercial quantities; and second, the potential market for a biodegradable alternative to the mountains of synthetic materials piling up in the industrialized world was huge—at least in the abstract. As luck would have it, a break in favor of Biomax appeared very quickly, but from a source that neither Fadem nor anyone else would have anticipated: the banana plantations of Costa Rica.

Steve Gleich was a senior technical researcher working at DuPont's Research Division for Agricultural Products. He was aware of the Biomax project and was familiar with work on biodegradables being conducted by a joint venture company owned by ConAgra and DuPont. One day, another packaging engineer told Gleich, "If you solve the banana bag problem down in Costa Rica, you'll be a big hero." Banana bag problem? Gleich had no idea what he meant. The engineer pulled a low-density polyethylene bag from his drawer. "They use millions of pounds of this stuff in the banana plantations," he said. "They put a bag over every banana bunch. Some are impregnated with pesticides, but most are simply used as little hothouses to ripen the fruit and protect it from bruises."

This bit of information flipped a switch in Gleich's mind. Millions of pounds of nondegradable polyethylene translated into two things: big revenues for the vendor and a massive waste disposal problem for growers. If a bag material could be designed to disintegrate and biodegrade at the right time, growers could eliminate major labor and waste-handling costs.

Working with contacts in Fadem's development unit, Gleich arranged to have fifty bags made from Biomax and sent down to a sales agent working with Delmonte's banana operation in Costa Rica. These bags were used to cover the fruit in the normal way and were observed over a three- to four-month period. As the bananas were harvested, the bags, now brittle, began to break apart into small strips and fall to the ground, where they could easily be raked up and composted. These first bags, however, turned brittle too soon in the cycle of fruit production, causing some bruising. So the enterprising researcher asked for another batch of bags—slightly heavier and formulated to come apart more readily. Unfortunately, because of an internal squabble between the field manager and his counterpart at the head office, the field manager refused to install the redesigned banana bags—and this application development effort stalled.

Other agricultural applications emerged, but each application development effort suffered a setback—nonperformance by an early adopter or loss of a key internal champion. Fadem, the head of corporate new business development, remained convinced that he had a potentially valuable radical innovation on his hands, but seven years after the start of the project, there was still no revenue in sight.

In 1996 Fadem convinced senior management to invest several million dollars in an advertising campaign designed to promote Biomax and to uncover potential customers. Response was sufficiently robust that Biomax was transferred out of development and into DuPont's polyester resins and intermediates business unit, although Fadem's organization remained involved. As of mid 2000, Biomax was on its second product manager, applications development remained a challenge, and revenue continued to be limited, but the product team believed they were on the verge of turning the corner.

RADICAL INNOVATION PROJECT TIME LINES

The DuPont Biomax story documents starts and stops, detours down application dead ends, waxing and waning of interest and funding, a changing cast of characters, near death experiences and revivals, and the eventual handoff to a business unit—which continued to be messy. The movement of the project from the laboratories of a disbanded business unit through the corporate business development organization and ultimately to one of the company's operating units took eight years. Ten years after start-up, the project's market success remained unclear.

This route is captured in the Biomax radical innovation time line in figure 2-1. The abundance of project discontinuities shown in the figure makes this project life cycle appear like chaos punctuated occasionally with periods of manageable, routine uncertainty. Discontinuities influenced the project's funding, staffing, tasks, management requirements, and relationships to the larger organization. For example, one of the most promising agricultural applications disappeared because of an internal squabble within the lead customer's organization. As a result, the project went from a full-time project to a skeleton crew working part time. The project team struggled to find the next market opportunity and barely survived on minimal, life-support-level funding. The implications of these stops and starts on project management are addressed more fully in chapter 4.

CHARACTERISTICS OF THE RADICAL PROJECT LIFE CYCLE

Time lines for each of the twelve projects in our study revealed similar patterns, though the mix of uncertainties and their specific characteristics varied considerably, as did the responses of the project

FIGURE 2-1

THE BIOMAX TIME LINE

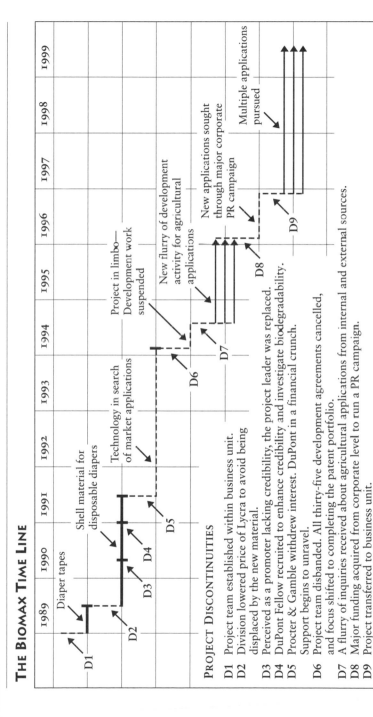

| | 1989 | 1990 | 1991 | 1992 | 1993 | 1994 | 1995 | 1996 | 1997 | 1998 | 1999 |

Diaper tapes

Shell material for disposable diapers

Technology in search of market applications

Project in limbo—Development work suspended

New flurry of development activity for agricultural applications

New applications sought through major corporate PR campaign

Multiple applications pursued

D1 D2 D3 D4 D5 D6 D7 D8 D9

PROJECT DISCONTINUITIES

D1 Project team established within business unit.

D2 Division lowered price of Lycra to avoid being displaced by the new material.

D3 Perceived as a promoter lacking credibility, the project leader was replaced.

D4 DuPont Fellow recruited to enhance credibility and investigate biodegradability.

D5 Procter & Gamble withdrew interest. DuPont in a financial crunch. Support begins to unravel.

D6 Project team disbanded. All thirty-five development agreements cancelled, and focus shifted to completing the patent portfolio.

D7 A flurry of inquiries received about agricultural applications from internal and external sources.

D8 Major funding acquired from corporate level to run a PR campaign.

D9 Project transferred to business unit.

Note: The variability of resource support is represented by the changes in the thickness of the lines. Thin lines indicate thin funding, and fat lines indicate sufficient funding. Each line represents the pursuit of a new application. The breaks (labeled "D" for "discontinuity") identify major changes or transitions in the life of the project.

teams and firms to these uncertainties.[4] From these time lines we have derived the following general characteristics of the radical innovation life cycle:

- long term—often a decade or longer;
- highly uncertain and unpredictable;
- sporadic—stops and starts, deaths and revivals;
- nonlinear—requiring a recycling back through activities in response to discontinuities and setbacks and a continuing application of all the key radical innovation project management competencies;
- stochastic—key players come and go, priorities change, exogenous events are critical; and
- context dependent—history, experience, corporate culture, personalities, and informal relations all matter, creating a mix of accelerating and retarding factors.

Experience with incremental innovation indicates something very different. A potential marketable improvement to an existing product is quickly placed within a clearly defined, time-tested process designed to prove or disprove its value to the corporation. This process, which typically encompasses six months to two years, has organizational sponsorship, funding, and the assignment of a development team. Development and commercialization are directed along a formal, orderly stage-gate process.[5] None of the radical innovation projects we studied could be described by this orderly process. Even though the radical innovation life cycle includes many of the same sets of activities and decision points, the reality of managing the process is strikingly different for radical versus incremental innovation. The key differences between the course of incremental innovation and the long and winding road followed by radical innovation are summarized in table 2-1.

MULTIDIMENSIONAL UNCERTAINTIES

The common way of defining radical innovation focuses on the amount of technical and market uncertainty that must be resolved.[6] *Technical uncertainty* includes issues related to the completeness and correctness of the underlying scientific knowledge, the technical specifications of the product, manufacturing, maintainability, and so forth. *Market uncertainties* include issues related to customer needs and wants—either existing or latent forms of interaction between the customer and the product, methods of sales and distribution, the

TABLE 2-1

INCREMENTAL VERSUS RADICAL INNOVATION

	INCREMENTAL	RADICAL
Project time line	Short term—six months to two years.	Long term—usually ten years or more.
Trajectory	There is a linear and continuous path from concept to commercialization following designated steps.	The path is marked by multiple discontinuities, or gaps, that must be bridged. The process is sporadic with many stops and starts, hibernations and revivals. Trajectory changes occur in response to unanticipated events, outcomes, and discoveries.
Idea generation and opportunity recognition	Idea generation and opportunity recognition occur at the front end; critical events are largely anticipated.	Idea generation and opportunity recognition occur sporadically throughout the life cycle, often in response to discontinuities (funding, personnel, technical, market) in the project trajectory.
Process	A formal, approved process moves from idea generation through development and commercialization.	There is a formal process for getting and keeping funding, which is treated by participants as a game, often with disdain. Uncertainty is too high to make the process relevant. The formal process has real value only when the project enters later stages of development.
Business case	A complete and detailed plan can be developed at the beginning of the process because of the relatively low level of uncertainty.	The business model evolves through discovery-based technical and market learning and likewise the business plan must evolve as uncertainty is reduced.

TABLE 2-1 (CONTINUED)

INCREMENTAL VERSUS RADICAL INNOVATION

	INCREMENTAL	RADICAL
The players	Assigned to a cross-functional team, each member has a clearly specified responsibility within his or her area of expertise.	Key players come and go during the early life of the project. Many are part of the informal network that grows up around a radical innovation project. Key players tend to be "cross-functional" individuals.
Organizational structures	Typically, a cross-functional project team operates within a business unit.	The project often starts in R&D, migrates into some sort of incubating organization, and transitions into a goal-driven project organization.
Resources and competencies	The project team has all the competencies required to complete the process. The project is subject to the standard resource allocation process for incremental projects.	Creativity and skill in resource and competency acquisition—from a variety of internal and external sources—are critical to the survival and success of the project.
Operating unit involvement	Operating units are involved from the beginning.	Informal involvement with operating units is important, but the project must avoid becoming captive to an operating unit too early.

relationship to competitors' products, and so forth. Radical innovation projects involve high levels of both types of uncertainty. Incremental projects are generally low in both dimensions of risk.

We quickly discovered that the two dimensions of technical and market uncertainties failed to capture the complex, dynamic, and shifting uncertainties that surround radical projects. Project teams had to contend not only with challenging technical and market uncertainties, but with organizational and resource uncertainties as well.[7] Many of these stem from a fundamental conflict between the mainstream organization and the radical innovation team, and the difficulty of managing the relationship between them. Here are some of the *organizational* uncertainties the project teams we studied had to struggle with:

- What capabilities must the project team embody?

- Who should lead the project team and who else should be part of the team? How do we recruit these individuals without making waves?

- How do we define relationships with the rest of the organization—the business units, central R&D, senior corporate management?

- How do we deal with variability in persistence and continuity of management support?

- How should we manage the expectations of senior management and of the receiving operating unit?

Few of these questions ever concern incremental project teams. The same applies to the *resource* uncertainties that periodically assail radical projects:

- What funding and competencies are required to complete the project tasks?

- Which of these are currently available to us?

- How should we acquire missing resources and competencies—through internal development or partnering?

- Who are potential partners, and how do we form partnerships?

- What is the smartest method to use for managing those relationships?

The two additional dimensions of uncertainty—organization and resources—created unanticipated challenges for project management. Personnel who joined a radical innovation project with preconceived ideas of how to do new product development found that traditional management approaches didn't fit.[8] Most of the people we interviewed were not prepared for the extent of the difficulties. Here is how the Biomax team experienced these uncertainties:

ORGANIZATIONAL UNCERTAINTIES: The project had three distinctly different homes and passed through the hands of a changing cast of laboratory scientists, technicians, and project champions.

RESOURCE UNCERTAINTIES: Financial support, provided by a variety of internal sources, fluctuated throughout the project.

TECHNOLOGICAL UNCERTAINTIES: These included issues related to degradability, biodegradability, formulation to achieve appropriate degradation characteristics, and manufacturability of the material and end products.

MARKET UNCERTAINTIES: The project was inundated with market uncertainties related to a number of applications, the actions of potential internal and external customers, and decisions by government agencies about environmental regulations.

Each of our projects had to contend with these same four dimensions, though the levels of uncertainty within each dimension varied with time and in unpredictable ways. For projects to mature, uncertainty must be reduced on all four dimensions. However, for the projects we studied, uncertainty within each dimension typically fluctuated dramatically over the course of the life cycle. The project managers we observed tended to ignore some categories of uncertainty at times, particularly those with which they were least comfortable, even though these may have potentially killed the project. In particular, project managers seemed more comfortable dealing with technical uncertainties than with market, resource, and organizational uncertainties.

The problem of multiple dimensions of uncertainty is complicated by the fact that the uncertainties interact with one another. For example, the resolution of a technical uncertainty may produce an insight that allows the delivery of new value to the market, just as the response from a customer trying out an early prototype may cause a technical redirection. The Biomax team initially set its technical formulation to satisfy a potential market application in baby diapers. This formulation had to change when the market application shifted to agriculture.

Each dimension of uncertainty contains one or more potential "showstoppers"—events or discoveries that will close down the project.[9] If these are not addressed and resolved, the project is finished.

In the GM hybrid vehicle project, underperformance in technical development by alliance partners led to project shutdown. In the case of Polaroid, it was a lack of financing. And in the case of Otis Elevator's bidirectional elevator, the delay in the initial order from a lead user—caused by the Asian economic crisis in the late 1990s—triggered project cancellation. Table 2-2 identifies the potential showstoppers we observed in our twelve projects. Members of the research community will find them familiar. Success in the game of

TABLE 2-2

TYPES OF PROJECT SHOWSTOPPERS

UNCERTAINTY DIMENSION	SHOWSTOPPER
Technical	Major setback in technology development, application development, or manufacturing process development
Market	Assumption about attractiveness of a particular application space turns out to be false Market test of prototype fails or has disappointing results Failure to successfully develop a relationship with an appropriate lead user
Organizational	Loss of champion (permanently or temporarily) Change of attitude in business unit Change of project manager Transfer of oversight responsibility to a manager who is opposed to the project Failure to close alliance deal Failure of partner in technical development or manufacturing Loss of a key team member who is difficult to replace Change in senior management and/or strategic intent of the firm Change in SBU management Transition in project phase Transition to relevant operating unit or spin-out
Financial	Major loss of funding because of a reversal in overall corporate performance or a change in senior management sponsor

radical innovation requires that team leaders and members be prepared to meet each changing set of challenges with a set of competencies drawn from within the team or acquired elsewhere in the
organization or from strategic partners.

We now move on to the seven managerial challenges that radical
innovators must face and the competencies they need to overcome
them. In chapter 3 we examine the fuzzy front end of innovation—
the set of activities that encompasses the transition from promising
ideas through opportunity recognition and evaluation to the decision
to form a radical innovation project.

CHAPTER 3

GRABBING
LIGHTNING

LARGE, TECHNOLOGY-INTENSIVE FIRMS TYPICALLY HAVE difficulty capitalizing on their deep reservoirs of technical knowledge. There is a gap between the firm's knowledge base and radical innovation projects. In our interviews, workshops, and seminars, practitioners repeatedly expressed frustration with the ineffectiveness of their efforts to bridge this *conversion gap*.[1] Overcoming this challenge—the subject of this chapter—requires generating radical ideas, identifying promising business opportunities enabled by those ideas, and creating sanctioned projects to pursue those opportunities.

Most firms in our study used ad hoc and intermittent approaches to stimulate and capture radical ideas; hence, radical innovation projects occurred unpredictably and infrequently. In a few cases, however, dynamic and visionary leaders had begun to create a culture that stimulated the flow of high-quality ideas. These firms established an organizational approach to radical innovation that we have characterized as an "innovation hub."

Hubs serve as home bases for the firm's cadre of experienced radical innovators. They are focal points for the development and commercialization of radical innovations and offer a practical approach for increasing the success rate of radical innovation projects. They serve as repositories for the cumulative experience of dealing with each of the radical innovation life cycle's seven management challenges. In this chapter, we explore how hubs can help implement mechanisms for capturing radical ideas and—in the words of DuPont's corporate business development director, Terry Fadem—"grab lightning everyday."

REDUCING FUZZINESS IN THE FUZZY FRONT END

Idea generation, opportunity recognition, and initial opportunity evaluation are three activities that companies use to bridge the gap between their reservoirs of technical knowledge and the formation of radical innovation projects. This set of dynamic activities—each one of which must occur before a project can move forward—constitutes the fuzzy front end of the radical innovation life cycle.[2]

IDEA GENERATION. Idea generation is the starting point for both incremental and radical forms of innovation. In the former, ideas generally come from ongoing interaction between a company and its customers. Ideas that lead to radical innovation, however, are much more likely to result from the synthesis of new and nonobvious insights from bits of disparate technical information. In some cases, radical innovation starts with a technical idea or set of technical ideas. The idea may be born out of the natural curiosity of a scientist or engineer, or stimulated by a challenging problem. The technical idea can take the form of a discovery of a novel technology, a new insight into an old problem, or a new way of linking existing technologies. In other cases, radical innovation has its roots in a market need, an industry "Holy Grail" (a great and unsolved challenge in the company's industry), or the strategic vision of the firm's leadership. Each of these can catalyze the development of technical ideas with the potential to be breakthroughs. Because ideas can come from so many sources, noticing them is difficult. Many are missed for lack of an alert listener.

OPPORTUNITY RECOGNITION. For a radical idea to move forward, someone must recognize its business potential—in other words, make a connection between a novel technical solution and a compelling market need. This seems obvious. But a scientist with an idea may not have a sufficiently deep understanding of the market to grasp the nature of the opportunity. To be an effective opportunity recognizer, one must have both technical knowledge and the business savvy and market sense to see the business potential in a radical idea.

INITIAL EVALUATION. Opportunity recognition triggers initial evaluation, the due-diligence process through which companies determine whether to commit the resources needed to develop the idea. Initial evaluation involves making explicit assumptions about how a technology will develop, how markets will unfold, and how the organization will respond to the opportunity. High uncertainty makes evaluation particularly difficult.

Two contrasting stories from our case studies illustrate what may go on in the front end of radical innovation. A project we observed at Analog Devices relied primarily on individual initiative at the start, following the pattern typical of radical projects. The second example from Nortel Networks showcases an alternative and more systematic approach. Nortel Networks established a radical innovation hub—a home for people *and* systems dedicated to capturing radical innovation—through a formal, internal venturing program. The hub played a pivotal role in the launch and development of the Nortel Networks project.

ANALOG DEVICES

In 1979, Steve Sherman coordinated an informal lunchtime meeting sponsored by his company, Analog Devices of Norwood, Massachusetts. A chip designer by profession, Sherman was drawn by the prospect of hearing about the research of the meeting's guest, a professor from nearby Boston University. The professor had written a paper on the manufacture of chips that incorporated mechanical devices within their designs—known today as MEMS (micro-electro-mechanical system) devices. The discussion at the luncheon motivated Sherman to experiment with the design aspects of this idea in the laboratory.

Through the early 1980s, Sherman bootlegged time and resources to work on the MEMS concept, even though he had no idea how it could be applied. The device he had in mind was much different from anything previously designed or produced by Analog Devices, which at the time derived most of its revenue from small-volume, specialized integrated chips designed for instrumentation. Sherman was confident that he could design a chip with a built-in mechanical system. But could the design be manufactured? Further, how would it be packaged on a board?

Sherman took his questions to Carl Roberts, a packaging and design expert. "Some day we're going to have a circuit with these moving beams in the center," he told Roberts. "You're going to have to figure out how to integrate them into a system." Sherman also approached Richie Payne, an R&D manager and Analog Devices Fellow with a reputation for creativity and an aptitude for business development. Payne had a strong network of contacts inside and outside Analog Devices and understood how to connect ideas with applications.

The evaluation process for this project was triggered when Payne took his story directly to CEO Jerry Fishman. Instead of utilizing formal evaluation criteria and evaluation teams, Analog Devices relied on the experience of its still-active founder, Ray Stata, and the judgment of its CEO. Fishman used his informal network of technology and market experts to assess Sherman's work and its market promise.

CEO Fishman reacted to the confluence of three factors: the technical progress Sherman had made in developing the technology; his conviction that the automotive industry would offer an attractive new market for this technology; and the availability of a project champion—Richie Payne. Sherman's work had demonstrated the potential of the new chips being used in sensor devices (called *accelerometers*), and another Analog employee believed that these could be used in the auto industry for a number of applications—for example, triggering dashboard air bags. Fishman knew that automotive technology was moving more and more toward electronics and believed Analog Devices could deploy its technical capabilities there. In early 1988, Sherman and Payne received formal project recognition from Fishman, an annual budget of about $500,000, and a small team of researchers to work on the MEMS device. At that point, Payne recruited Bob Tsang, an accomplished process development engineer. Introduction of the accelerometer opened a huge new market for the company.

In this case Steve Sherman was the idea generator, and Richie Payne filled the role of opportunity recognizer and champion. Payne articulated the business opportunity to the CEO, who formally established the project with a team and a budget. Sherman and his team had made it through the fuzzy front end, but it took nine years to complete the journey.

Nortel Networks's NetActive

In 1996, the management of Nortel Networks's Residential Broadband Division wanted to stimulate demand for its new broadband service targeted at homeowners. Management reasoned that a large number of practical uses for the broadband service would make it more attractive and encourage mass subscribership. To identify potential applications for broadband communications, an "idea sandbox" was established, with a clear mission: investigate ideas for new products and services that would require broadband hookups. After nine months, division management sent Jeff Dodge to join the group and to harvest the result of its work.

Dodge was a Nortel Networks engineer with an entrepreneurial bent and a computer science background. His job was to sift through the ideas that the small technical team had developed, identify those with potential commercial merit, and move them forward. To Dodge, the most attractive of these ideas was a concept for renting software over the Internet. For one-time or occasional services (e.g., tax preparation, travel planning, or games), consumers might prefer to rent rather than buy software. The problem was that broadband Internet was not required to make this idea work, so a new source of development financing would be required.

As Dodge was working on his assignment, another Nortel Networks employee, Joanne Hyland, was establishing a venture development unit within Nortel Networks R&D. When she and her team issued a request for proposals, Dodge submitted his rental software concept—now called NetActive—for evaluation.

Hyland's team was prepared for a flood of proposals. It had developed a fast-track screening process for deciding whether an idea warranted further attention. Dodge's concept passed this screen and qualified for a small amount of funding and assistance in preparing a business proposal to take to the venture investment advisory board. There, too, the concept passed muster. The business proposal for NetActive was accepted by the board in January 1997, and an official development team was formed with significant funding. The project had made it through the fuzzy front end and was off and running.

The NetActive project worked through many of the uncertainties and discontinuities described in the previous chapter, including major shifts in corporate strategic context, changes in team composition, financing crises, and several generations of business models. A major external financing deal was consummated in June of 1999, and the venture was spun off. Nortel Networks remained a major shareholder with 45 percent of NetActive's equity and with three representatives on the venture's board of directors.

In this case, radical idea generation was accomplished by the creative engineers in the idea sandbox. Jeff Dodge served in the role of opportunity recognizer. And Joanne Hyland's New Ventures Program, the radical innovation hub of Nortel Networks, triggered initial evaluation of the software rental concept. The venture development unit had established a mechanism for systematically receiving ideas and working with the idea generators to refine the nature of the opportunity.

THE ANALOG AND NORTEL NETWORKS EXAMPLES ILLUSTRATE how different organizations approach the initiating activities of radical innovation projects: idea generation, opportunity recognition, and initial evaluation. The three sections that follow describe the challenges inherent in effectively executing these activities and offer ideas for improving practice.

GENERATING AND CAPTURING RADICAL IDEAS

The ratio of raw, untested ideas to commercially viable outcomes is anyone's guess and is probably company- or industry-specific. One source[3] puts them at three thousand to one, but any such ratio begs the question, What is a raw idea? Managers in technology-rich companies assume that the floors of their research laboratories must be littered with innovative technical ideas. But Craig Wynett, director of the Corporate New Ventures program for Procter & Gamble, put it this way: "I challenge those managers to reflect on whether they are talking about the volume of ideas, or the volume of *good* ideas." From Wynett's perspective, good ideas are those that lead to radical innovations with the potential to create major new business opportunities for the firm. Data from our study supports his assessment. While there were many ideas floating around the R&D-intensive firms in our study, truly game-changing ideas were few.

To understand why idea generation leading to radical innovation is so difficult, recall the differences between radical and incremental innovation. In the case of incremental innovation, goals are specific and clear, the product line a new idea will join is defined, and sources of ideas (salespeople, customers, and competitors) are known and understood. Idea generation in these cases is directed at improving the performance of the mainstream business. Systems are well established for responding to these kinds of ideas.

It's a different story for radical ideas. The creative individuals that initiate radical innovation look at things in new ways and make unusual connections. These individuals are typically referred to as "out-of-the-box thinkers" and represent a small minority of technical employees in most organizations. One senior technologist told us: "Not more than 3 percent of our researchers can think outside the box." The challenge for the firm is to support and encourage these individuals and their brand of thinking.[4]

RIPENING AND MATURING RADICAL IDEAS

Some breakthrough ideas are serendipitous. Most, however, are the consequence of extended efforts to accumulate in-depth technical knowledge and ad hoc approaches to enhance and work the idea. It's not usually a light-bulb, "aha" experience, and even in the rare cases when it is, the flash of light is just the beginning. Ideas evolve, and confidence is built through "fleshing out" the ideas.

Joe Bittar, vice president of product strategy for United Technologies's Otis Elevator Division, focused his thinking over one weekend on a challenge put to him and other senior managers at a monthly staff meeting convened by J. P. van Rooy, the division president. The challenge was to "solve the problem of the mile-high building," a "Holy Grail" for the elevator industry. Over 50 years ago, Frank Lloyd Wright designed a mile-high building that could be constructed with available materials and technologies. However, this building could not be constructed until the problem of moving the people was solved. A single elevator shaft was not a solution due to the weight of the cable. Multiple shafts consumed too much available "real estate" of the building. Bittar actually did have an "aha" experience during his noodling over possible solutions, though it seemed too costly. Why not allow the elevator cab to detach from the shaft and move horizontally to a second shaft? This would require much less "real estate" of the building for shafts or cars than previous solutions had required. His immediate action on Monday morning was to arrange for a two-day retreat with his "ten best engineers" to work the idea, to test it's validity, and to develop it more fully. When they came away from that retreat, the singular idea had evolved into multiple possibilities for horizontal and vertical people movers. They had, in fact, "broadened the problem," and two years later, according to Bittar, "The patent lawyer is still writing."

All this is to say that ideas evolve, and they don't evolve in predictable ways. Psychologists call the activities associated with idea development "loose associative thinking" processes.[5] Associative logic is *not* sequential. It's jumpy. For a time, the maintenance of uncertainty is important. Closure is a killer; it strangles associative thinking in favor of arriving at "an answer." Early in the process, leveraging uncertainty, riding it, and valuing it are critical to developing robust ideas.

Radical ideas come from creative individuals, such as Otis Elevator's Bittar, who have deep technical knowledge and who think outside the constraints of the firm's current business. They are stimulated by curiosity, by challenges from the firm's management, or by specific techniques that firms employ to encourage and support them. They draw on both firm-specific and external reservoirs of technical knowledge.

Approaches to stimulating radical idea generation generally fall into two categories: motivational tools and organizational mechanisms. We will take a look at both.

MOTIVATING RADICAL IDEA GENERATION. *Strategic intent* is senior management's primary motivational tool for idea generation. The concept, as described by Gary Hamel and C. K. Prahalad, embodies a "misfit between current resources and corporate aspirations."[6] Senior management motivates idea generation when it actively encourages the quest for new opportunities. In projects we studied, some radical ideas emerged in response to a general call for growth, to counter competitive pressures, or to improve the financial performance of the enterprise. For example, the CEO of Texas Instruments exhorted his employees to "find new businesses in the white spaces" between existing business units. DuPont scientists were asked to help the corporation "invent its way" out of financial tough times.

In other cases, the aim was to move the firm beyond the constraints of current customers, current business models, and current technologies.[7] In these cases, employees were urged to explore growth in new directions in order to do the following:

- get into a new industry (the automotive industry in the case of Analog Devices);
- lead the next industry-transforming breakthrough (in the case of Air Product's gas separation technology); or
- pursue an industry "Holy Grail" (to find a way to move people up and down a mile-high building in the case of Otis Elevator).

Senior management can inhibit or expand the search for radical ideas through its articulation of strategic intent.[8] Some executives are very good at thinking about the future in disciplined ways and communicating their visions to their managers and employees. Executives with deep technical knowledge and the wisdom that comes with years of industry experience can inspire others to think boldly. Jerry Meiling, who recently retired as Corning's vice president of R&D, was one of these visionaries. In the late 1980s, he foresaw the intersection of two areas of science—materials (Corning's specialty) and molecular biology—and was thinking through the consequences for Corning's future. At the time of his retirement, he was influencing investments and hiring laboratory scientists with backgrounds in human genetics to take advantage of the new "fertile field" of opportunities.

ORGANIZATIONAL MECHANISMS FOR IDEA GENERATION. Executives have a number of organizational mechanisms for translating strategic intent into action. Few are new. These mechanisms aim at getting idea generators out of standard routines and connecting them to new pockets of knowledge. These include think tanks, corporatewide requests for proposals, technology forecasting, slack time for "doodling," periodic transfer of personnel from one unit to another, and technical forums geared to scientific cross-pollination. In one of these exercises at IBM, research manager Steve Depp was asked to forecast the development trajectories of three key technologies: displays, computer memory, and efficiencies in power utilization. By systematically integrating his thinking about these three technologies and their anticipated paths of development, Depp envisioned their convergence in the form of an "electronic book," at the time a new format for storing, displaying, and manipulating text and graphics. Depp believed that such a device could be useful in a number of applications. Today, the "e-book" concept is widely accepted, and several commercial versions have already appeared. Depp's insight, however, occurred in the late 1980s and resulted in the project we studied.

Idea generation is also stimulated by connecting idea generators to *external sources* of new knowledge. Specific techniques we observed include sending idea generators to technical conferences; being alert to suggestions from customers and suppliers; deciphering product breakthroughs in other industries; and bringing in outside experts from universities, federal labs, and even other corporate labs to interact with R&D personnel. These mechanisms were useful not only for stimulating idea generation but also for giving the idea generators the opportunities to validate their ideas through professional colleagues.

GOOD IDEAS NEED A PLACE TO GO

Firms that lack a systematic approach for capturing radical ideas play a waiting game. They believe that creative people are irrepressible and that they can count on the passion and persistence of those individuals to get their ideas recognized. This is true in some cases but not others. Bernie Meyerson, who was instrumental in the development of IBM's super-fast silicon germanium chip, would not give up on his idea even though it contradicted the accepted technical wisdom, fell outside the strategic boundaries of the firm at the time, and met with substantial organizational resistance. His battles to get his idea heard ended up with, in his words, "lots of blood on the walls," but his passion and perseverance eventually won out.

By comparison, the initial idea for the GE digital X-ray project came from Jack Kingsley, the manager of a small group of scientists working on the development of display technologies for aircraft. Kingsley thought the aerospace display technology might be applicable to medical imaging. After talking to other scientists on his team, he contacted one of the technical people at GE's Medical Systems business unit (GEMS), who was extremely negative about the idea. According to Kingsley, "because we were busy with other things, I didn't push it any further. I don't know if I had pushed it harder whether anything would have happened or not."

The idea reemerged four years later, but this time Kingsley enlisted his boss, Bruce Griffing, to help make the case to GEMS. Griffing proved to be an impassioned champion. When asked why he was more successful than Kingsley in getting GEMS to take notice, Griffing responded: "I thought it was important—that it really had the potential to change the game. I pushed it a lot harder than he did."

Some idea generators prefer to focus on exploratory research and avoid being drawn into the business development process, which they view as a drag on their time. At one firm, a senior manager from a business unit showed up periodically in search of ideas with the potential for creating growth in his division. Initially, researchers were thrilled by his interest and laid their ideas on the table. But they quickly found that promising ideas provoked intense pressure to resolve technical issues and to convert the ideas into manufacturable products. More interested in scientific exploration than commercialization, these researchers resisted being drawn into the grunt work of product development and learned to be circumspect in their future dealings with the business unit manager. This situation underscores the need for developing a capacity within the firm for receiving ideas and carrying them forward.

KEYS TO GENERATING MORE AND BETTER RADICAL IDEAS

While everyone acknowledges the importance of the mechanisms just described, companies still struggle to get the job done. To summarize, our recommendations for stimulating idea generation are as follows:

- create and sustain strategic momentum for radical innovation;
- proactively implement organizational mechanisms for getting radical innovations out of the lab and into commercialization projects; and
- develop a "receiving" capacity for radical ideas so that creative people have a place to go with their ideas.

This last recommendation points us to the next section. As one respondent put it: "Our firm does not have a system for identifying ideas as opportunities. If there isn't a buyer for a research project out there among the business units, then the idea just starts to smell."

RECOGNIZING OPPORTUNITIES

Idea generators need a place to take their ideas for quick back-of-the-envelope assessments, for help with ripening their ideas by extending or redirecting their thinking, and for assistance in articulating the potential for their ideas.[9] To get radical ideas moving forward, receivers need to be adept at recognizing opportunities. In the general innovation literature, a good idea is equated with the recognition of a promising business opportunity. This may be the case for incremental innovation, where the gap between idea and opportunity is narrow. The technical and market uncertainties associated with radical innovation, however, make it difficult for idea generators to perceive potential business opportunities. Opportunity recognition for radical innovation requires special skills and talents, which we describe in this section. In ten of our twelve case studies, the individuals who generated the ideas did not recognize the opportunities. That job fell to others.

OPPORTUNITY RECOGNIZERS AS HUNTERS AND GATHERERS

The individuals who come up with radical ideas usually have only a vague idea of application domains; their market knowledge does not reach the threshold of understanding and judgment required to bring opportunities into focus. On the other hand, opportunity recognizers have market knowledge and organizational positions that help them connect ideas with application possibilities. They have the ability to think broadly about potential connections among different fields of science and about social trends, markets, and customers. They perceive opportunities that others fail to see or see them before most others do. In our case studies, opportunity recognizers were generally low- to mid-level research managers. These individuals viewed laboratory work through lenses not commonly used by either bench scientists or typical business people. In this sense, they served as critical links between idea generation and initial opportunity evaluation.

Opportunity recognition is highly dependent on individual initiative and less dependent on routine practices and procedures. It can be either reactive or proactive. On the one hand, individuals may be alert and ready to react to promising ideas. We call these "gatherers" of radical ideas. On the other hand, individuals may take responsibility for actively seeking out ideas with business potential. We call these opportunity seekers "hunters."[10]

Gatherers are embedded in the flow of technical creative activity; they hear the continual background hum and see its steady glow. But they also hear the thunder—and see the bolt of light-ning—when someone in their organization comes up with a radi-cal idea that breaks the continuum. They don't see it as a distraction from the continual flow of creative activity, but rather as an oppor-tunity to create something that is radically new. In fact, they view it as their responsibility to help the idea generator access resources he or she needs to further develop the concept.

Gatherers have the experience, skill, judgment, and motivation to be alert and receptive to ideas that bubble up from R&D activ-ity or that appear from other sources. Effective gatherers have the technical sophistication to assess what they encounter. In addition, their life experiences have engendered a certain cosmopolitanism—an awareness of markets and social and scientific trends. In many of our case studies, first-line and midlevel research managers and senior scientists played the role of gatherer.

At Analog Devices, the first signs of success in developing a micro-actuator on a chip told researcher Steve Sherman that he was onto something important. Sherman considered the business implications as chip designers all do at Analog. Payne assumed the role of radical idea gatherer by recognizing the business opportunity and bringing it to the attention of the organization.

Hunters take a more active approach to idea recognition, seek-ing out ideas with business potential. They go out into the organi-zation looking for out-of-the-box thinkers, ask questions to uncover latent ideas, and make connections between people, programs, and ideas that might not occur without their intervention. They are the catalysts for the thunder and lightning of radical idea generation.

Like gatherers, hunters have technical training, but they are more likely to be experienced in marketing or business develop-ment. Perhaps as important, a successful hunter knows how to articulate the opportunity in compelling terms that gain the atten-tion of higher management—something that few bench scientists are skilled at doing. One IBM opportunity hunter described his job this way:

> I started looking through our research organization to uncover intel-lectual property that I could leverage into the marketplace. I was actively scanning and knew [that one scientist] had been running

around evangelizing the technology for two or three years. He hadn't been able to build a case that got it recognized and funded. What we had here was a [corporate research] Fellow, one of the smartest guys in the world, but he couldn't get the attention to tilt this thing up.

THE CHAIN REACTION OF OPPORTUNITY RECOGNITION

The recognition of opportunity by a gatherer or hunter does not necessarily trigger the evaluation process. As in idea generation, a single "aha" is insufficient. A chain reaction is usually required.

Given the high uncertainty associated with radical innovation, a front-line recognizer may be unable to articulate the opportunity to management in a compelling way. In some circumstances the recognizer may be uncomfortable about sticking his or her neck out before others have expressed their opinions. The recognizer may also lack the political clout to gain the attention of the organization. Hence, other individuals need to make the same connection between the idea and the business opportunity.

At DuPont, the evaluation process did not begin until *several* people recognized the potential of a technical discovery by Don Coates, a DuPont researcher. Coates noticed unexpected properties in the fiber material he was testing for composites applications. Under certain conditions the material emitted electrons. One of the senior technologists recognized a potential electronic display application and invited Terry Fadem, director of corporate business development, to an informal demonstration and review. "I get daily notices of all the technical reviews going on here," Fadem recollected, "but I have so many other things to do that I do not go unless somebody tells me to." Acting on the research manager's advice, Fadem went to the review and was sufficiently impressed by what he learned that he contacted John Hodgson, general manager of the electronic materials business, the unit that would inherit the project if and when it was ready for commercialization. Fadem had known Hodgson for more than twenty years and had previously worked for him. Given his confidence in Fadem, Hodgson took a look at the material and recognized the potential of Coates's discovery. His familiarity with competing technology helped him visualize a market application. Working together, Fadem and Hodgson speculated about how they would overcome the problems that were bound to crop up.

In this case, Coates was the idea generator. The series of opportunity recognition events that led to formal evaluation and formation of the project started with Coates's fellow technologist (the gatherer in this case) and extended to Fadem and Hodgson, who were in positions to support it.

By virtue of his position and training, Terry Fadem is the prototypical opportunity recognizer. Nevertheless, he chose not to engage the company's formal evaluation process immediately. Given the uncertainties associated with the technology, he first tested the idea within his informal network. "Because of the way managers have grown up around here," he told us, "there are all these internal networks and webs, and I work them. My call to another guy, and then to another guy, is how it happened." In this case, as in most others, the informal network of individuals with the capacity for opportunity recognition helped bridge the gap between idea generation and the initial decision-making process. Hunters and gatherers are important elements in any system of opportunity recognition.

Keys to Enhancing Opportunity Recognition

Senior management's commitment to radical innovation is as important for opportunity recognizers as it is for idea generators. Their visible commitment sensitizes and challenges everyone to be alert for ideas with business potential. But more must be done. Our field research suggests recommendations for improving opportunity recognition, as follows:

- Senior management should establish a corporate vision and objectives that stimulate and guide opportunity recognition.

- The R&D organization should encourage its senior scientists and low- to mid-level research managers to take on the role of radical idea gatherers.

- If the company has a business development unit in place, its personnel should serve as radical idea hunters.

- Hunters and gatherers should establish informal networks to identify ideas and to test initial assessments.

- Opportunity recognizers should be connected to one or more radical innovation hubs. Hunters and gatherers who are not part of a broad network of other people dedicated to radical innovation are lone voices in the wilderness.

- Finally, the radical innovation hub should trigger the evaluation process, as described in the following section.

INITIAL EVALUATION

Initial evaluation is the third component of the front end of innovation, and as such, it must be a "fuzzy" evaluation. When senior managers talk about how to evaluate radical innovations, they often mention gut instincts. One retired Hewlett-Packard manager bristled at the idea of a disciplined evaluation process for radical innovations, saying: "All we needed were Bill [Hewlett] and Dave [Packard]." That manager's experience is not unique. At Analog Devices, the initial evaluation of the accelerometer project depended on the insight and judgment of its founder, Ray Stata, and its CEO, Jerry Fishman. Even today, ten years after the launch of that project, Analog Devices continues to rely on founder Ray Stata for decisions on whether to pursue accelerometer-related business opportunities.

Founders and early leaders of technology companies—if still active—can be powerful forces for opportunity recognition and evaluation. They have first-hand experience with breakthrough innovations and enjoy tremendous credibility among employees. Their support for a radical project can galvanize commitment to its development. Unfortunately, the founders of most established technology firms eventually depart, taking their capacity for deep insight into the potential of radical innovations with them. When evaluating radical innovations, most mature firms cannot and should not rely either on the gut instinct of a single

powerful individual or on a set of rigid evaluative criteria designed
for evaluating incremental innovations. Rather, new systems and
new metrics are required.[11]

GETTING THE RIGHT PEOPLE TO
CONDUCT THE EVALUATION

Establishing an effective evaluation team for radical innovation
ideas is a major challenge. The natural tendency is to engage senior
managers, but there is an inherent conflict in this practice. On the one
hand, some senior corporate and business unit managers have strategic vision, credibility in the organization, and a deep understanding of
the firm's business model. However, in general, their experience base lies
primarily in established lines of business. Few have experience with
highly uncertain radical projects. As a consequence, most have not
developed judgment about these types of projects. Further, their judgment may be influenced by commitments to established business units
whose products may be displaced by the innovations they are being
asked to assess. Hence, when mature firms assemble evaluation boards
composed of senior managers with little or no experience with radical
innovations, failure avoidance may dominate the evaluation process.

A radical innovation evaluation board must include individuals whose *combined* capabilities bring both credibility and wisdom
derived from experience in evaluating radical concepts to the task.
The board should also include members with specific expertise
related to the underlying technologies and potential market applications. This implies that the composition of the oversight evaluation board may change over the course of the radical innovation life
cycle. The initial evaluation panel might include the following:

- senior corporate and business unit leaders who have strategic
  vision, deep understanding of the firm's business model, credibility in the organization, and courage to look beyond the firm's
  current strategic vision and business model;
- savvy business development managers;
- highly respected senior technologists (e.g., research fellows with
  deep knowledge in the relevant technical domains); and
- veterans of past radical projects.

Outsiders who have specific knowledge and experience lying outside the firm's area of expertise can bring significant benefit to the evaluation panel. In several of our projects, executives of small high-tech firms, university researchers, and consulting firms played important roles. For example, Intel has developed an external network of venture capitalists through its program of coinvesting in external ventures. If Intel chooses, it can selectively draw from this network when it assembles an evaluation board. Likewise, if it chose to do so, Texas Instruments could call on its relationship with venture capital partner Hambrecht and Quist for representatives on a radical innovation evaluation board. Of course, if a firm opts to engage outsiders in the evaluation process, it must implement mechanisms to protect proprietary information.

The objective is to ensure that members of an evaluation panel are sophisticated with respect to evaluating high-risk, but potentially breakthrough, opportunities and that they have the credibility and authority to get the organization to take appropriate action in response to their decision.

CHOOSING THE RIGHT CRITERIA

The first formal evaluation of a radical project generally takes place when the project applies for funding. Too often, evaluators measure the project with the same calipers used to assess more familiar and less uncertain incremental projects. When this happens, the radical idea is confronted with a set of "tyrannies":

- the tyranny of served markets—"Our current customers won't like this";
- the tyranny of the established business model—"This doesn't fit within our familiar routines for making money";
- the tyranny of current strategy—"We're not in that business";
- the tyranny of the current organizational structure—"If this can't be adopted by one of our business units, we won't be able to manage it";
- the tyranny of arbitrary financial hurdles—"If it cannot generate revenues of $250 million within three to five years, it's not worth our time"; and

• the tyranny of language—"This is business mumbo jumbo to us." (Scientists and research managers speak the language of science and cannot always articulate their case to senior management review boards.)

In our study, most managers acknowledged that the criteria used to evaluate a radical concept should differ from those applied to evaluating incremental innovations. In practice, however, members of formal evaluation boards view radical projects from the perspective of the mainstream business. As a result, they expect to see specific project goals, early market research on new features, and detailed financial projections. The high uncertainty associated with radical innovations makes them nervous and encourages them to insist on even greater rigor in analysis and a more careful application of traditional evaluation methods and criteria. Generally these methods are inappropriate or counterproductive. Either they give a false sense of security, or they lead to premature rejection of promising ideas. It is easier to say "no" or to require more detailed information than to defend a decision to invest resources in the absence of "hard data."

When radical project teams are compelled to apply conventional criteria during initial evaluation, the result is predictable: "blue sky " numbers based on questionable assumptions. In one case, the project manager who worked up a funding proposal to present to the firm's new business board solicited input from the appropriate business unit. The resulting proposal made assumptions about product specifications and presented a profit and loss statement in which every line item was rendered in detail: sales revenues, manufacturing costs, sales and administrative overheads, expenses for R&D and product planning, and so forth. The business unit even helped develop a product pricing schedule and estimated sales volume over time.

According to the project manager, "Our target was to break even . . . [but] when we took this to the new business board, they said: 'This is not a good business case. It doesn't make enough money.'" Indeed, though this first business case projected a $2.5 billion market for the proposed product application, short-term profits were not sufficiently attractive. "So," said the project manager, "we revised it." Using more favorable market assumptions, the project team arrived at numbers that met the new business board's expectations. "I can't say that this is a real business case," the project manager admitted. "On the other hand, it's a logical business case." Technical champions who view the rules by which they are forced to play as unreasonable and inappropriate often subvert them, undermining the purpose of the evaluation process.

The purpose of initial evaluation is to determine whether there is enough promise in an idea to warrant the next step: making a limited commitment of resources to a small team that will test critical assumptions and further explore the opportunity.[12] Hence, initial evaluation should answer a couple of simple technical and market questions: What is the technical "wow" associated with this innovation? and, Is the market big enough?

THE TECHNICAL WOW. Technical evaluation focuses on how the innovation differs from known technologies and who is likely to benefit from those differences. Don Coates, the scientist in DuPont's explosives division, read an article in a magazine about a discovery at Sandia National Laboratories in New Mexico, in which diamond coatings were applied to fibers to enhance their strength. Coates knew the Sandia researcher and decided he'd like to work with him on the project. So he proposed a Cooperative Research and Development Agreement (CRADA) between DuPont and Sandia Lab. Eventually it was approved, and he began working with his Sandia colleague on the problem of strengthening composite materials. At a professional conference, the Sandia researcher had learned about diamond-coated fibers emitting electrons, and on returning to the lab, he tested the material for this property. In tests at Sandia and back at DuPont, the carbon fiber emitted electrons at a higher rate than any other known material. They realized that their material was a much better electron emitter than it was a composite-strengthening material.

DuPont's Terry Fadem recalled: "We had no desire or interest in pursuing its electrical properties at that time until this 'aha' occurred. We were sitting in a conference room in Building 356 . . . and there were several of us listening to this presentation. Suddenly it became apparent that we could make flat panel displays and other things where electron emission was required."

Similarly, at IBM, the technical wow was Bernie Meyerson's discovery that the accepted understanding of the oxidation properties of silicon was wrong. This insight enabled a dramatically different and more efficient manufacturing process. That, in turn, allowed silicon germanium to be a high-performance material for next generation chips.

In general, project teams and their supporters used the following technical questions to assess whether the project was worth pursuing:

- What will this technology enable to happen? Does it create new value?

- What are the potential applications?

- What impact could it have on people's lives?

- Can we demonstrate technical feasibility? (Projects we studied used lab-based mathematical analysis experiments and other kinds of technical feasibility analyses to establish the technical wow and to gain confidence in the relative benefits of the technology.[13])

Cost, as an element in the customer value calculation, is a corollary issue. Even if the new technology is viewed as superior to the established technology, can it be produced at a cost that will induce current users to switch? Two projects in our study faced this question. The General Motors team charged with early stage development of a hybrid power source vehicle had to determine if that innovation would be both functionally and economically competitive with current internal combustion vehicles. The team at Air Products was struggling to develop a new method for producing oxygen in manufacturing plants. Both the market for industrial oxygen and its price were known. What the Air Products team had to determine was whether they could design and build an on-site oxygen-generating unit that would both deliver the goods and deliver them at a price that would cause customers to switch to the new technology. They knew from their history and familiarity with this market that a cost reduction of at least 30 percent would be needed to get their industrial customers to switch.

Questions like these cannot always be answered in advance. Research teams must often travel some distance down the development path—even down a dead-end path—before the answers become clear. Thus ongoing evaluation is part of the game. "As it turns out," one scientist told us, "everything that the program got launched off of was a mistake. When we critically examined the technology, we found that we had no competitive advantage." A dead end.

IS THE MARKET BIG ENOUGH? The next question that project members and evaluators must answer is whether the market is big enough to justify investing in technology development.[14] Given the daunting odds against any early stage project making it to commercialization, and the cost of getting there, a large market is often a must. Few long-term projects get the green light from management without it. As one scientist told us: "We can't get a project off the ground if it has less than $250 million in market potential." Joel Birnbaum, recently retired chief scientist for Hewlett-Packard, told us that $200 million was the threshold number for innovations that addressed "near or adjacent" business. Procter & Gamble's CTO Gordon Brunner pointed to a minimum threshold of only $100 million in the U.S. market, but noted that his company can leverage that revenue figure into $500 million through P&G's global reach.

Some researchers know from the very beginning that they are addressing large markets and do not feel compelled to answer the market size question. For example, when Nucor Corporation decided to build a new steel mill based on a previously unproven technology for continuous casting of thin-strip steel, it was pursing a century-old Holy Grail of the steelmaking industry. There was no question that success with the new technology would give the company unchallenged cost leadership. Otis Elevator's J. P. van Rooy did not have to ask his company's market researchers and number crunchers to estimate the financial consequences of cracking the 130-story barrier. He and everyone else in his business understood that doing so would be a *very* big deal.

Likewise, when researchers are working on a breakthrough technology capable of cannibalizing an existing one, they don't need to spend a lot of time asking whether the market is big enough. They already know within an acceptable range.

By comparison, in cases with high market uncertainty, the concern about market size is critically important. In some cases, the evaluation boards rigidly adopted a threshold for market size or revenue projections, and the projects jumped through hoops to meet expectations. In their drive to try to extract funding from these boards, the project teams engaged in a certain amount of hyperbole in representing market size, playing with the numbers in order to satisfy the rigid criteria of the evaluation board. Off the record, they had very little confidence in the numbers they were representing to management. However, they rationalized their gamesmanship with the understanding that any numbers used early in the game would be grossly inaccurate in any case. Not surprisingly, we found no evidence of a systematic process for substantiating the size of the markets for radical innovations early in the life cycle. Thus, there was a fundamental disconnect between the criteria of the evaluation board and the reality of the project's business case.

In those cases where the project team worked around the formal evaluation process and acquired funding through alternative sources, the funding usually came through the support of a senior manager. The evaluation process in these cases was different from that used by formalized evaluation boards. Interestingly, the innovators and their senior management supporters seldom if ever asked the following questions for which professional marketers would want answers:

- How fast is the market growing?
- What must the firm's role be in market development?
- What feature set will appeal most to customers?
- What price will the market bear?
- When will we start to see profits?
- How should we position our product?
- What is the best approach to distribution?
- How soon will we be able to start collecting revenue?
- What are our competitors doing, and how will they react? (In fact, the word "competitor" rarely enters the dialogue of early stage researchers and evaluators.)

It was belief in the robustness of the technology and the potential for numerous attractive applications that bolstered the confidence of the manager. The manager's gut instinct about "Big M"—a market that would be big enough—emboldened that individual to take the risk and to support the project. In the DuPont electron emitter case described earlier, lead scientist Kurt Fincher told us: "The display market is at $8 billion dollars right now . . . and will be in the ball park of maybe $20 billion by the year 2000. Who knows where it's going, but displays are one of maybe three or four absolutely positive things that are going to be technology driven and going to be enormous. To be a part of that is real exciting."

KEYS TO EFFECTIVE INITIAL EVALUATION

The following are the crucial steps in an initial evaluation of a radical idea:

- Build an evaluation team that includes senior business and corporate managers, business development managers, veterans of radical innovation projects, and, when appropriate, outside experts.

- Focus on the commitment of human and financial resources to take the next step, assuming that evaluators like what they see. In most cases, the next step is to attack the most critical uncertainties, questions, and assumptions uncovered during the initial evaluation. According to Nortel Networks's Joanne Hyland, the effectiveness of the initial evaluation process can be enhanced through attention to risk identification and mitigation.

- Develop an evaluation protocol with criteria appropriate for assessing radical innovations. Initial decisions about a growth opportunity should not be based on projections of financial cash flows, market share gains, or the measures typically applied to incremental innovation projects. Rather, the focus should be on the deliverable benefits of the technology—how rich and robust they might be—and on whether the market will be "big enough" if the benefits envisioned for the new technology are delivered. The initial evaluation process is unlikely to answer any of these questions and will probably generate more questions than it answers. Management will be justifiably uncomfortable. But the process should uncover what is known and some of what is unknown about the radical innovation and the perceived business opportunity.

A More Systematic Approach to Grabbing Lightning

The capabilities to generate an abundance of ideas, recognize the few with real business potential, and implement a realistic process of initial evaluation are three competencies that every company needs if it hopes to capture the benefits of radical innovation. Independently, each contributes to better results. These competencies are most effective, however, when they are joined together and embedded within the organization.

We advocate that competencies for idea generation, recognition, and evaluation—and their associated activities—be organized within a structure we call a *radical innovation hub*. A larger company may need a network of hubs. The radical innovation hub would link people with ideas, hunters and gatherers, opportunity evaluators, and key people in corporate functions and operating units. Figure 3-1 is a graphic representation of the radical innovation hub and its links. In this figure, opportunity *gatherers* are located in Business Units A and B and in Corporate R&D. (Of course, they can be established in other parts of the organization—even within alliance partners—that might be a source of radical innovation ideas.) These individuals serve as listening posts—ready, willing, and able to react to radical innovation idea generators. The hub may also assign one or more opportunity *hunters* who proactively seek out promising ideas. In the diagram, the hunter is going after idea generators in Business Unit A and in Corporate R&D. Again, hunters could be sent out to any part of the organization to poke around and to uncover new ideas. With respect to capturing radical innovations, the subject of this chapter, the hub can perform a number of critical functions, which are listed in the box labeled "Radical Innovation Hub." Among these are convening an evaluation panel to consider one or more radical innovation ideas. Four possible outcomes of the evaluation process are indicated in the diagram.

FIGURE 3-1

A RADICAL INNOVATION HUB

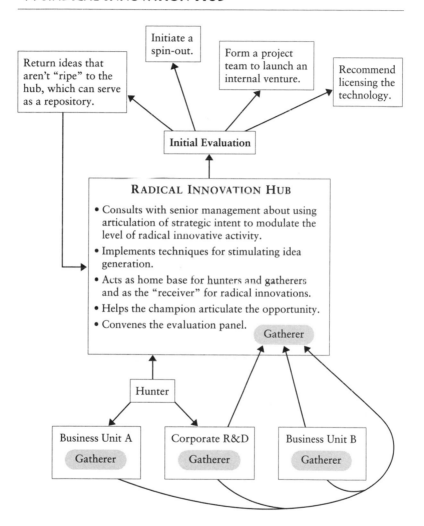

Why a hub? Experience has shown that informal, ad hoc systems leave too much to chance, as illustrated in our earlier discussion of the initial false start in the case of GE's digital X-ray project.[15] Informal networks are short-circuited when key people change positions, leave the company, or retire. Consider these two examples:

One of the companies in our study designated a single new business development manager—an individual with broad experience—and located him in central R&D. There he served as both hunter and gatherer, floating from project to project within R&D. Ultimately, he became so enamored of one project that he joined it as a full-time team member. This effectively ended his usefulness as a wide-roaming hunter on the lookout for promising ideas. The firm lost the benefit of his experience and had to start over with an inexperienced individual. The firm viewed the position as rotational rather than as part of a web of experienced, capable individuals who could reinforce, support, learn from each other, and build an opportunity recognition competency for the organization.

Another company relied heavily on two R&D managers and a research engineer for opportunity recognition and initial evaluation. These three men met periodically over lunch to discuss technical ideas submitted from outside the firm. When the three retired, the function they performed ended.

Unlike these informal approaches, hub structures take responsibility for fuzzy front-end functions. They impose continuity and a system on a catch-as-catch-can set of activities. Hub teams also create a network of idea generators, hunters, and gatherers and actively develop their skills. People like Terry Fadem and internal venturing programs like the one we described at Nortel Networks are critical information nodes for receiving, evaluating, and passing on information to key personnel. Most companies have not formally established idea-receiving nodes.

Each hub acts as a receiver of ideas. It stands ready to respond with quick, back-of the-envelope assessments, and connections to others in the organization who can help innovators explore the viability of their ideas. In this organizational arrangement, a core group of innovation experts implements a systematic approach to evaluation, using a pool of qualified people inside and outside the organization who are skilled at evaluating radical concepts. An appropriate evaluation team is assembled for each radical idea as needed, and hub personnel manage the evaluation process.

At Nortel Networks, Joanne Hyland's New Ventures Program was established to serve as a radical innovation hub. In addition to using a request for proposals to stimulate idea generation, Hyland's hub organization developed a Web site that helped employees get started on articulating ideas. The initial contact person in Hyland's group would engage the idea generator before the idea was fully formulated and help that individual sort out what was known and what was uncertain about the concept.

Once the idea was formally submitted, Hyland's team performed a preliminary screen. If the idea represented a compelling opportunity, a business development specialist worked with the idea generator for a week or more to further define it. Eventually, a three-person team judged the attractiveness of the opportunity, and Hyland decided whether to fund it. Funding at that point did not sanction a formal project; instead, it represented a commitment of resources with the goal of developing a business case for evaluation by senior management. That commitment ranged from several weeks to several months. "The overall competency that we brought as a team," according to Hyland, "was the ability to take technology and translate it into compelling business propositions."

If the business case evaluation resulted in a sanctioned project, the venture development organization was available to provide business incubation services, as described by Hyland:

> There's a supporting skill set that goes into making that happen— including business development, marketing, financial management. There's also the whole softer side—understanding what it means to put a team together, putting the right combination of people together, and the coaching that's necessary to help the team develop the capability to do it on their own. We don't sit on a team, or tell them the way it's going to be done. We're there to coach them and help them to deliver.

DuPont's innovation hub operated less formally than its Nortel Networks counterpart, but implemented many of the same functions. This hub had a very active system of hunters and gatherers. As director of new business development, Terry Fadem operated with a small staff in the heart of the corporate R&D group. Fadem had more than twenty years' experience in business development with DuPont and had done this type of work in many of its business units. The technical grounding he needed to be effective came from his formal science education as well as his experience, which had introduced him to all the relevant science and technology bases of the company. Fadem's greatest value may have been his access to an informal network of scientists, sales representatives, and business unit managers, who regularly phoned him with news about important developments. This made him a central information node and a link between emerging technologies and commercial markets.

To keep track of technologies and markets, Fadem maintained a room with four list-covered white boards. The lists included the following:

- an inventory of key science and technology projects within DuPont;
- all markets in which the firm had a presence and the potential needs in those markets; and
- business concepts currently being pursued within DuPont and the information needed to continue funding.

"It's messy," he concluded, "but it has a lot of discipline to it."

In describing his role, Fadem said: "I function as the catalyst inside R&D. I'll say to a scientist: 'I know you just invented this yesterday, but I see a market for this thing. Let's sit down and talk about it.' Because our new business development unit is out here close to the experimental activity, we can have those daily interactions and promote an awareness of 'what's the world view' versus 'what's my project.'"

BEYOND THE FUZZY FRONT END

A radical project that emerges intact from initial evaluation has moved beyond the fuzzy front end. But it quickly finds itself under pressure to resolve uncertainties and provide convincing evidence that the commercial promise that attracted attention initially is not smoke and mirrors. Reducing uncertainties to permit the transition from project to commercialization is typically the task of project management. However, we found that traditional project management approaches were inadequate for coping with the chaos of the radical innovation environment. A new set of project management capabilities is required. This is the focus of chapter 4.

CHAPTER 4

LIVING WITH CHAOS

MANAGING RADICAL INNOVATION PROJECTS

During the past several decades, relentless global competition has driven established firms to make great strides in the science of project management. Consultants, researchers, and practitioners have compiled a substantial project management knowledge base.[1] They have developed management systems and tools that enable project teams to move big, complex undertakings along quickly and efficiently. As a result, leading firms have become much more adept at continual improvement and incremental innovation related to their existing products and processes. Management of radical innovation projects, however, remains more art than science. Because radical innovation projects are faced with high uncertainty on multiple dimensions, the sophisticated management tools that work so well in the incremental innovation environment are not adequate. Hence, new tools must be added to the traditional project management toolbox. In this chapter we explore project management approaches that—rather than reflecting the command-and-control structures of traditional project management—address the uncertainties and complexities of radical innovation projects.

Traditional approaches to project management are based on planning and controlling resources (people, equipment, material, and financing).[2] They operate on the premise that managers can predict future results based on their wealth of past experience and knowledge. Common tools used in project management are Gantt charts, which plot resource requirements of activities along a time scale; PERT/CPM, which map multiple tasks and identify relationships and conflicts among related activities; and stage-gate systems, which provide review and decision-making opportunities at milestones along the project path. Uncertainties can be treated as exceptions to the well-defined development path. The project manager focuses on applying resources appropriately, completing the tasks according to plan, and achieving the project objectives on time and within budget. Deviations from the plan are considered poor performance.[3]

The complex set of uncertainties in the radical innovation environment makes "management by exception" impractical. Dealing with the chaos of radical innovation requires different project management systems and competencies, as illustrated by the GE digital X-ray project story that follows.

THE GE DIGITAL X-RAY PROJECT

In 1993 Bruce Griffing was on the verge of resigning as project manager of the GE digital X-ray project. The project had hit a stone wall. GE Medical Systems (GEMS) had initially provided its blessing and financial support, but along the way, the division head had become an obstructionist. He was focused on increasing his division's short-term financial performance through efficiencies and cost containment and saw the digital X-ray project as a major distraction and a drain on short-term cash flow. As a result, he backed away from the project.

With GEMS's financial support gone, Griffing struggled to keep the project going. The digital X-ray system had proven its technological feasibility, but the project lacked the funding to build and test a prototype. Griffing needed resource acquisition skills that generally would not have been necessary in a fully funded incremental innovation project. Fortunately, he received the support of his boss, Lonnie Edelheit, head of GE corporate R&D labs. Edelheit took the case to CEO Jack Welch, who agreed to support the project out of discretionary corporate funds—an unusual step.

Griffing had to depart from traditional project management procedures again when R&D funding from DARPA and the National Cancer Institute (NCI) became available for breast cancer research. Griffing redirected technology development activities to mammography applications in order to acquire this funding. Still later in the project life cycle, the project's manufacturing partner was unable to achieve the target for manufacturing yield. Since the project was not ready to transition to the business unit, Griffing was forced to adopt an unusual strategy: establishing a manufacturing capability within GE Central Research & Development.

Had the digital X-ray project been part of an incremental innovation, it would likely have been dead the moment the head of GEMS withdrew his support. The normal budget process would have killed it. The stage gate–like project management system that had been developed, refined, and deployed with great success throughout GE's business units would have flashed a red light as soon as the manufacturing partner failed to achieve acceptable yields. Traditional project management did not provide mechanisms for getting around these roadblocks; Griffing had to improvise and take tactical detours. Any one of these unanticipated discontinuities could have killed the project, if traditional project management thinking had been applied.

In spite of all the organizational and resource uncertainties faced by the digital X-ray project, Griffing and his team had it relatively easy compared with other projects in our study. Technical development in this case, while challenging, proceeded reasonably smoothly. And given the long history of involvement of GE Medical Systems in medical imaging, market uncertainty was relatively low. Still there were numerous potential showstoppers among the organizational and resource challenges.

Radical project managers normally confront uncertainties and discontinuities as central aspects of functioning, rather than as reasons to disband. Overcoming project discontinuities and progressively reducing uncertainties are the overarching goals of the radical innovation project team and its manager. They are successful to the extent they can prepare the project for acceptance by an existing business unit, a new unit, or a spin-off company for commercialization. But no one will take the handoff until major technical and market uncertainties are reduced or eliminated. The receiving unit must be confident that the technology will work, that it has the features and attributes desired in the marketplace, and that it can be produced reliably. It must also have assurance that customers and applications are well enough understood so that sales, marketing, and distribution functions can be implemented successfully and that projected revenues and profits can be achieved.

As we note later in chapter 8, it is difficult and unusual for radical innovation projects to reach the level of maturity expected by most business units before handoff. There are typically lingering uncertainties needing to be resolved. Hence, in chapter 8 we advocate the use of a "transition team" to accelerate the project through the final stages of the maturation process. Even so, before the transition team takes charge, the project team must get the project ready. There must be a high level of confidence, built by the project team, that the market promise is there and that the technology, in the form and application domain chosen, will deliver a fundamentally new and valuable set of benefits.

The greater the understanding of the complex mosaic of uncertainties, the more effective the project team will be in undertaking its tasks. To set the context for understanding the keys to effective project management, we characterize the chaotic nature of the environment that is the world of the radical innovation project manager as follows:

THE REDUCTION OF UNCERTAINTIES IS NEITHER PROGRESSIVE NOR SEQUENTIAL. Although the general trend in successful projects is uncertainty reduction, the accumulation of learning and the occurrence of unanticipated crises cause the levels of the four types of uncertainty to rise and fall throughout the project. Sometimes a project reaches a level of development and then regresses to a less mature level. Thus the project manager's job in the radical innovation context is less one of listing tasks, delegating them, and controlling progress, and more one of monitoring where the project stands on each uncertainty dimension and making decisions about which uncertainties to attack at any point in time. In most cases, at most times, the project team will not pay attention to all of the four dimensions simultaneously. The project manager must lead the team in adapting and redirecting its focus as necessary to keep the project moving.

CONFRONTING ORGANIZATIONAL OR RESOURCE UNCERTAINTIES REQUIRES DIFFERENT PROJECT MANAGEMENT CAPABILITIES FROM THOSE NEEDED TO DEAL WITH TECHNICAL AND MARKET UNCERTAINTIES. In the fuzzy front end, the project teams we studied typically operated within R&D and were composed mostly of R&D personnel. These individuals were prepared to deal with technical uncertainties and often were sufficiently cosmopolitan that they could engage in early market learning. However, they were usually ill-prepared to deal with the high levels of organization and resource uncertainty that arose because of the need to manage interfaces with a wide variety of internal and external partners.

THE UNCERTAINTIES ARE INTERACTIVE. This is true for all product development projects, but it presents greater challenges for management of radical innovation projects who must deal with more and higher uncertainty. For example, the reaction of a lead user to a prototype may cause minor changes in the implementation of an incremental innovation but a major redirection in the development of a radical innovation.

COPING WITH PROJECT DISCONTINUITIES CAN TEMPORARILY SWAMP EFFORTS TO REDUCE UNCERTAINTY. Major crises require rapid and aggressive responses. The project team must deal with them quickly and successfully or run the risk of losing organization support. The Otis project provides an example.

THE OTIS ODYSSEY ELEVATOR PROJECT

The Otis Odyssey bidirectional elevator project was going along just fine. The technology had been developed quickly, and a demonstration system was already set up in a company facility. Market uncertainty was likewise reduced when Asian builders indicated their interest in putting up a very high building for which the Otis elevator system would be the people mover. Then the Asian market crashed, putting the project's first installation on hold. The project team was unable to quickly respond with a proposal for alternative applications for the technology, and Otis's CEO decided to delay additional investment in Odyssey pending the receipt of a firm order.

RADICAL INNOVATION PROJECT MANAGEMENT TOOLS

As indicated in chapter 2, the set of uncertainties will vary in makeup and intensity from project to project and within any given project over time. Hence, radical innovation project management tools must be selected and adapted to fit the situation—in itself a project management challenge. Not all projects will need to use all the tools in the radical innovation project management toolbox, and the tools that are selected may need to be modified to fit the specific situation the project team faces. The set of tools offered in this chapter is merely representative of the possible tool range. Project managers may find that some are appropriate to their situation and others are not.

SET THE EXPECTATIONS OF RADICAL INNOVATION TEAM MEMBERS

Team members who are excited about the promise of technical discovery are highly motivated to work on development of radical innovations. Yet, they are often unaware of the nature of the radical innovation life cycle. As indicated earlier, they may be unfamiliar with the multidimensionality of the challenges that they will face and not be prepared to recognize and deal with them. This lack of preparedness increases the likelihood of project crises, making project management that much more difficult.

Project managers and radical innovation veterans associated with the radical innovation hub, as discussed in chapter 3, can jump-start projects by educating team members about the radical innovation life cycle. Setting expectations about the nature of the context—both within the project and with respect to the interface with the rest of the organization—can help team members accept the ambiguity that characterizes most radical innovation projects—especially in the fuzzy front end. Ensuring that team members are well aware that they will have to deal with all four types of uncertainties, not just technical uncertainties, is critical to increasing the effectiveness of the project's team. It can also help catalyze the intensity and focus needed to attack crises quickly and decisively. Finally, this is a critical first step in preparing the team to use the next project management tool.

IDENTIFY AND TRACK UNCERTAINTIES

This may seem like a contradiction in terms. After all, if a project team can identify, define, and catalog the uncertainties, are they really uncertainties? Without doubt, a firm that has a radical innovation hub and accumulates learning will become increasingly adept at understanding and dealing with uncertainties. However, implementing this project management tool will always be a daunting challenge, even for the most sophisticated of radical innovation teams. The projects in our study revealed that there is a big difference between identifying an uncertainty and resolving it. For example, the project team may know that its seed funding will run out in six months, but not know where it will find the funding to continue the project. Likewise, it may be an absolute certainty that the project will not survive the next progress review unless a manufacturing partner is secured, but the team may be uncertain about the characteristics of an ideal partner, may not yet have identified a short list of candidates, or may not have devised a mutually acceptable partnering arrangement. The project may have a mandate from senior management to attack a new market with the radical innovation, but have little or no knowledge of the market and how to enter it. It may be clear that significant technical breakthroughs must be achieved in one or more technical areas, but how to do that may be highly uncertain. Each of these examples occurred in one or more of the projects in our study.[4]

Cataloging uncertainties is the first step in confronting the chaos of radical innovation projects. It provides a foundation that allows the team to begin to explore and identify alternative paths to resolving the uncertainties. The project team can rank them with respect to importance and criticality of timing and can make decisions about allocation of time and attention to dealing with them. All four categories of uncertainty—technology, market, resource, and organization—should be considered. Active and ongoing monitoring will enable the team to assess the degree to which each uncertainty has been reduced, add new ones that have appeared, and reprioritize uncertainty reduction activities.

The natural human tendency is to confront uncertainties with which we are more comfortable and put the others on the back shelf. This is a dangerous problem for teams composed mostly or solely of scientific or engineering personnel, who may prefer to focus on technical challenges. In one of the projects we studied, the team succeeded in signing up one of the firm's major customers to serve as an early test site for the prototype system. But they were so focused on technical feasibility that they hadn't thought through nontechnical issues and what questions should be asked. Hence, they neither prepared the lead user for the nature of the prototype nor provided guidance regarding the feedback they sought—beyond technical feasibility. As a result, the results of the prototype test were unsatisfactory, which in turn put the brakes on the development of the innovation.

Technical challenges are without a doubt important, but they are only part of the puzzle that must be resolved. Failing to recognize and confront resource, marketing, and organizational uncertainties increases the difficulty of managing radical innovation projects and the likelihood that one of these uncertainties will turn out to be a project killer.

Capable project managers will recognize the difficulty—perhaps impossibility—of confronting all the project uncertainties at the same time. By identifying and tracking them, the project team can focus its efforts on addressing some uncertainties while choosing to delay dealing with others, or even to outsource them to an internal or external partner. However, the team must understand and evaluate the trade-offs when *choosing not to learn* in a particular domain for some period of time. Generally, because there is interaction among the uncertainties, there is danger in avoiding or being disconnected from the resolution of an uncertainty.

One of our project participants chose to focus on manufacturing the radical innovation and to outsource market development to partners. Because the project team missed out on the hands-on experience of interacting with lead users, the project stumbled when the market didn't respond to the initial form of the product. The project team had a difficult time sorting out whether the problem was the product form itself or the manner in which the partner was developing the market. When teams choose to partner to compensate for missing capabilities or resources, they need to stay sufficiently connected to the experience of their partners to be able to absorb and incorporate their partner's learning.

It would be reassuring to be able to point to one or more of our case studies in which uncertainty identification and tracking were successfully implemented. But this idea grew out of our observation that most teams neglect—or are "fuzzy" about—many of the uncertainties that show up across many projects. (Perhaps this difficulty is the origin of the phrase "fuzzy front end.") The inability to get their arms around the full set of uncertainties contributes to the ad hoc, crisis-oriented management practices that dominate radical innovation projects.

DEVELOP AND IMPLEMENT A LEARNING PLAN

Typically for incremental innovation projects, a business case and project plan are developed, replete with Gantt charts and stage-gate decision-making criteria. They are used to guide and control the activities of the project team and to assess progress. Requiring the same kind of plan and business case is counterproductive early in the radical innovation lifecycle due to the high uncertainties experienced.

Our case studies revealed several creative approaches used by project teams to cope with the inappropriateness of traditional formal project plans. In one case, the team changed the plan's revenue projections on the fly to meet management's requirements for funding. In another case, the project manager told us he kept two sets of plans. One was for the team's internal use only. It included stretch goals and connected responsibility for tasks with team members. The second plan was used in discussions with management. It had much more conservative goals and didn't associate tasks with names of team members in order to protect them in case projections couldn't be met. Finally, several teams led by exceptionally maverick champions simply did not keep any such planning documents.

A *learning plan*—an alternative to a typical project management planning tool—is a more appropriate and useful tool for radical project management.[5] A learning plan does the following:

- incorporates the results of uncertainty cataloging;
- spells out assumptions about each uncertainty;
- presents approaches for testing each assumption and resolving each critical uncertainty through experimentation and learning;
- prioritizes the assumption-testing tasks and defines a path for moving forward as quickly and as inexpensively as possible; and
- serves as a log of the project's history—serving to guide not only the project but also the development of the database for the radical innovation hub.

Just as uncertainty identification and tracking must be a continual process, a learning plan must be revised on an ongoing basis to reflect what has already been learned and what remains to be discovered. In this sense, this tool is more for monitoring and guiding progress rather than for rigidly controlling and directing the completion of tasks. Progress against plan should be monitored by checking off assumptions that have been tested. The learning that has resulted, the decisions that have been made, and the redirection that has occurred as a consequence of that learning should be documented. The idea behind a dynamic learning plan is reflected in the comment of one project member: "We're going through a learning curve for improving the performance of the technology and reducing the cost. The technology is being designed differently and built differently as we learn."

Even a temporary increase in the uncertainty inventory that comes from a clearer understanding and definition of uncertainties can be seen as progress. According to one of our respondents, evaluation in a learning plan is based on "learning per dollar spent" rather than tracking task completion against budget and schedule.[6] An improvement in the team's understanding of the underlying uncertainties can accelerate progress toward project maturity, even if sometimes progress is uneven—two steps forward, one step backward.

The respondents from our participating companies and the senior technology managers who participated in our workshops and think tanks generally assume that once uncertainties are reduced sufficiently, the project team can adopt tried-and-true project management techniques. However, we found that radical innovation projects have surprisingly high residual uncertainty—even during and after the transition to operating status. The project team needs to retain a strong orientation toward learning and redirecting, and a healthy caution about relying completely on traditional project management tools. This is so counterintuitive that we have devoted an entire chapter (chapter 8) to the challenges of managing the transition process. Even late in the radical innovation life cycle, a learning plan is more appropriate in most cases than a traditional project plan.

ADOPT A RESOURCE ACQUISITION STRATEGY

Radical innovation projects often operate with minimal financial resources, as we saw in the DuPont Biomax case—especially early in the radical innovation life cycle. The traditional budget *allocation* process used in the mainstream operating environment doesn't get the job done for radical innovation projects. Rather than simply vying for a budgetary allocation, project managers must have a *resource acquisition* mentality.[7] Often this starts with bootstrapping—using slack resources available to team members or provided by their formal and informal sponsors. Resource acquisition demands much more attention and greater intensity from project managers than they anticipate. Identifying sources of available resources, figuring out how to get them, and procuring them are all aspects of a radical innovation project manager's job. In every one of the projects in our study, acquiring resources from outside the firm was as important as accessing internal resources. Again, this project management task is so critical to the survival and ultimate success of the project—and its difficulty is so commonly underestimated—that we dedicate chapter 7 to an in-depth discussion of this topic.

MANAGE INTERFACES WITH THE MAINSTREAM ORGANIZATION

In addition to dealing with technical, market, and resource uncertainties, project managers were often confronted with the need to manage a difficult—sometimes apathetic, sometimes hostile—organizational context. Because of the underlying conflict between radical innovation and mainstream activities, there is a popular assumption that radical projects should be isolated from the mainstream organization, if only for their own protection. More than a few innovators who have abandoned big corporations for smaller, more entrepreneurial firms are outspoken in the conviction that radical innovation within established companies is next to impossible. Some researchers concur and recommend locating innovation projects far from the mainstream, and, if they are successful, keeping them far away. If the new business displaces the old, so be it.[8]

For projects that are self-contained and have organizational validity and guaranteed support, isolation may be a good option. But few radical innovation projects fit this profile. For the rest—the great majority—project teams have significant deficiencies in knowledge, skills, and resources. The sponsoring organization is often the best place to find and acquire those missing ingredients. Isolation may protect the project from the counterproductive forces within the mainstream, but it also cuts the project off from important skills and resources. Further, it eliminates the opportunity for the firm to assimilate the learning and stretching that the radical innovation project team has achieved.[9] In spite of conflicts with the mainstream, every project in our study benefited from interactions with the rest of the organization. The connection helped them to survive and succeed.

A large firm is an amazing storehouse of accumulated know-how, which can be tapped through informal networks that bring together scientists, business unit managers, sales people, marketers, and people who control financial and laboratory resources.[10] Radical innovators who have been around their companies for a while build up extensive informal networks of people who will support them—either because they believe in the importance of the innovation or because they have faith in the innovator.

Virtually every manager we interviewed spoke about the informal networks that allowed their projects to reduce uncertainties and gain needed capabilities and resources. As one manager put it: "There's a secret way the company operates. Because of the way in which managers have grown up around here, we have these internal networks. That's what makes this place work." A project manager at another firm underscored the importance of his informal network within R&D when he said: "Basically we have no budget. But I can use my network to get help from people within central R&D. They don't cost me any money. As long as I don't spend any money, I can get access to brains and bodies."

If the project operates within the organization (and not as a remote skunk works), the project manager must protect it from the destructive elements of the mainstream business while making the most of the mainstream resources. If this sounds like a case of having your cake and eating it too, it is. It can be accomplished if the leader is skillful at positioning the project so it can benefit from the munificence of the parent firm while avoiding the drag on the project created by organizational resistance.

A radical innovation hub with a track record of success can be highly effective in helping the project leader manage the interface between the project and the rest of the organization. A hub that has been around for a while will have its own informal network that can complement the network of the project leader. The hub can be a conduit for money, human resources, advice, facilities, and legitimacy flowing to the project—through both informal and formal channels.

BUILD PROJECT LEGITIMACY

One key difference between incremental and radical projects involves legitimacy in the eyes of the organization.[11] Incremental innovation projects enjoy high organizational legitimacy. They are generally funded through normal budgetary allocation processes and are viewed as activities that will soon contribute to the bottom line. Radical innovation projects don't enjoy this legitimacy, or its advantages. It is not hard to see why. They will not contribute to the bottom line any time soon, if ever. They don't help with Job One—doing current activities cheaper, faster, and better.

Legitimacy is important because it provides access to the resources and capabilities that every radical project needs, as Bruce Griffing discovered when CEO Jack Welch signaled his interest in the digital X-ray project. Legitimacy also counters organizational resisters to radical innovation.

One of the objectives of the leaders who manage the organizational interfaces should be to work toward establishing formal legitimacy to complement the informal legitimacy embodied in informal networks.[12] Here are some things that project managers in our study did to enhance project legitimacy.

COMMUNICATE. Effective project managers kept up a steady stream of communication with key supporters and team members. At Texas Instruments, the rapid growth of the Digital Light Processing (DLP)[13] project created a tremendous communication challenge—both within the team and between the project and the rest of the firm. The project manager contracted with an outside firm to establish a sophisticated and secure internal communications system to keep key constituencies abreast of technical and business developments. Aside from providing typical project status reports, effective communication casts the inevitable setbacks and little failures as steps in the learning process and highlights successes—even small ones. Internal forums to keep scientific and business people informed of the technology and its potential applications can also contribute to establishing legitimacy.

SELL THE DESIRABILITY OF PREEMPTING OTHER INNOVATORS. A project gains legitimacy when the larger organization is convinced that it is an important defensive move—in other words, "If we fail to seize this opportunity, one of our competitors will." It was for exactly this reason that Air Products established a consortium to respond to a Department of Energy (DOE) request for proposals. If a competitor had received DOE funding to develop the ceramic membrane technology sought by the agency, those technological advances could have been used to encroach on Air Products's primary business. Air Products was unwilling to take that chance.

DRIVE TOWARD DEMONSTRABLE RESULTS TO PROVIDE JUSTIFICATION FOR FUNDING. IBM's Bernie Meyerson was famous for proclaiming "data wins." When the resisters within his firm waved their arms in protest, he waved hard data in their faces. Progress in reducing uncertainties not only quiets the naysayers, but also establishes legitimacy for those in the organization who want to be supporters. Similarly, the test results from the composting facility confirming the biodegradability of DuPont's Biomax contributed to Terry Fadem's willingness to adopt the orphaned project and to provide the funding to keep it going.

To the extent that an early-stage project can bootstrap its activities through a small core team of dedicated volunteers, it may be seen achieving results without visibly consuming resources. IBM's Meyerson and his band of renegades were able to make tremendous progress using bootlegged time and resources in the development of the silicon germanium chip technology during a time when the technology was outside IBM's strategic framework. When CEO Lou Gerstner dramatically shifted corporate strategy to include the sale of chips to external customers, Meyerson's project quickly gained legitimacy. A track record of results makes formal funding an easier decision for senior management.

Finally, converting the technology into a prototype that can be demonstrated can help establish legitimacy. At Texas

Instruments, the demonstration prototype was called the "lab queen." Project team members were used to "hauling out the lab queen" to show to senior management, potential customers, and marketing partners. This was important for convincing key supporters that the radical innovation was technically feasible, thereby contributing to the legitimacy of the project. At Air Products, an early demonstration unit was placed in one of the firm's own plants to prove to senior management that oxygen could be generated using this novel technology. That action strengthened the organization's commitment to continue to fund the project.

ATTRACT THE SUPPORT OF LEAD USERS. The testimonials of potential lead users—particularly if they are well-known or prestigious firms—lends the imprimatur of legitimacy to projects and reduces market uncertainty. In the IBM silicon germanium case, Meyerson got the attention of researchers at several firms when he presented the results of his early scientific experiments at a professional conference. After preliminary discussions, members of those firms began to see the applicability of Meyerson's work to their own innovation trajectories. Meyerson asked them to provide testimonials to that effect to IBM's senior management. Although the work that Meyerson was doing was not within the strategic framework of IBM at the time, the enthusiasm of such prestigious firms was enough to get Gerstner's attention and to help IBM's senior management understand the implications of Meyerson's discovery for IBM's future.

LINK UP WITH A "BRAND NAME" PARTNER. A connection with a partner organization that management respects may solve more than half of the legitimacy problem: "If XYZ Corporation is taking this project seriously, maybe we should too." If the partner has deep pockets, so much the better. TI technical champions went outside of the firm to seek technical validation of the applications envisioned for DLP technology. This team engaged a current TI customer and potential user of the DLP technology and validation was provided. As a result of this engagement a TI product group picked up the challenge and with it a set of product requirements as a roadmap causing the highest management levels within TI to track DLP technology's progress. The DLP technology rapidly evolved to the current architectural success.

ASSEMBLE AN INFLUENTIAL BOARD OF ADVISERS. A board of "brand name" people provides legitimacy, even as it provides their insights and support. Including key managers from the operating unit helps assure "buy in" and resources. As indicated in chapter 3, adding credible external members to the board can provide additional legitimacy. This approach was implemented at Air Products by project manager Doug Bennett. Bennett staffed his advisory board with senior managers from the appropriate operating units and from corporate R&D, as well as a key manager from Ceramatec, Air Products's primary external technical development partner.

BUILD BRIDGES TO THE BUSINESS UNIT THAT WILL BE THE EVENTUAL HOME OF THE PROJECT'S TECHNOLOGY OR PRODUCT. For those projects that are likely to transition into an existing business unit, effective project managers find appropriate ways to make connections to that unit. The advisory board approach mentioned earlier is just one. The business unit can be formally solicited for advice or for recommendations of customers who might be candidates to try out a prototype. Even better, the members of the project team can develop a deeper relationship by fostering an informal network that can become a huge asset when it is time to transition the project into the business unit. In the case of the GE digital X-ray project—even though the GE Medical Systems division head was a resister, not a supporter— the project team had an extensive working relationship with marketing and engineering personnel in the business unit who had contacts within lead user firms.

ATTRACT "SUPERSTARS" TO THE TEAM. Superstars enjoy an aura of legitimacy, and that aura can rub off on the teams they join. In the Biomax case, there were serious concerns about whether the new material would satisfy evolving standards for biodegradable material. Since the original project leader was viewed with skepticism as a promoter with limited credibility, respected

DuPont Fellow Henn Kilkson was recruited to the team. It was understood that Dr. Kilkson would not lend his good name to the project and its claims unless his high standards were met.

GET THE RIGHT PERSON FOR THE JOB

We have been looking at suggestions that any project manager can use to reduce the four uncertainties surrounding every radical innovation project. Now let's examine the personal traits and capabilities that allow project managers to effectively lead radical innovation projects.

In eight of our twelve cases, technical champions assumed project management roles in the earliest stages. These individuals generally had lots of energy, enthusiastic optimism, commitment to their work, and an incredible ability to sell their vision. These traits are powerful assets for any project manager, but are insufficient. There are other equally important traits and capabilities required for long-term project success. Managers of radical projects must be comfortable with uncertainty, they must be capable of setting a course and getting others to buy into project goals, and they must have sufficient flexibility so that they can handle course corrections as progress unfolds. They should see the job as one of learning and leading, rather than controlling and managing. Effective project managers bring technical know-how, personal credibility, and informal networks to their projects. Organizational skills are just as important as enthusiasm and leadership; a project manager must be adept at the organization game.

Project managers need a deep understanding of the dynamics of the radical innovation life cycle. Some project managers we interviewed were clearly unprepared for the stops and starts and the seemingly chaotic course of events they experienced. Many were surprised, frustrated, confused, and often overwhelmed by the morass they were charged with managing, and they struggled to learn as they moved forward. As educators, we cannot help but think that the capabilities of project leaders could be improved through training.

KEYS TO EFFECTIVE RADICAL INNOVATION PROJECT MANAGEMENT

Implementing some or all of the project management tools described in this chapter, as appropriate for each project, is critical to success. We summarize them here as seven keys to effective radical innovation project management:

SET THE EXPECTATIONS OF RADICAL INNOVATION TEAM MEMBERS. This lays the foundation that enables the team to counter the difficult challenges of a radical innovation project.

IDENTIFY AND TRACK UNCERTAINTIES. With a sophisticated understanding of the radical innovation life cycle, the project team will be able to identify and track the full range of uncertainties confronting the project and will incorporate them into the project's learning plan.

DEVELOP AND IMPLEMENT A LEARNING PLAN. A traditional project plan isn't suited for managing a radical innovation project. It is designed for a command-and-control situation, in which there is limited and manageable uncertainty. By comparison, the radical innovation environment requires a rapid and inexpensive probe-and-learn management approach. A learning plan that promotes adaptability in response to learning is more useful.

ADOPT A RESOURCE ACQUISITION STRATEGY. An effective project manager will be skillful in accessing and procuring sources of project financing and missing competencies—from both informal and formal internal sources, as well as external sources.

MANAGE THE INTERFACES BETWEEN THE TEAM AND MAINSTREAM ORGANIZATION AND EXTERNAL PARTNERS. The project manager and team members will be aware of the critical impact on project success of their relationships with internal and external partners, which will likely change dramatically over the course of the project. They will be adept at managing interfaces—fostering positive exchanges and blocking or deflecting the negative elements that can slow or stop their project.

BUILD PROJECT LEGITIMACY. An effective project manager will protect the project and facilitate the flow of support by building legitimacy in the eyes of the mainstream organization. This can be accomplished through a variety of means, including attracting individuals to the project team with high personal credibility, appropriating the credibility of internal and external partners, and communicating the accomplishments of the team in implementing the learning plan.

GET THE RIGHT PERSON FOR THE JOB. It is critically important to get the right person for the job of project manager, whether it is the technical champion who accepted the role of project manager in the fuzzy front end when there was no one else to take it on; the radical innovation hub personnel who facilitated idea generation, opportunity recognition, and the initial evaluation that led to formally establishing the project; or someone from senior management who took on the role of project sponsor. Given that the job may change as the project matures, it may also be important to change project managers when a different skill set is required to keep the project moving toward commercialization.

Successful implementation of the seven keys to radical innovation project management increases the likelihood that the project will stay alive and continue moving forward. In most projects, early progress is marked by resolution of technical uncertainties. As confidence in technical feasibility increases, market issues take on increasing importance. The project team must find ways to learn about markets that don't yet exist. Traditional market research approaches aren't up to the task. A new set of market learning capabilities is required—the focus of chapter 5.

CHAPTER 5

LEARNING ABOUT MARKETS FOR RADICAL INNOVATION

THE MARKET LEARNING CHALLENGE NEEDS TO BE FACED VERY early on in the project, for several reasons. First, market insights and choices impact the direction of technical development. Second, market understanding is critical to the development of the business model—in other words, how the firm intends to make money from its innovation. Third, funding decision makers are wary of a technology in search of a market. They are more likely to support a project team that can show progress in identifying promising applications possibilities. Fourth, for those projects that have an obvious eventual home within an existing business unit, demonstrating market understanding enhances the receptivity of the business unit to support the project. This chapter deals with the challenge of understanding markets that may not yet exist or that will be fundamentally transformed by the introduction of the radical innovation.

Some important distinctions about different types of radical innovations and their relationships to current operations were identified in chapter 1. Those types include innovations that take the organization outside its current strategic boundaries; those that operate in the white spaces between existing business units; and those that strengthen the firm's position in familiar markets through significant technological advances.

With respect to market learning, projects working on the first two types of innovation are very similar, but those working on the third type face very different challenges. For projects that are leaps forward in the current business, market uncertainty is considered rather low. There are presumably no serious changes considered in the business model; it is aligned as closely as possible with the operating unit's current operations. The infrastructure for contacting customers, understanding markets, setting prices, and delivering products is well developed.[1]

Our discussion of market learning issues focuses primarily on challenges facing firms moving into unfamiliar and undeveloped markets—the first two types of radical innovation described above. We caution, however, that the tyranny of known markets can easily cause complacency in market learning activities for firms operating in familiar markets. In every case we studied, at some point project team members recognized that, in order to leverage the opportunity to the fullest, new market domains would have to be developed.

Once initial opportunity evaluation has taken place and initial technical feasibility has been established, myriad questions arise about markets, such as, Who's likely to benefit from this advance? What performance and cost level must we meet before any market will consider us? These must be considered in order to build confidence in the viability of the opportunity, to gain internal support, and to clarify the numerous options that the technical development trajectory might take.

The Air Products case illustrates three main points about how radical innovation teams learn about new markets. First, the team did not start by studying *the largest market*, but rather by studying a market that they believed *would benefit most* from their technology. Second, traditional market research techniques were not used; instead, the company relied on anthropological, experiential techniques and moved quickly from market to market. Third, through its observations, Air Products derived a set of measures that helped assess the usefulness of its technology in various applications.

AIR PRODUCTS: EXPLORING NEW MARKETS

In the mid 1980s, Mike Carolan, a research scientist in the Gases Group of Air Products and Chemicals Corporation, recognized the potential impact of applying ceramic membrane technology to the production of oxygen. This insight came from reading the many scientific journals that crossed his desk. Ceramics technology offered the promise of highly selective oxygen removal from ambient air. A significant percentage of Air Products's business derived from the large-scale production of oxygen for use in manufacturing. If this technology could be made to work at an industrial scale, it could conceivably meet a long-term objective of the company: to significantly reduce the price of tonnage oxygen generation.

Though the opportunity was clear, the technological path was not. Air Products eventually drew up an agreement with Ceramatec, a small firm with competencies in ceramics research and manufacturing. Interestingly, Ceramatec had developed an idea similar to the one pursued by Air Products, but had conceived of a much different application: the generation of oxygen for small-scale users. The small-scale application represented a totally new market opportunity. Here, the benefits afforded by ceramics membrane technology were distinctly different from the dramatic cost reduction identified as the key benefit for tonnage oxygen users. For these small-scale users, a portable oxygen-generating unit that provided process oxygen on demand at any work site would eliminate the need for ordering, delivering, inventorying, and moving heavy oxygen cylinders—the established industry infrastructure of the time. It would also eliminate associated dangers and chances of shortages in the supply of cylinders at critical times.

Thus, Air Products found itself with a technology capable of serving two distinctly different markets: big industrial customers and small users. It decided to approach each through a different project: the first, MEOS (Mixed Electrolyte Oxygen Separation), would seek industrial-level, on-site applications for tonnage oxygen; the second, SEOS (Solid Electrolyte Oxygen Separation), would concentrate on a portable, small-scale version of the same technology. Since the SEOS application appeared to be the easier of the two, it was attacked first. SEOS had the potential to destroy a mature industry infrastructure and encourage new application markets to emerge. But where should the team begin in tapping that potential? Who would benefit? What conditions would maximize the technology's advantage? And which application areas experienced those particular conditions?

While Air Products's scientists set out to prove the technical feasibility of the small-scale oxygen generator, other team members began generating application ideas. Most were in established markets involving the existing pool of customers for stored oxygen. These included scrap yards that had to cut metal, metal cutting shops, and hospitals. Other markets that had no connection to Air Products at the time (e.g., restaurants) were also added to the list as logical beneficiaries of this technology.

The team's next job was to learn more about how these markets currently used oxygen and to evaluate the conditions under which the differences that SEOS offered were perceived as valuable. A new member, Jeff Knopf, was added to the team to explore potential applications for the technology. Knopf had a chemical engineering degree, but had migrated into sales and account management. He had been successful at understanding user needs and developing insights, based on his technical training, for solving customers' problems. He had also demonstrated business acumen in developing new customers.

Knopf made scrap yards the initial focus of his hunt for applications. Scrap yards did not represent the greatest commercial promise, but they gave Knopf a chance to understand the value of the technology. As he observed metal cutters in local scrap yards, several things stood out. First, these workers did not leave the oxygen tanks on continuously, but turned them on and off as needed. They also moved them about the yard to get to the pieces of metal that needed cutting. SEOS could not maintain necessary flux levels unless oxygen flowed continuously. And frequent movement required that the unit be turned off. Knopf brought SEOS's chief engineer, Steve Russek, along on his scrap yard forays so that he could see the problem and consider its implications. They drew a set of graphs that expressed the envelopes of value the scrap yard market would perceive. These detailed the flux rates and purity levels needed by a market if it were to find SEOS valuable. This insight had been gained by watching scrap yard workers in the course of their workday.

Metal cutting shops were Knopf's next sector for investigation. These shops represented a larger market, and one where the unit was on constantly. His investigative approach was the same: observation of work coupled with discussion with shop employees about the value they perceived from the potential new delivery system. Similar investigations followed as new commercial development personnel joined the team and as the team learned more about where the technology was and was not valued. The more promising application areas were analyzed for size and potential market value.

Over the next two years, more than ten possible applications, ranging from metal cutting to medical uses, were investigated. Throughout the period of exploration, a tight linkage was maintained between the technical and the commercial development sides of the team. Since the direction of technology development was heavily dependent on market-based discoveries, every insight that the commercial development people drew from their fieldwork was discussed at length with the scientists.

This case describes how market learning in new or unfamiliar markets really happens. No surveys of large samples of customers were used. Instead, the team carefully observed numerous small samples. No market research department was involved. Instead, the work was done by experienced market listeners and their technical counterparts on the project team. Instead of immediately focusing on big markets, the team aimed at discovering the characteristics of a market that valued the innovation highly. These characteristics of market learning in the project reflect common patterns we observed throughout the projects in our study.

MARKET LEARNING:
DIFFERENT QUESTIONS, DIFFERENT METHODS

Radical innovators generally have only the outlines of a very big picture. While incremental innovators benefit from early customer input, their radical counterparts must operate in the dark, since customers seldom have a context for understanding the product or its capabilities. Neither the final product nor its applications can be described reliably. Furthermore, contacts between innovators and the corporation's marketing professionals (and their methodologies) are generally nonexistent early in the development process. Laboratory researchers aren't even sure what questions to ask prospective customers. Technical project team members who aren't trained in marketing don't use formal methods to secure market feedback. More often than not, their probing is more toward other technical specialists who might be able to provide them with feedback about potential uses or value.

There are few forays into the market early in the radical innovation life cycle, little customer contact, and no concept testing. Rather, the process we observed was more introspective, thoughtful, and imaginative and based on pasting trends together. Steve Depp of IBM, for example, painted a robust picture for us of how an electronic book could change peoples' lives. The descriptions of the possibilities were rich and provided the groundwork for the continued motivation to move the project along.

Even while the project team is working to prove the technology, market exploration needs to begin in earnest. From our case studies and interactions with other companies pursuing radical innovation projects, it was apparent that market learning—particularly in the fuzzy front end of the radical innovation life cycle—is based on nontraditional questions. Traditional market research often focuses on segmenting the market, positioning the product, estimating potential market share, and projecting overall market growth rate.[2] This is reasonable and appropriate for incremental innovations, where the market is already established and the business model is set. By comparison, the higher market uncertainty for radical innovations leads project team members to focus on the following questions:

- What are the potential applications and which should we pursue first?
- How can we confirm technical feasibility? (Our respondents cited this as one of their key market-related questions.)
- How can we demonstrate the technology?
- What is the fundamental technical value offered by the radical innovation? What benefits can it offer to potential customers?
- What is a gross estimate of potential market size? Will the market be big enough to justify moving forward with the project?

As the radical innovation life cycle progresses, the traditional market research questions increase in importance. Even so, radical innovation project team members reported that these exploratory questions continue to be important for extending market learning.

It's not surprising that traditional market research methods designed to answer traditional market research questions are used infrequently in radical innovation projects. Few of our respondents reported using written surveys, concept testing, focus groups, or secondary research. Instead they pursued market learning via these nontraditional approaches:

- Project team members attended trade shows to compare their ideas with other innovative technologies—especially those being introduced as next-generation products.
- Professional technical conferences and meetings provided access to peers from other companies, universities, and government labs who could provide feedback.
- Internal networks were used to request feedback from peers in other parts of the company. According to DuPont's director of corporate business development Terry Fadem: "The DuPont Company knows everything about almost every product and every market in the world. We just have to ask. I can find 80 percent of the knowledge I would ever need within the DuPont worldwide organization."
- Team members relied on their own past experience in thinking through market-related questions. (This points to the value of creating a radical innovation hub organization as a repository of expertise and cumulative knowledge.)

- A prototype was used to demonstrate the technology—even if it was very crude (the most frequently cited market learning mechanism).

- The team established a development partnership with a potential lead user (the second most frequently cited approach). (See chapter 7 for a discussion of the importance of external partnerships, spotlighting the critical impact of Analog Device's market learning partnership with BMW.)

- Customers' interactions with the technologies they already used were observed in order to identify potential markets for radical innovations.

Because prototyping was the most frequently used vehicle for market learning, the next section focuses on how firms in our study engaged this approach and why prototyping is different in the context of radical innovation versus incremental innovation.

A DIFFERENT ROLE FOR PROTOTYPING

In the domain of radical innovation, prototypes are first and foremost instruments of market learning. This runs counter to the conventional wisdom of incremental innovators: that the purpose of a prototype is to iron out wrinkles near the end of the design phase. For the radical innovator, a prototype is a mechanism for *teaching the market* (which sometimes is internal to the company) about the technology and for *learning from the market* how valuable that technology is in that application arena.[3] Here are three examples:

> Otis Elevator built a full-scale, operating elevator system in the demonstration facility of its North American Operations business unit. In the process of assembling the prototype, the project team was able to identify and work through many of the system's integration problems. But more important, the prototype facility provided the opportunity for interaction with and learning from a steady stream of potential customers. It helped potential customers develop an understanding of possible novel uses for the technology, including isolation systems for moving

prisoners, solutions for urban traffic congestion to aid in city planning, and others.

Air Products set up a demonstration unit of its SEOS technology in one of the firm's own facilities. The object was to gain experience with the new method of oxygen generation and to gain senior management's buy-in.

In the case of IBM's e-book development, a prototype of the high definition display was placed in one of Boeing's facilities for several months to evaluate its usefulness in applications such as reading maintenance manuals.

Radical innovators are much more apt than their incremental innovation counterparts to develop an early prototype—even a crude one—as a device for market learning. The potential customers who interact with these prototypes may have trouble evaluating them, as with all innovations that are fundamentally new. This is a perennial and well-known problem for marketers. If potential customers do not understand a technology, or if they lack a frame of reference for understanding it, they may be unable to provide useful feedback. In these cases, researchers may encounter the following impediments to learning:

CONFUSION. The innovative product does not fit into the potential customer's experience or product classification system. They do not "get it."

A FOCUS ON IRRELEVANT ATTRIBUTES. Product developers are often dismayed when potential customers ignore key attributes of an innovative product and focus, instead, on those thought by the developers to be irrelevant.[4] As one development manager pointed out, "When you're developing a new product based on a new technology, you have to make sure your product does not give customers reasons to immediately reject it no matter how irrelevant an item may seem to those involved in developing the product."

PROBLEMS OF USER-PRODUCT INTERACTION. Early prototypes are usually crude or clunky devices that reflect little or no attention to user interfaces. If managed inappropriately, they can be off-putting to those charged with testing them and giving feedback.

If customers are clear about the objective, however, they can be an important early source of information to validate the product's value. For example, when Motorola was developing its first pager, the prototype unit was heavy and transmitted a lot of static along with the voice of the user. A hospital agreed to serve as a test site. The building was hard-wired to allow transmittal since the radio wave infrastructure was not yet built. Administrators and doctors were given the clunky pagers for 60 days. When the Motorola team tried to get the system back after the trial period, hospital administrators and doctors refused! The concept had been validated through this extended-use test.[5]

Prototypes that can be readily understood can greatly enhance the value of early evaluations. Since customers have no previous experience with radically new products, the team has two choices. One is to work hard *to design prototypes that are easily learned and operated*. This reduces the chance of the prototype being misused or rejected altogether. Unfortunately, few project teams have the resources to add elegant user interfaces to their prototypes. Getting the innovation to work—and for several different applications—is challenge enough.

The second alternative is to *condition customers* to understand what it is you want them to evaluate. Customers should be asked not to focus on design interface issues. Instead, their attention should be directed at identifying and validating the key benefits that the technology promises. Another critical input of value is the user's experience with any other aspects of the technology that they see as valuable, which the project team may not have expected or imagined. For example, the Odyssey team at Otis Elevator didn't foresee that a different aspect of their solution would catch one market's attention. Since the innovation required that elevator cars disembark from the vertical shaft, any single car's journey could be customized to navigate through a building or series of buildings and tunnels. That concept appealed to correctional facilities as a mechanism for moving high-risk prisoners from one area of the facility to another, or even to a courthouse. Originally, the customized routing and security aspects of the technology were not explicitly considered by the Odyssey development team. Market contacts brought the value of those features to the Odyssey team's attention.

Early market learning needs to lead to tentative decisions about initial applications in order to provide guidelines for further technical development. Prototyping, when implemented appropriately, can be a powerful tool for soliciting valuable feedback for the project team as it struggles with identifying promising initial applications.

Selecting Initial Target Applications

How does a project team choose the first application? The temptation is to choose the one that promises the largest market or to choose an application domain where the company has existing customers. But neither may be the optimal approach.

We can see that in Air Products's exploration of new markets, Jeff Knopf and the development team were much less concerned about choosing "the right" application (i.e., the one that would have the largest market) and much more concerned with choosing one that would help them learn.[6] For this reason, Knopf selected scrap yards as the first places to visit. Further, he did not focus on the industrial gases market, in which Air Products had a number of close relationships.

Fertile fields for application ideas are generally found among those *likely to benefit the most* from a new technology. These are rarely large mass markets, since early versions of the technology may not yet offer the total set of benefits needed for the mass market.[7] The troubled Iridium project, which promised global satellite comunication and was sponsored by a coalition of firms led primarily by Motorola, is a case in point. The ultimate vision of equipping everyone on the planet with a device that allowed them to communicate with anyone, anywhere was and is truly radical. The question is, Where to begin? The press reported: "You can dial from any point on the globe, including a boat in the middle of the ocean, or on a camel's back in the middle of the desert."[8] Perhaps these specific high value targets, as opposed to mass market mobile telephony, would have been the best initial applications for the purpose of market learning and, ultimately, market development.

In contrast to the market learning approach adopted by Jeff Knopf at Air Products, few of our subjects went looking in niches for applications. Instead, lack of time and resources, and pressure to produce big results quickly, encouraged them to seek application ideas from the people most likely to talk to them—individuals and companies with whom their firms already had relationships. Going to friendly parties for help is a natural human tendency. Unfortunately, these are not always the best sources of market insights—and that must be the sole driver for early partnership choices.[9] We witnessed cases where the first partner was chosen on the basis of convenience: a long-standing relationship between the two firms existed. One research manager offered this justification: "As a researcher, my job is to demonstrate that the technology will work. It's the job of marketing to find the applications. I do not have the resources to pursue many applications." Unfortunately in this case, the partner did not perceive enough value to get excited, project team members did not choose to explore other application markets, and project momentum fizzled.

To prove the robustness of a technology, it is important to generate and pursue numerous application paths.[10] Air Products pursued applications for its new oxygen separation technology not only in its traditional market of industrial gases, but also in new markets that would displace oxygen cylinders, such as restaurants, scrap yards, welding businesses, and medical applications. Likewise, Texas Instruments explored potential applications for its digital light processing innovation in digital printers, large-screen projection systems, and table-top conference room video projectors. And DuPont probed the attractiveness of potential markets for its biodegradable polymer ranging from packaging to agricultural applications and composting. At one point, DuPont was exploring thirty distinct application opportunities. In each of these cases, any single early market may represent only small revenues. Together, they can add up to a large business with enormous growth potential. The quest for the "killer app" in the early stages is not likely to produce good results—unless the focus is on rapid learning rather than growing revenues.

Still, we observed that R&D project teams perceive their job as demonstrating the value of the technology in *one or two* application domains. They probe and test serially, learning and redirecting each time. This is logical from their perspective, but we have observed cases where a team simply gave up when a probe did not connect with a promising market. It would be more fruitful to generate and pursue multiple applications, not so much to test the size of success in any one, but to validate that the technology has many promising avenues for development.

Who Does Market Learning for Radical Innovations?

Market learning is obviously important, but who is responsible for it? Technical researchers find it easy to say: "I'm a scientist [or engineer]—market research is not my job." But this does not reflect the reality we encountered in the field. Early in the radical innovation life cycle, scientists are, in fact, talking with potential customers and business unit leaders to get early validation of benefits. They do not think of these activities as market learning, although they are. The truth of the matter, as it stands today, is that early market learning is the responsibility of radical project teams.[11] If they fail to do it, it will not be done. Cases in which market learning was outsourced to strategic partners or consultants ended in disappointment and regret.

Once projects moved past the point of demonstrating technical feasibility, a business development person or two are often added to the project team, as was the case with Ted Foster and Jeff Knopf at Air Products. While these individuals generally have technical backgrounds, either through education or experience, most also had many years of experience with the firm in a variety of marketing and business development positions. They had contacts and relationships with customers and business unit personnel, which allowed them easy access to useful information. They were more strategic in their thinking than market researchers—who are tactical and analytic—and more consultant-like than a typical sales person. Fellow project teammates characterized them as skillful at observing and drawing insights. They are inductive rather than deductive thinkers.

We see another opportunity for the radical innovation hub group discussed in chapter 3 as a third source for leaders in market learning. At DuPont, for example, corporate business development director Terry Fadem launched an ad campaign about the company's new biodegradable polyester material, Biomax. The ads were rich in detail about the features of the material and were printed in trade journals in a variety of industries. These ads included a return card and phone number so that interested companies who saw application possibilities could register their ideas. This campaign provided Fadem with a list of at least thirty potential applications and thirty willing partners. Texas Instruments did something very similar with its Digital Micromirror Device display engine.

KEYS TO SUCCESSFUL MARKET LEARNING

In this chapter, we have described the market learning issues that confront radical innovators and have shown the range of practices found in our studies. The primary question is, How can companies do a better job of learning about the markets for radical innovations? Here are some alternative approaches for better practice:

DON'T EXPECT MUCH FROM TRADITIONAL MARKET RESEARCH. It tells us what exists, not what could be or should be.

PROBE AND LEARN. A big corporation rarely jumps into anything until it has practically studied it to death. This is a good way to avoid costly mistakes, but also a good way to avoid doing anything really new. It is also expensive and time-consuming. Entrepreneurs, in contrast, get into the game quickly and try to figure it out on the fly. This appears to be a pattern among companies at the forefront of new industries. These companies and their employees know that their forecasts may be wrong, that there will be many surprises, and that the new technology and its applications will unfold in ways that neither they nor anyone else can imagine. So instead of gathering and analyzing more and more data, they pursue opportunities through a practice of "probe and learn,"[12] often with early prototypes.

FOCUS ON MARKETS THAT MAXIMIZE RAPID LEARNING. Don't allow a "mega-markets-only" mentality to deter interest in smaller markets. In choosing the application areas to probe, focus on those that stand to benefit the most from the innovation. Some of these applications may be small relative to corporate expectations, but if potential customers in those domains place a high value on the innovation, they represent market entry points that may, one day, support large and growing businesses.

Project teams will learn more from these users than from any others. Other application domains may be judged to be too far afield from the innovator's current business, leading corporate executives to sell or license the technology to others. But, as many have learned to their regret, slavishly serving existing customers can be a dead-end strategy. Think beyond products to product platforms.

DEAD ENDS ARE LIKELY, SO TEST MULTIPLE APPLICATIONS SIMULTANEOUSLY. Pursuing applications in series eats up time and can frustrate researchers. Keep many irons in the fire at once; doing so will increase the likelihood of hitting on a real opportunity quickly. This multiapplication approach appears to work best for materials-based and component-based innovations that can become part of many things. Like all prescriptions for radical innovation projects, there are exceptions. For example, one of our study companies, General Electric, required serial probes for its medical imaging technology project because each probe brought about technical learning that was then built into the next experiment.

SELECT EARLY CUSTOMER ALLIES WHO HAVE POWERFUL REASONS FOR EXPLORING WITH YOU. For example, firms that are in the number three or four position in their industry, who are playing competitive catch-up, are likely first partners. Work with them to ensure that they understand what you need from them in terms of evaluating the concept or prototype.

BE PREPARED FOR SURPRISES. When it comes to applications, project teams should never allow themselves to think that they've totally figured it out. Scotch tape was invented to insulate refrigerated railroad cars. Radio's initial purpose was for point-to-point communication—not for the broadcast application that is its main use today.[13]

One chief scientist we interviewed described what he termed "application migration":

> You start off with one set of customers that you may have with this one property that you've targeted, and what happens is that somebody else comes up with a lot of other uses, and they grow. It just spreads out. What started as a material to make one set of things ended up as a completely different product. I still don't know what we'll ultimately end up with.

TRAIN AND EDUCATE PROJECT TEAM MEMBERS TO EXPECT THAT MARKET LEARNING IS PART OF THEIR JOBS. Traditional market research people—either corporate staff or business units—are not trained to operate in the radical innovation environment. The project won't progress without market learning, and, hence, the project team will have to find a way to get it done. The project team needs people who are willing to subject themselves to the discomfort of undertaking tasks that normally are outside their purview. They need to be open to learning about and implementing nontraditional approaches to exploring potential applications for their radical innovations. They need to understand that their efforts, at least initially, are not likely to provide definitive answers but rather directions for further exploration.

As indicated in chapter 4, when discussing project management capabilities, we saw that competencies for reducing market uncertainties were important, especially after the project team gained sufficient confidence in technological feasibility to warrant moving ahead. Even though the project team would rather continue its focus on technical issues, it is forced to demonstrate the existence of a market, if only to validate the importance of the innovation. However, market learning and a demonstration of technical feasibility are not enough. A radical project finds itself under pressure to resolve uncertainties and provide convincing evidence that the commercial promise that attracted attention initially is not smoke and mirrors. The firm, as investor, wants to understand the business model. What is it? What new competencies must be developed or outsourced to make the model work? And what about customers? Who are the customers most likely to be attracted to the innovation? Does the innovation represent real value to them? And most important, the firm wants to know when the nascent venture will make money. The next chapter focuses on the process of business model development.

CHAPTER 6

BUILDING
THE BUSINESS
MODEL

A RADICAL INNOVATION TEAM CAN EASILY BE CONSUMED WITH technical development. Technologists, after all, love technology and are motivated to discover and develop fundamentally new ideas. Yet, most of them understand the importance of finding an early answer to this question: How can we make money with this innovation? Even an incomplete answer can help guide technical development and market learning, define the relationships with internal and external partners, and provide a case for continued funding. Answering this fundamental question, however, requires that a number of others must be addressed:

- What sort of value chain must be built before this innovation can be successfully commercialized?
- What will our role be in the new value chain?
- Who else will participate in the value chain and what will be their roles?
- Who will pay whom and for what?

These are business model questions. A business model is a broad-stroke picture of how an innovative concept will create economic value for the ultimate user, for the firm, and for its partners. It considers the infrastructure required to move the product to the market in a manner that is both easy and convenient for customers and profitable for the firm.

Business model questions rarely arise in traditional product development projects targeted at incremental innovations to existing products. For these projects, customers and markets are known, and a set of practices for determining price, distribution partners, and delivery systems is already in place. So too are forecasts regarding the product's potential for helping the firm achieve revenue and profit objectives. The same cannot be said for radical innovation projects. For radical innovators, market and technical issues must be considered in tandem, as they impact each other. Consider the case of Monsanto, a company that has reinvented itself.

In the 1970s, Monsanto was a textiles and specialty chemicals company. Today, it is known as a company that applies genetic engineering to improve agricultural and pharmaceutical products. Monsanto struggled with the challenge of building the business model for one of its breakthrough products—a genetically engineered tomato—with mixed results.

In the early 1990s, the company's scientists successfully engineered a tomato resistant to insect strains that had wiped out crops in previous seasons. Monsanto executives were struggling with the issue of how to make money from this technical breakthrough, especially since widespread adoption of the new tomato would cannibalize its thriving pesticide and herbicide business. If the company sold seeds that grew bug-resistant tomatoes, farmers would harvest the seeds and plant them the next season—and the next, and the next. Monsanto's revenue stream would dry up. That market insight led to a major technical change. Laboratory scientists reengineered seeds to reproduce only once; farmers would have to buy new seeds every two years. They labeled this reengineered product "The Terminator."

Had the business model issue not been considered, technical development would have taken a different course. But, as it turned out, the new business model was not entirely "bug resistant." Farmers sued Monsanto on the grounds that Terminator seeds planted in neighboring fields would cause their own traditional plants to stop reproducing. In addition, the ongoing controversy about bioengineered foods threatened to restrict the market opportunity for the Terminator. After ten years, Monsanto had achieved the technical breakthrough, but was still looking for a business model that would deliver the pot of gold.[1]

Even as innovators learn about markets and continue technology development, they must conceptualize a business model through which application choices can create future cash flows. There are typically many choices and many unknowns. Nortel Networks's spin-out project called NetActive—which is based on a proprietary software locking system also called NetActive—is described in the following case study. This case study offers several insights about key issues in defining a business model:

- Radical innovations frequently disrupt current ways of doing business for the members of the value chain.

- Figuring out how to structure the value chain requires probing and learning just as evaluating early market application choices did.

- Building the value chain requires systems thinking.

NORTEL NETWORKS SEARCHES FOR A BUSINESS MODEL

Nortel Networks had assigned a small team of innovative engineers to what was called an "idea sandbox" (as discussed in chapter 3). Their goal was to identify potential applications for broadband communications technology. Jeff Dodge, a Nortel Networks senior business manager with a technical background, was given the job of sifting through the sandbox of ideas for the nuggets with commercial merit.

"This one really kicked back" is how Dodge described the idea of making various popular entertainment and applications software products available online through a rental arrangement or pay-per-use. Few people who want to see a movie are willing to purchase it outright, he knew, but thousands more will put up $3 to rent a videocassette version for a day or two. The same might apply to gaming software, tax preparation programs, and others. The Nortel

Networks team's innovation was a method of encoding software in such a way that a customer could use a piece of software for a specified period of time, after which time the software would automatically reconnect to the NetActive system that would demand additional payment.

Dodge had a rudimentary business model in mind when he presented the software rental concept to Nortel Networks's newly formed Ventures Program. The ventures group liked what it heard but had reservations. No one had thought through a win-win arrangement for all the parties that had to be enlisted to execute this particular concept. Software publishers owned the rights to the software—how could they be compensated in a way that would secure their participation? Would software publishers be concerned that rentals would cannibalize their traditional sales? Customers would use the software, but how much would they be willing to pay, and what mechanism would be used to collect their money?

To confront issues related to the definition of a business model, Laura Dierker was added to the project team as VP of sales and marketing. Her responsibility was to seek out arrangements with the third parties who might be involved in implementing Nortel Networks's plan. Working with e-commerce distributors appeared to be the way to go. These distributors were the people that most computer users turned to on the Web to buy hardware and software products. Most were enthusiastic about the Nortel Networks idea, as it represented a new distribution channel for their wares. But none actually owned or were interested in obtaining content. They were interested in playing in this new game once it was up and running, but none wanted to get involved in the process of commercialization.

Dierker saw software publishers—the game producers—as the next logical group to approach. "Here's a new way for you to distribute your products," Dierker told twenty-one of these producers. For small publishers facing the battle for shelf space in other channels, the rental approach had lots of appeal. Again the response was favorable, but without commitment. These contacts did generate a new idea, however: Since few people have broadband cable and downloading software titles through a standard phone line Internet connection takes too long—often several hours—why not provide customers with free disks loaded with the program in order to bypass the download problem? Each NetActive program can be opened only through the Internet via NetActive's unlocking mechanism, which is activated once the Internet connection has taken the user's name and credit card information. Pricing could be determined on a per-play basis or by the number of days the program remains unlocked and available to the customer. A portion of the rental fee could be credited to the account of each of the parties in the value chain, for example, NetActive, the software's distributor, the copyright holder, the e-commerce merchant handling the Internet site and credit card transaction, and so forth.

This approach had lots of promise, but raised new questions: How would the customer obtain the disk—through the mail? At a video rental outlet? At a computer store? Also, would this strategy provide enough revenue to NetActive to qualify as a stand-alone business? Dodge, Dierker, and the others on the team had to create a chain of value-adding activities that produced a clear benefit for customers and a win-win situation for each of the players in the chain (see figure 6-1).

Nortel Networks's venture board saw merit in this business model, but determined that it did not play to any of the company's strengths. So the project was targeted for a spin-out as a stand-alone business unit, with Jeff Dodge as its president. NetActive publicized its technology as an innovation that offered benefits different from those the team had originally perceived as key innovations, such as substituting for purchase of a single-use piece of software. These more enriched benefits included:

- new pricing models including pay-per-use, rental, limited-time evaluations, TBYB (try-before-you-buy), rent-to-own, and purchase;
- broader distribution with no threat of piracy; and
- one-to-one consumer marketing.

FIGURE 6-1

THE RENTAL SOFTWARE VALUE CHAIN

Software publisher	NetActive encoding	Disk distributor	e-Site transaction manager	Other	Customer

With NetActivation, software publishers and resellers are able to get 100 percent registration of anyone who tries or buys their software. NetActivation can provide pay-per-use access to the titles and build individual, interactive relationships with customers.[2]

Finding a Place in the Value Chain

The Nortel Networks story underscores several important aspects of building a business model around a radical innovation. The project team needs to understand and define the entire value chain as a system of interrelated players; find a place in the value chain that is profitable and has long-run promise; and recruit and develop partners who will excel at the parts of the value chain in which the firm chooses not to participate.[3]

In the Nortel Networks NetActive case, what the customer pays must provide returns to a number of different players. If rental rates are anything close to those of video movies, there will be only a small revenue pie to carve up and serve to several value chain participants; NetActive's share may be measured in pennies per rental. If that proves to be the case, the new venture will achieve major business status only if rental volume is huge. The one-to-one market may, in fact, represent a higher value proposition than rental royalties. This opportunity is yet to be fully explored, however. Finally, any investor would naturally ask, "Is NetActive's locking technology so proprietary that a competitor could not move in and challenge its position in the chain? Has it set an industry standard? What strategy must it pursue in order to ensure that it does set the standard?"

Bridging the Gap between Technical Innovation and Business Success

Radical innovators are generally technical in background and interest and may not realize that the direction of technical development and the eventual business model are bound together. The choice of where and how the firm will participate in the value chain is, in part, determined by early decisions about the direction of technical development and vice versa. These very important decisions may not be sufficiently considered by technical innovators. Early in the life of the Digital Light Processor project, TI determined that its OEM partners would adopt the technology more readily if it arrived in the form of a system component—the engine of the end product—rather than just a chip. This technical choice helped define the parts of the value chain that would be assumed by TI and its partners. Later on, new applications emerged for which other OEMs were prepared to take on different parts of the value chain. This allowed TI to concentrate on technical development for which it had superior capabilities.

The task of developing a business model is very different from the tasks most scientists, technicians, and engineers are trained to do. And for many, it is not something they *like* doing. Nevertheless, the rudiments of the early business model are sometimes inadvertently determined by scientists through their conceptualizations of how the technology will work and through their interactions with early application probes. Most scientists and engineers are not cognizant of the impact of these decisions. And high levels of uncertainty in the technical and organizational realms may motivate them to favor familiar market models and to ignore alternatives.

Once business development people are added to the project team, economic models are more easily developed and tested to determine the range of price-value options that might be offered. This is one of the earliest steps toward developing a business model. For example, when Hank Zorman, Ted Foster, and others in Air Products's business development organization began to assess the business model for the new oxygen separation membrane technology, it became clear that the economics for industrial applications would be much more attractive if the waste heat that was generated as a by-product of the oxygen generation process could be used to generate electricity, which the customer could either sell to the local power grid or use to power its own plant facility. As the example above indicates, identifying assumptions about who would value the innovation, and at what price, begins the work of developing the business model at a more sophisticated level. These assumptions, along with technical assumptions that need to be made, form the basis of the *learning plan* discussed in chapter 4. Testing this set of assumptions becomes the work of the project team.

As with market learning, the challenges to business model development vary depending on where the opportunity may be found relative to the firm's existing business. Is it in one of the firm's existing markets, or is it a new line of business, either in the white spaces or outside the firm's current strategic context?[4]

RADICAL INNOVATIONS THAT FIT WITHIN THE MAINSTREAM BUSINESS

Our project participants typically believed that innovations falling within their current lines of business would present no major business model challenges. They assumed that the infrastructure for contacting customers, understanding markets, setting prices, and delivering products was well developed. However, the following key business model challenges emerged as the radical innovation life cycle unfolded:

HOW WILL WE MANAGE THE CANNIBALIZATION OF OUR CURRENT OFFERING(S)?[5] This involves managing the marketplace *as well as* the resistance of the operating unit to doing things differently. One of many examples of the kind of organizational resistance that radical innovations encounter with new business models is Monsanto's move into genetically engineered seeds, discussed earlier in this chapter. The transition has been fraught with surprises. One is the reluctance of the sales force in the company's agricultural division to adopt the novel, highly beneficial, bug-resistant seeds to sell to the farmers and cooperatives they'd serviced for so many years. Why? Because Monsanto's business model included selling those seeds every other year—which was a different pattern from what the sales force, and the farmers, knew from experience.

HOW DO WE OVERCOME CUSTOMER RESISTANCE TO ADOPTING THE NEW TECHNOLOGY, ESPECIALLY IF THEIR USAGE PATTERNS MUST CHANGE? The 30 percent cost decrease that Air Products's MEOS project promises to current industrial oxygen customers will surely appeal to their wallets. But the cost savings will be realized only if they sell the resultant cogenerated power to utilities—which will require that they build in additional administrative systems to manage that sale. It is unclear the extent to which the new requirement will be readily adopted by Air Products's customers.

HOW DO WE AVOID THE TYRANNY OF THE CURRENT BUSINESS MODEL? The business model that the SBU is familiar with has tremendous power to shape and constrain the innovation. One engineer expressed it this way: "To the greatest extent possible, our projects try to stick with known business models and routines to help get the SBU to adopt them." In other words, reduce risk by sticking close to the operating unit and its business model. The trade-off is the increased probability of less than rousing success because the project is forced to grow within the constraints of the current business model.

For example, GM's hybrid electric vehicle was proposed as a new car model that would be targeted and sold just like any other vehicle. At the proposed price of $35,000, it was more expensive than most conventional compact vehicles, yet delivered no commensurate benefits to customers. The price of gasoline was so low that it offered no economic benefit, especially when the very expensive biannual battery replacement was factored in.

Thus, even for "familiar markets" projects, every project we have observed has encountered important and unanticipated business model issues. Experimentation with business models is just as critical as experimentation with technological paths in the radical innovation domain. The biggest challenge we identified for innovations in current lines of business is complacency in understanding and tackling this issue.

APPLICATIONS WITHIN THE WHITE SPACES OR OUTSIDE THE STRATEGIC FRAMEWORK

As described in chapter 1, these are innovations that leverage combinations of technologies across business units or technology domains, or innovations that take the firm completely outside its current market and technology spaces, as in the case of Nortel Networks's NetActive project. While the initial promise of a large market may have driven the project, how to develop it, capture it, and ensure that the returns are worth the effort is more than just an intellectual exercise. There is no existing business model. While these innovations are riskier than those developed for existing business units, they have the potential to stretch the organization in new directions and provide platforms for growth. Project teams that attempt to develop business models from scratch need to address the questions discussed in the following sections.

HOW CAN WE LEVERAGE THIS INNOVATION TO MAKE MONEY? The project team must identify the best mechanism for generating revenue. Should we sell or lease? Should we aim to make money on the razor or on the razor blades? Should we try to make money on the hardware, on after-sales service, or both? Should we charge per use or charge a lump sum? The business model must identify a cost/features formula that will support and sustain high margins. It also should provide barriers to entry by competitors. In our cases, we found little evidence that this second factor was heavily considered. The implicit assumption was that the technical prowess of the innovation would keep competitors at bay.

WHAT SUPPORTING INFRASTRUCTURE IS NEEDED BEFORE ANYONE CAN USE THE INNOVATION? The cellular telephone was a great invention, but its commercial success depended on development of switching software and equipment, service providers, and forests of microwave towers. These were necessary elements of the cell phone business value chain that, at the time of the technical invention, did not exist. Motorola had to help in the development of a number of these ancillary businesses before its vision of mobile telephony could be realized. Similarly, NetActive's project team had to figure out who would handle rental payments and who would distribute the disks.[6] Finally, alliances with the title producers were key, as they would need to submit their disks to NetActive for encoding.

WHERE DO WE FIT IN THE VALUE CHAIN? Innovators must determine which portion(s) of the total value chain they can handle on their own and which must be handled by suppliers or strategic partners. NetActive, for example, had to decide whether or not it would handle the rental payment transactions. It ultimately decided against it. As another example, TI had to decide if it was going to produce desk top presentation projectors, or the projection optics component (the engine), or just the Digital Light Processing chip. The following story, based on one of our twelve projects, illuminates the "where to play" issue.

IBM's SiGe Chip: Fitting into the Value Chain

In October 1998, IBM announced a major technological breakthrough in the field of semiconductors—mass production of the first standard, high-volume chips fabricated from silicon germanium, or SiGe. Project leader Bernie Meyerson discovered that an alloy of silicon and germanium could become the basis for new high-performance transistors with switching speeds up to four times faster than those of traditional semiconductors. An important added benefit was their ability to operate using only a small fraction of normal power requirements for competing technologies. IBM's ability to mass produce silicon germanium would make it possible for hardware manufacturers to substitute chips made from this material for more costly, power-hungry, and exotic alternatives, such as gallium arsenide (GaAs). SiGe semiconductor technology offered a breakthrough price-to-performance ratio not available from these existing component technologies. Best of all, the new chip material could be manufactured with the same costly fabricating equipment used to make conventional silicon chips, potentially avoiding billions in new capital investments.

The burgeoning wireless communications market, in which SiGe technology could be applied, was huge. Cellular phones, wireless local area networks, direct-to-home (DTH) satellite services, and satellite-based communications all depended heavily on low-cost, power-conserving, high-speed integrated circuit technology.

The business potential of SiGe was very unclear early in its development. Like most other new scientific discoveries, the gap between experimental laboratory work and a revenue-generating business was initially very large. It took many years of hard work and tremendous persistence on the part of the innovator to get the right people in the organization to recognize the opportunity. The company had a long history as a volume producer of memory chips, an arrangement in which other firms provided the higher value application design functions. Meyerson was aware of that history and knew that acceptance and funding of his project would probably lead to a similar outcome: IBM would get the high-volume chip fabricating part of the value chain, while someone else would handle the smaller but higher-profit business of design.

However, Meyerson believed that IBM should go after more of the value chain associated with the silicon germanium chip and expand IBM's chipmaking activities beyond its traditional foundry operations. He and the project's first business manager pushed for broader involvement in the value chain. They resolved to work only with companies that were willing to let IBM in on the chip design issues relevant to the application. Meyerson hoped to learn these skills and eventually co-opt that part of the business for his company. He wanted IBM to use the development of the new chips as an opportunity to expand its design capabilities. In the end, he accomplished his objective with IBM's acquisition of CommQuest, which was slated to design silicon-germanium-enhanced chip sets for next-generation cellular phones. Other efforts were ongoing, such as hiring a workforce trained in the specialty design coding work that was needed.

Firms struggle with the trade-off of speed to market with an existing capability versus taking the opportunity to grow new capabilities. Bernie Meyerson pushed IBM to capture more of the value chain. He pushed to have them develop the complementary capability of chip design to add to IBM's traditional competence of chip manufacturing. Most projects have had to adjust their positions in the value chain as the market developed.[7]

Who Pays Whom, and How Much? The answer to this question is not always clear in the early stages of development. Frequently early on there's a focus on the ultimate end user without regard for the rest of the value chain. Initially, while all of the players expressed the sentiment that the software rental concept had promise, most were not willing to pay money to NetActive for the encoding. The NetActive team finally figured it out. "The title producers did not want to buy our technology . . . they were buying a new marketing program from us. Therefore, we had to build the rest of the program before they would talk with us." Once it was clear how each member of the value chain could contribute, the payment scheme began to fall into place.

It is important to develop and test alternative revenue models and payment schemes. Ultimately, a successful revenue model must (a) generate enough revenue for the innovating firm, and (b) be acceptable to all members of the value chain. In the case of NetActive, the revenue flow's most recent iteration involves the customer purchasing a CD at a price up to one quarter of the price of a conventional CD at a local movie rental house. Then the customer is required to pay for initialization of the software and its rental, via the Internet, to an e-commerce provider.

WHAT CHANGES WILL CUSTOMERS HAVE TO MAKE IN ORDER TO USE OUR INNOVATION?[8] Imagine the risk a company such as NetActive is taking in trying to convince customers to rent software. These customers must pay a video rental store a small amount for the CD, then load it into their computer, initiate an Internet call to a Web site, make a series of choices about the length of time they want to use the software, and make a second payment, this time via the Internet.

The movie theater projection systems that Texas Instruments has recently announced will require theater owners to purchase new equipment costing many times that of conventional projectors. Celluloid film and film reels on which they have received movies for decades will be replaced with digital videodisks. Eventually, movies would be distributed from studios to theaters by satellite or fiber-optic cable.

The changes created by this innovation also create issues about who gets the savings. There are great savings in digital projection technology. But most will accrue to the studios as savings in shipping costs of large reels of film, not to theater owners. Theater owners are currently warning that digital video will not succeed without some sharing of those savings.

KEYS TO EFFECTIVELY BUILDING BUSINESS MODELS

Radical innovation project team members face a number of challenges for which they are usually not prepared by training, experience, or inclination: finding the best application; collecting market data and making market probes; demonstrating how the firm will make money; and developing an initial entry strategy (a market niche). When an application probe appears promising, the project team needs to consider how the value chain could be structured and how the nature of that envisioned value chain could (or should) alter the technical direction of the project. The following keys will help project team members determine the business model that will enable the firm to generate satisfactory revenues, profits, and a return on its investment in the development of the radical innovation:

ENVISION AND UNDERSTAND THE ENTIRE VALUE CHAIN. It's not enough for the project team to develop a deep technical understanding of the radical innovation and to identify potential customers, although this is a great starting point. The team needs to use a systems approach to figuring out all the activities that must be completed to bring the innovation to market. It is unusual for someone with the skill and experience to accomplish this key activity to be on a radical innovation team in the fuzzy front end. It is also difficult for most individuals embedded in a firm to overcome the tyranny of the firm's prevailing business model. This presents an opportunity for the firm's senior management to exercise leadership by bringing skill and experience to bear on the project. This can be accomplished in one—or better yet a combination of—the following ways: assign a radical innovation veteran who fits the project and is compatible with the project team to be the project manager; charge the radical innovation hub with finding a strategic visionary to be an adviser to the project; and work with the radical innovation hub to assemble an oversight board that can challenge the project team to develop this vision. The hub, working with the project oversight board, should help guide and monitor progress as the team develops and evaluates alternative business models.

DETERMINE THE FIRM'S PLACE IN THE VALUE CHAIN. Start with the firm's current set of assets: competencies, resources, and relationships, but don't stop there. It's not enough to figure out what role the firm can play today. The project team needs to determine what parts of the value chain will be most highly valued by customers. It also must assess the vulnerability of the firm's success to inadequate performance by a questionable value chain partner. Insights about these issues may cause the project team to propose to the firm that new competencies need to be developed or acquired.

PROBE AND LEARN. Just as project teams need to generate many application ideas, they must also develop and evaluate alternative options for making money. The "probe-and-learn" approach works as well here as it does in dealing with the other uncertainties that must be resolved to achieve project maturity. Business model development is a like a logic puzzle. The best way to solve the puzzle is to (a) determine what customers want and are willing to pay for, (b) think through the elements of a value chain that will deliver it to them, (c) determine where one's company will fit in the chain, and (d) determine how it will work with partners to deliver value. The project needs to aggressively engage with both potential customers and potential suppliers and to follow the trails to other potential customers and suppliers as they emerge from the probe-and-learn process. When the logic of the business model doesn't work on the first try, try again.

PREPARE FOR WAR, PARTICULARLY WHEN CANNIBALIZATION IS A POSSIBILITY. If the radical innovation is likely to displace an existing product line, the project team should expect resistance from the established operating unit. Even when that is not the case, the project will be competing with other activities in the firm for resources and attention of senior management. The unsophisticated project team that isn't prepared risks being blindsided and forced to divert its own energy and resources to defensive action. The best defense is a good offense. If possible, the internal resisters should be co-opted and recruited to join in and share in the success of the radical innovation. When that isn't possible, the project needs to develop the political power—through senior management champions, the radical innovation hub, and its oversight board—to counter the resistance.

As the last key suggests, radical innovation projects are critically dependent on internal and external partners who provide missing resources and/or capabilities. In chapter 4 we highlighted managing interfaces—particularly with the mainstream organization—as a critical project management competency. In the next chapter, we address the challenge of acquiring resources and competencies from external partners.

CHAPTER 7

ACQUIRING RESOURCES AND CAPABILITIES

CONVENTIONAL WISDOM TELLS US THAT BIG COMPANIES HAVE plenty of resources for the pursuit of innovative ideas. This is both true and not true. It is true when an innovative idea is very close to the money—in other words, when it will pay off in the short term. The conventional wisdom is *not* true for a radical innovation. Faced with high uncertainty about when the payoff will come, if ever, decision makers who allocate resources are reluctant to support a project that may turn out to be a "black hole." Hence, the challenge of acquiring resources and missing competencies is a big part of radical innovation. This chapter focuses on how radical innovation project teams overcome the uncertainty of acquiring resources.

In chapter 4, we discussed seven keys for effective management of radical innovation projects. Among those were *skill in resource acquisition* and *ability to manage interfaces with the mainstream organization and with external partners*. Both of these project management capabilities are important for overcoming deficiencies in resources and competencies, a challenge faced by every one of the project teams in our study. Attracting the necessary financial support was a continuous challenge, and for most projects, external financing made the difference between project continuation and being put on the shelf. The story is the same when we consider competencies. In all projects save one, the companies we studied lacked one or more competencies critical to the successful pursuit of their respective opportunities. As a result, project teams—and especially their champions—spent extraordinary amounts of time dealing with resource and competency acquisition activities.

In the GM case study that follows, the project used established routines to secure R&D funding for early development. But when the cost of sustaining the project began to increase, the normal R&D budget allocation process wasn't up to the task. The project team had to creatively and aggressively manage interfaces with another technology development group and with senior management to win continuing funding. This case also illustrates the importance of managing interfaces with external partners. Eventually the project was successful in securing major funding from a government agency, which allowed the project to go forward.

FUNDING GM's HYBRID ELECTRIC VEHICLE PROJECT

General Motors had been researching hybrid vehicles for several decades, but in 1989, a technical insight motivated a renewed investigation of its potential. There was a realization that various engine, electrical, and battery technologies had matured enough to make a hybrid vehicle possible. This insight emerged from a discussion among two research managers and a senior engineer. The senior research manager decided to commit discretionary funds under his control to set up a technology evaluation team. After several weeks of exploratory analysis, the results of the evaluation were sufficiently positive that he in turn approached the head of the research division with a proposal to establish a formal project with a team and a budget. That proposal was approved.

After three years of effort, part of the overall hybrid vehicle development effort was in danger of losing its funding. In an effort to save it, the project team staged a technology demonstration for GM's corporate executives. Although the demonstration was impressive, it failed to produce continued funding. "You put on a good show," the director of GM's development group informed the project team, "but we've received orders to close you down. Our budgets can't handle you."

It looked like curtains for the hybrid vehicle. But later that day, one of the senior executives who had attended the demonstration called the development group director to say, "That's great stuff. You've got to keep them going." Miraculously, the project was resurrected the following day, albeit under very tight budget control.

Serendipitously, a month later, a GM manager found himself sitting on an airplane next to a U.S. Department of Energy (DOE) official, whom he had known for some time. The GM manager described the hybrid vehicle project to the DOE official. He liked what he heard, and agreed to recommend the project for federal funding. Approximately one year later, that funding was authorized. GM participated in the Partnership for Next Generation Vehicle (PNGV) consortium of the Big Three U.S. automakers, each member of which was working on a hybrid vehicle. The GM project was significantly increased in scope by the funding, and effort at R&D and the development group was consolidated under one project heading.

GM decided to outsource significant parts of the technology development effort. This included development of two competing engines, both of which possessed a degree of risk. By 1998, it became clear that neither of these engines had the technical maturity to meet expectations within the timeframe of the contract.

There it was. No engine, no hybrid vehicle as planned. GM closed the project. The hybrid vehicle was down but not out, however. A small group of believers proposed resuscitating the project with a more conventional engine. Actually, the corporate interest in hybrids changed direction because, based on lessons learned during this experience, GM was fulfilling its PNGV commitments with different hybrid architecture.

The hybrid vehicle case illustrates the role of internal funding in getting projects through the fuzzy front end and early development, and the difficulty of sustaining internal funding as these projects require increasing commitments. In most of our cases, project teams were forced to scramble for follow-on funding, often to the exclusion of most other development activities.

External funding—including federal support—played a major role in nine of the twelve projects in our study. So too did the collaboration with external partners, although these often had disappointing results. In 50 percent of our case studies, including the GM project discussed above, the failure of external partners to meet performance expectations caused major setbacks.

THE FIGHT FOR FUNDING

Most big, established firms have deep pockets. That's the good news. The bad news is that most of those resources are committed to lower-risk efforts of incremental innovation. Further, resources are not unlimited. Getting money, facilities, and people out of those deep pockets is universally difficult for radical innovators, and they spend an inordinate percentage of their time and energy chasing resources. Our business culture takes it as an article of faith that rational decision makers allocate resources to the greatest opportunities on a risk-adjusted basis. However, decision making in established firms is notoriously risk averse. Breakthrough opportunities are difficult to discern, and the risks that surround them cannot always be sorted out or quantified. The corporate budget allocation process is primarily geared toward the firm's ongoing business needs. It is not designed to fund radical innovation projects—whose outcomes are uncertain— from beginning to end. As a result, people with game-changing ideas who think they will find an open door to corporate coffers are sorely mistaken. So how do radical innovation projects get funded?

Funding in the fuzzy front end is typically informal. A project champion either prevails upon a research manager for discretionary funds or bootstraps the project through his or her informal network, scrounging for the discretionary time of researchers and for the use of supplies and facilities.

Even when a radical project is formally established, it is not out of the woods. It has a formal budget, with funds coming from a new business development organization, a business unit, corporate R&D, or from the CEO's discretionary account, but these funds are generally unstable over time. Support for the project may decline or disappear in the face of a downturn in corporate fortunes. The length of time it may take a technology or market to mature will test the patience of corporate funders anxious for return on their investment. Furthermore, radical innovation projects based on new technologies often require inordinate amounts of development funds, far beyond normal budget allocation limits. Decision makers and sponsors come and go. Key supporters retire or take transfers. Because the radical innovation life cycle typically lasts a decade or longer, a project can expect to see its supporters and sources of funds change two or three times. Consequently, project champions must scramble, approach a variety of potential funding sources, and even reorient the direction of their projects to suit the interests of whoever holds the purse strings. Acquiring resources is a dynamic process. Those who wait passively for funding—perhaps believing that the world will always beat a path to the door of a great new idea—will come up empty. In all twelve projects in our study, the persistence of project champions in acquiring resources was critical to the continuation of their ventures.[1]

The majority of projects in our study paid a substantial price for their resource-hunting efforts. Time spent chasing resources was time not spent on project development, which lengthened the beginning-to-end project life cycle. On the other hand, the fight for funding is not entirely a bad thing, because it forces the radical innovation team to sharpen its case for funding. The due diligence of potential investors exposes assumptions to intense scrutiny and injects questions that stimulate new thinking. Also, if the project team is effective in presenting its case for funding, others will recognize the opportunity and be inspired by the team's vision and commitment. These individuals can directly, or as intermediaries, help the project team access resources. The sudden resurrection of the GM hybrid vehicle project provides just one example. The challenge for the firm and for the project team is to find the right balance. Ideally, radical innovation projects should engage in an appropriate level of fundraising activity—enough to gain the benefits just described, but not so much that good projects are hamstrung.

FUNDING RADICAL INNOVATION PROJECTS:
THE SENIOR MANAGEMENT PERSPECTIVE

Figuring out the optimal level of funding for a radical innovation project as it evolves is exceedingly difficult. On one hand, if there is too little funding, the project is starved for fuel. The project team spends too much time chasing support, slowing the development and introduction of the innovative product. At best, the firm delays reaping the financial rewards of commercializing the innovation. At worst, the innovation misses the window of opportunity, or the project dies.

On the other hand, too much funding—especially too early in the radical innovation life cycle—can also create problems.[2] Even though inadequate funding is a much more common problem for radical innovation teams, in two of our case studies, too much funding dramatically increased organizational and managerial stress and slowed progress. One case, which involved major funding from a government agency, is discussed in the following section about external funding. In the other case, overcommitment of funds early in the project life cycle caused expectations to be raised too high, too soon. The initial project manager in this case—an empire builder—took advantage of the political support of the firm's CEO to attract major internal funding. The project moved into its own building, outfitted with a state-of-the-art information system. The head count ramped up to several hundred people very quickly, even though the project was still in early market development. Tremendous organizational inertia was created by the commitment of tens of millions of dollars per year in pursuit of an untested business model. When the project team ran into resistance in initial markets, the project was forced through a painful restructuring, and the initial project manager was reassigned. For several years the project barely survived in the "land of the living dead" until a new champion got it back on track.

As this example suggests, overcommitment of resources to a particular path reduces the willingness and capacity to be flexible. It increases an escalation of commitment to the original path, increasing the likelihood that there will be resistance to abandoning the project, even if that is the appropriate decision. Inevitably some paths pursued will not pan out, and the project team will need to back off and redirect. One radical innovation hub manager lamented his inability to convince senior managers to allow him to kill loser projects. The message from senior management was, "We've already made a substantial investment. We're Corporation X and we don't fail. You have our authorization to invest additional financial resources. Pursue this path until you achieve success." Fully funding the radical innovation project up front or overcommitting is not the solution to the resource acquisition challenge. Instead the team needs to be able to acquire the right amounts of funding at the right times in the life of the project.

EXTERNAL FUNDING: TWO-EDGED SWORD

As indicated earlier, in nine of our twelve cases, external funds spelled the difference between project continuation and termination. In fact, in eight of the nine cases receiving external funding, government agencies were significant contributors. Clearly, those examples illustrate the importance of external financing. But external financing is often a two-edged sword. Projects may receive critical financial infusions, but then often find themselves saddled with excessive administrative burdens. One of the companies in our project chose to establish a cooperative R&D agreement (CRADA) with a federal laboratory. This turned into an administrative nightmare—requiring months and months and lots of legal fees to finalize the CRADA agreement. As the technical champion told us, "We'll never use this approach to funding again. The costs in time and dollars of negotiating the agreement were horrendous."

In other cases, the price of external funding may be a redirection of technical development. The original intent of the Air Products project was, first, to be the leader in next generation gas separation systems for the production of high purity oxygen for industrial customers and, second, to displace oxygen cylinders. When the DOE issued a request for proposals to develop gas separation technology for application to synthetic gas (syngas) production, Air Products decided that it had to pursue the funding for two reasons. First, it wanted to preempt potential competitors from developing the core technology. If a competitor won the DOE contract, it might be able to leapfrog Air Products in the production of oxygen for industrial use. Second, Air Products saw an opportunity to leverage the DOE funding for development of other strategic products (syngas, hydrogen, and carbon monoxide).

The consortium led by Air Products won the grant from the DOE. As expected, this required a significant adjustment—dramatically broadening the scope of the overall effort. Sustaining the original application development and ramping up a major new technology development effort absorbed a significant amount of management attention. Air Products rose to the challenge and succeeded in gearing up to take advantage of the government funding. Air Products views its capacity for acquiring and managing government funded R&D projects as an important competency. The combination of this competency and the dedication of senior management attention enabled Air Products to meet the challenge and seize the opportunity presented by unanticipated government funding.

In most of the cases we observed, external funding was a desperate attempt to keep a project going when internal funds fell short, or it was forced on the project team for strategic reasons, as in the Air Products case. And success in obtaining these external funds never led to entirely satisfactory outcomes. Firms need to figure out how to strategically access external funding—so that the benefits outweigh the downsides.

ORGANIZATIONAL PATHWAYS FOR RADICAL INNOVATION INVESTMENTS

The quality of senior management decision making about radical innovation varies from company to company and over time within the same company.[3] During our five-year study, we saw changes in senior corporate and business unit management in nine of the ten companies. These changes accelerated some projects and retarded others, depending on the orientation and capabilities of the new managers. Imagine the problems created by executive turnover for projects that last ten to fifteen years (the length of some projects in our study). In one case, the executive champion of a project was promoted and then retired during the period of our study. According to the project leader, decision making under the new executive became more arbitrary and less effective. Further, under this new executive the funding board experienced 30 percent turnover from quarter to quarter. The consequences of these personnel changes created a significant problem of commitment continuity. The challenge and opportunity for firms is to develop an effective process for making investment decisions about radical innovation projects—and to sustain effectiveness in the face of inevitable changes within the decision-making team.

Clearly there are significant problems with the ad hoc, catch-as-catch-can approaches to project funding described thus far. Some firms are actively working toward more rational and reliable processes that identify projects with the greatest strategic potential and fund them in progressive stages, which they identify as internal venture capital models. These models incorporate venture capital industry practices. They include a comprehensive due diligence process, partnering with outside expertise to improve decision making, and a portfolio orientation.

In addition to data gathered as part of our twelve project study, we conducted in-depth interviews with venture capital fund managers at four firms: Nortel Networks, Lucent, 3M, and Procter & Gamble. The approach that was used by Nortel Networks, described in the next section, is based on a venture capital fund model, and various forms of this approach are being used by other U.S. corporations.[4] (Note: Descriptions of funding approaches used by Lucent Technologies, Nortel Networks, 3M, and Procter & Gamble are included in the Appendix.)

THE VENTURE CAPITAL MODEL AT NORTEL NETWORKS

In chapter 3 we discussed how Nortel Networks's NetActive project was evaluated, supported, and funded through the Ventures Program. Here, we review the venture capital funding approach developed by Nortel Networks, which integrated venture funding into its corporate structure.[5] Primary responsibility for this investing activity was assigned to a senior vice president, whose other tasks included corporate strategy and alliances, as well as the company's Business Ventures Group. Besides this senior vice president, the venture board's six-to-ten members included the CEO, the company's top legal counsel, and the chief mergers and acquisitions specialist.

This venture board considered acquisitions, mergers, divestitures, spin-offs, and strategic partnerships. The senior vice president approved internal venture investments, and the director of the Business Ventures Group approved seed investments. Additionally, each venture had its own board of directors to provide advice and direction.

The venture-funding process was stage-focused. A three-member venture qualification team evaluated ideas and recommended which "new business opportunities" (NBOs) should receive seed capital, in other words, "a minor amount of money . . . to actually get more information to make a better decision." Approval of these recommendations rested with Joanne Hyland. The seed capital allowed the Business Ventures Group staff to work with the innovator to explore new business opportunities and assess investment worthiness. As Joanne Hyland explained, "We invested seed dollars to conduct research—to get some answers about whether we actually wanted to turn an NBO into a venture."

The venture qualification team then assessed seeded projects and recommended which should go forward for further development as an official innovation. The senior vice president was empowered with final approval of those recommendations. If an NBO idea aligned with one of Nortel Networks's existing businesses, staff specialists articulated its value for that line of business and urged adoption of the project.

Only truly radical ideas went on to stage two: new business commercialization. In projects that reached this level, Nortel Networks looked for a team with demonstrated leadership capability and the right skill set. In addition, the target market had to be $100 million or greater, with a potential for 15 percent annual growth. Finally, the venture was required to show the promise of sustainable and differentiated products. Any radical innovation venture that fit within the strategic focus of a business unit was referred to the business unit for further funding past seeding, although Hyland's business development organization could provide additional incubating services, if needed. Projects that successfully moved through

Nortel Networks's two-stage process, but which were not appropriate for any of the operating units, were groomed to become separate, independent businesses. Nortel Networks retained an equity stake in these spin-out businesses, as they have with NetActive.

KEYS TO EFFECTIVE FUNDING OF RADICAL INNOVATION PROJECTS

Strategically, every firm should decide which approach or combination of approaches it will implement in funding radical projects. Will it rely on the bootstrapping ability of project champions? Will it set up an internal venture fund? For example, TI set up a totally owned internal corporate venture project to fund the DLP effort. Will it identify potential external funding sources, such as government agencies? Will it partner with external venture capital firms, as Intel and TI have done? Our observations of many projects—both in our cross-industry study and in studies of other firms that are members of the Industrial Research Institute—suggest that there is no single best way to fund radical innovation projects. However, some or all of the following will be useful to most firms and projects committed to improving the radical innovation funding process:

ENSURE THAT THE TEAM INCLUDES ONE OR MORE INDIVIDUALS WITH RESOURCE ACQUISITION SKILLS. Even in a relatively supportive environment, radical innovation projects struggle to get the resources they need. The project team must be entrepreneurial, creative, intense, and persistent in seeking resources, rather than expecting the budget allocation process to deliver the funds it needs.[6] However, given that radical innovation project managers normally do not have resource acquisition skills, firms need to ensure that the project team has access to the resource acquisition skill set. There are several options: First, an individual who already has a track record of success in acquiring resources for radical innovation projects can be assigned to the team. Second, the project manager or a team member can be trained or mentored to develop the skill set. Third, the firm or the radical innovation hub could assign, on an as-needed basis, a skilled "resource acquisition specialist" to the project—someone who can identify sources of financing (internal and external) and help develop funding proposals.

MAKE RESOURCE ACQUISITION THE PRIMARY TASK OF ONE INDIVIDUAL. If the team is assembled with at least one resource acquisition expert, then the task isn't left to a highly motivated but inexperienced band of fundraising amateurs. The rest of the team can focus on the tasks that take advantage of their capabilities. This approach is common in venture-capital-backed companies. In the early rounds of financing, the CEO usually is required to take the lead. In later stages, the venture typically has matured to the point where it has a CFO who takes the lead in the acquisition of financing. When Air Products was pursuing major funding from the Department of Energy, all hands were on deck—writing the proposal, forming the consortium of partners required to compete for the grant, negotiating deals, and so forth. All other project tasks were put on hold. By comparison, the project manager for Nortel Networks's NetActive project, Jeff Dodge, worked closely with experts in Nortel Networks's radical innovation hub to pursue funding. This allowed the rest of the team, to their great relief, to focus on tasks aimed at reducing technical, market, business model, and organizational uncertainties.

COMPILE A LIST OF ALTERNATIVE SOURCES OF FINANCING. Firms—ideally through their radical innovation hub—should develop an inventory of internal and external financing sources. Identifying them in advance of need will reduce the inefficiencies resulting from scrambling for financial support when the team is confronted with a funding crisis. It will also provide a starting point for the team's resource acquisition expert.

ASSESS THE TRADE-OFFS IN ACCESSING EXTERNAL VERSUS INTERNAL FUNDING. The decision to pursue and accept external funding should take into account both practical and strategic ramifications. What are the trade-offs? What is the administrative burden associated with acquiring the funding? What are the administrative costs of managing the relationship with the source of external funding? In what ways—positive and negative—will external funding change the nature of the project or redirect it toward different applications or markets?

STAGE THE FUNDING. Because of the nature of the radical innovation life cycle, firms should commit the minimum resources necessary for engaging in a "probe-and-learn" strategy, as discussed in chapter 5. Early in the radical innovation life cycle, more frequent and smaller commitments will support the need for rapid learning and redirection. The decision-making entity—whether an individual or the board—should be matched to the maturity of the project and the size of the funding decision.

PREPROJECT FUNDING. Move initial funding decisions to people closest to the action—research managers and/or innovation hub managers—who would have a small fund for seeding radical innovations. The goal should be to make timely decisions about the commitment of small amounts of seed money to conduct technological and opportunity assessment, to gather information, and to allow the project team to prepare its case.

INITIAL PROJECT FUNDING. The case for project funding should be presented to an individual or small board with experience in evaluating radical innovations. The case should include all uncertainties, identifiable risks, and assumptions, with a plan for attacking each.

RAMP UP FUNDING. The firm should determine the threshold funding authority of a radical innovation hub manager. Any requirement above that level should trigger a review and decision-making process that engages senior management.

TRANSITION FUNDING. It is critically important that sufficient funding is provided to complete the transition to operating status. There must be a clear understanding among all the parties involved in completing the transition—the project team, the transition team, senior management, the radical innovation hub organization, and the receiving operating unit—of the sources of the funding to support transition activities.

ASSEMBLE AN APPROPRIATE DECISION-MAKING BOARD FOR RADICAL INNOVATION INVESTMENTS. To enable objective decisions for ramp-up and transition funding, the investment board should involve people who are independent from the pressures of the operating units. There is no more certain way of making a venture funding board irrelevant than staffing it with managers who are driven only by the narrow, short-term interests of their own business units, or who lack the skill and judgment to make appropriate decisions. Senior management must be involved in making decisions on radical projects because of strategic considerations, but the decision-making team can and should include individuals who are experienced and sophisticated with respect to radical innovation and the specific technologies in question. As described in chapter 3, these may be veterans of radical innovation projects, managers from a new business development or radical innovation hub organization, and even outsiders who have specialized knowledge and expertise appropriate to the project and who are removed from the political pressures of the organization. Firms might consider including people with venture capital experience to be part of the board's decision making process, as was done at Lucent (see Appendix).

EXPLORE ALTERNATIVE VENTURE CAPITAL MODELS. During our five-year study, we witnessed firms experimenting with a variety of approaches to engaging in venture capital funding. Firms are grappling with two sets of choices. The first choice is the *eventual home of the fledgling business*. We observed investments directed at ventures that would be housed within the corporation's boundaries, and those that were targeted to be spun out from the company and operate as stand-alone organizations. Firms benefit financially from the spin-outs, but do not leverage the learning and competency stretching that comes as a result of working in the white spaces.

The second decision has to do with the *source of expertise* that firms rely on as they get involved in investing venture capital funding. In some cases, such as with Nortel Networks, Lucent, and Procter & Gamble, the firm opted to develop an internal venture capital investment capacity. These firms have either developed and promoted people within the corporation, or hired members of the

VC or consulting community to direct the company's investment efforts. Investments are typically focused on opportunities that originate from within the company. In other cases, such as with Texas Instruments and Intel, the firm chose to partner with external venture capital firms to make investment choices. Under this scenario, the firm may end up investing in opportunities that originate outside the organization, which come to their attention via the external VC firm. Firms that make a strategic decision to pursue radical innovation can learn from the experience of others and choose an approach that is consonant with their objective.

ACCESSING MISSING COMPETENCIES

Money is not the only resource that radical projects find in short supply. They are often short on technical and business competencies. Three approaches can be used to address missing competencies: internal development, acquisition of an outside firm, and partnering.

Competencies that were already in place within the parent company and that could be accessed by the project team were used for technical and market development in all twelve projects covered by our study. When competency gaps were large and could not be filled through internal partnering, these firms routinely opted to partner with other firms to fill them; they did not attempt to develop them internally. In only one case—the IBM silicon germanium chip project—was acquisition of an outside firm used to address a competency gap. That strategic action occurred at the end of the project life cycle.

Partnering played a critical role in all twelve of our projects. The decision to secure partners was often imposed by senior management as a condition of project continuation. However, corporate direction and oversight of partnership choices with respect to the firm's portfolio of partners was noticeably absent.[7] Finding and consummating a partnership were typically left to the project team.

These observations reveal an opportunity to improve effectiveness in partnering. For those firms that make the strategic choice to engage in radical innovation in a systematic rather than ad hoc approach, experience with monitoring and decision making will accumulate and be reflected in radical innovation hubs and oversight boards, for both the hubs and for individual projects. Rather than rely on project teams alone to identify and negotiate with potential partners, firms can use that cumulative experience to implement a strategic portfolio approach to partnering.

The partnering experiences of our dozen radical projects are not unusual. One study found that almost 30 percent of high tech firms used alliances for the development of their most recent substantial innovations.[8] Firms are increasing alliance activity for many reasons, including increasing their cross-national boundary presence,[9] preempting competitors from entering markets,[10] ensuring sources of supply, and, finally, absorbing new capacity.[11] This latter practice, in particular, is increasing as firms feel market pressure to act quickly and often aren't prepared to invest the time and resources required to develop needed competencies internally.

THE PARTNER CONNECTION

In addition to supplying capital, partners helped our projects address the following four competency gaps:

MARKET LEARNING AND BUSINESS MODEL DEVELOPMENT. As discussed in chapters 5 and 6, learning about markets that don't yet exist or that will be dramatically changed by the introduction of a radical innovation is a daunting task. Traditional market research techniques are generally ineffective. Learning about markets is especially difficult when the firm is exploring an opportunity outside the innovator's current strategic framework. Partners can help. For example, Analog Devices had the good fortune to have a European marketing engineer who sent an accelerometer test chip to his customer, Siemens, which evaluated it. Siemens recognized the value for their air bag applications and the potential of the technology. They worked with Analog to define the functions and performance of the final product and became the first customer for the accelerometer.

TECHNOLOGY DEVELOPMENT. Lead users and technical development partners provide innovators with an arena in which to methodically experiment with design and manufacturing approaches and gain valuable feedback about what works and what does not. They provide a relatively safe learning environment wherein the innovations can be tested iteratively and product designs can be modified. Each iteration refines the product and reduces uncertainty as a project moves toward commercialization.[12] As one project manager summarized: "We wanted to get quantitative feedback from a lead customer on the value of the product's capability in a real customer environment, doing real customer tasks."

TECHNOLOGY ACQUISITION. In some cases, the technical knowledge that is a core part of the innovation is acquired or developed through partnering, rather than through internal research alone. Air Products established a strategic relationship with Ceramatec to access its knowledge and skill base related to ceramic membranes. Likewise, in the GM case at the beginning of this chapter, GM adopted an aggressive approach to contracting for technology development.

MANUFACTURING EXPERTISE. In over half of our projects, teams sought out partners who would take on some of the production work. Firms without the requisite manufacturing expertise for producing the innovation were reluctant to develop that expertise in-house and had a strong preference for partnering.

The critical contributions of external partners to progress in these radical innovation projects should be apparent. But, they come at a cost. It's important for radical innovation teams to recognize and manage the trade-offs in partnering.[13]

THE PARTNERING TRADE-OFFS

Partnerships can be used to learn and internalize new skills and knowledge, in particular those that are tacit, collective, and embedded.[14] The years it often takes to develop these skills and knowledge—about technology or markets—makes the idea of partnering with those who have them extremely compelling.

Firms in our study frequently chose partnering to overcome

substantial competency gaps rather than invest in internal development of those competencies. They were more comfortable with the former approach. It is difficult to predict the time and cost required for internal development. Many firms have a track record of success in partnering for manufacturing and market development related to mainstream products and believe that the experience in the radical innovation environment will be comparable. However, even when the competency gap is large, the best solution is not always partnering.

It is impossible to determine, even through hindsight, whether internal development of missing competencies would have been preferable to outsourcing. However, it is clear that the firms in our study underestimated the difficulties associated with partnering in the radical innovation arena. Also, in many cases there did not appear to be a careful consideration of the trade-offs.

An orientation that favors partnering where appropriate is part of the acquisition mentality that radical innovation teams need to adopt. It also fits with the approaches to capturing radical ideas and radical innovation project management discussed in earlier chapters. These approaches recognize the value of partnering for gaining access to additional sources of information that in turn help project teams uncover and test assumptions. Further, a partnering orientation helps build the network of internal and external partners who can provide support when a project runs into difficulties and who can lead the project team to other partnering opportunities.

When partnering is successful, it is a quick and efficient way to resolve the competency gap. It can reduce time to market and avoids the risk of missing a window of opportunity in cases where internal development of competencies or acquisition takes too long or, worse, never produces the competency. When the partner is recognized for its competence and the partnership is productive, then the project team gains credibility and trust internally. Hence, at first glance, partnering looks like the low-cost, rapid solution. Unfortunately partnering is not a panacea. In several of our projects, unsatisfactory performance by partners or difficulties in managing the partnership created serious setbacks; these increased rather than reduced uncertainty. In no case was that clearer than in the GM case cited earlier. Nonperformance by technology development partners killed the project.

Unanticipated problems with partners were the norm in the projects in our study. Failure to manage three critical challenges—beyond the well-known relationship management challenges any partnership faces—increases risk. The three critical challenges are the time required to identify candidate partners and to consummate the partnering agreement; control of intellectual property; and decision making about ownership of segments of the value chain.

TIME REQUIRED FOR IDENTIFYING PARTNERS AND CLOSING AGREEMENTS. In about half our cases the time investment for identifying partners and closing agreements was substantial—dominating the project management effort for extended periods of time. In some cases, the novelty of the technology seriously limited the pool of potential partners. In others, the project team lacked experience in establishing partnership relationships.

In most of the projects we studied, the project manager had responsibility for finding and linking up with potential partners. This task diminished the time available to work on other priority tasks—often for months at a time. For Kitty Knox, leader of DuPont's electronic materials project, this task consumed her attention during the two years before the project was adopted by a business unit. Her initial preferred manufacturing partner decided to pass on the opportunity at the end of a yearlong courtship. After an extended period of pursuing an alternative candidate, she decided that the original candidate was preferable and returned to the negotiating table. In the intervening twelve months, DuPont's perspective on acceptable terms of a partnership had changed as a result of the evolution of the technology and the project. With a new approach and a new offer, she struck the deal. Likewise in other companies, a major commitment of time was required for setting up partnerships. IBM's Bernie Meyerson spent three months screening and performing due diligence on hundreds of potential partners. The TI senior executive who originally headed up TI's DLP project traveled the world negotiating with potential market development partners.

CONTROL OF INTELLECTUAL PROPERTY. Radical innovation development will almost certainly produce new intellectual property. Therefore, determining issues of ownership and control is an important part of the partnership negotiation process. As one veteran of alliance management stated: "These arrangements are notoriously leaky." This was a more difficult issue in situations where the partnership was structured as a supplier relationship in which the supplier retained rights to the technology. In one case the firm and its supplier operating under a technical development contract had an adversarial relationship. The supplier misled the firm about its setbacks and the real status of development until the shortfall in progress could no longer be hidden. Though the contract was terminated, the damage was done. This was less of a problem in cases where the firm funded the partner's development work and the agreement specified that the firm owned the output. Technical notebooks were open, technical learning was shared, and there was a sense of collaborative development.

Most people simply push forward, do their best to structure the partnering arrangements appropriately, and try not to worry about future consequences. Said one manager, "Frankly, I don't think we had a choice. We couldn't grow that expertise in-house." The trade-off is access to missing technical competencies versus the potential loss of control of proprietary knowledge.

OWNERSHIP OF SEGMENTS OF THE VALUE CHAIN. There is significant risk in partnering early in the life of the project when the business model is still highly uncertain. When the project is ready to go commercial, the innovating firm may be poorly positioned with respect to the most attractive parts of the value chain. The natural tendency is to retain the parts of the value chain that require competencies the firm already has and to outsource the rest. However, the marketplace may assign the major portion of the total value of the innovation to the parts that are outsourced.[15] It may also turn out that production of the parts that are retained will face severe competition, driving down profit margins. The computer software/hardware dichotomy illustrates the point. In the early years of the development of the PC, IBM saw itself as a hardware manufacturer and decided to outsource development and production of the operating system software. Imagine the impact on IBM's performance if it had successfully acquired or developed internally the operating system for its PCs.

At the inception of a partnership, the project team would like to clearly define and firmly establish the contractual relationship. However, because of the multiplicity of uncertainties at the front end of the radical innovation life cycle, there is a high probability that the relationship will need to be modified or, in the case of nonperformance, terminated. Thus the partnership relationship needs to be both highly structured—to reduce uncertainty—and highly flexible—to permit adaptation to unanticipated outcomes. This paradox is reflected in the following comment from one project manager:

> The choice of the right partner is really essential. The difficulty is that the choice has to be done in a kind of fluid fashion because, at the front end, you don't know what you have invented. The things that we're doing now have really modified our initial view of who would be the correct partner. As we drive down the development path from where we are today, I think that we'll continue to modify our notion of the perfect partner.

Careful analysis may indicate that partnering is the most attractive approach. But, in the cases we studied, managerial trade-offs and the strategic issues related to the value chain were of secondary importance compared with uncertainty reduction. We were surprised that we did not see more crash programs to develop missing competencies internally. In some situations internal development, or acquisition, might be the preferable strategy, particularly if the firm decides there is merit in stretching its strategic frame and expanding its competency base. Still, in most radical innovation projects, partnering will be an important option for dealing with missing competencies, and therefore, developing strategies for dealing with partnerships under high uncertainty is critical to the success of these projects.

KEYS FOR EFFECTIVE PARTNERING TO
ACCESS MISSING COMPETENCIES

Given the issues we have described and the problems associated with partnering, how can radical innovators do better? Here are our suggestions:

SELECT PARTNERS STRATEGICALLY. The decision should be made at two strategic levels. First, firms should consider which approach to resolving missing competencies is best: partnering, acquisition of another firm, or internal development. Second, if partnering is the preferred option, then the team should take into account the firm's portfolio of strategic partners when selecting a partner. In our study, we saw most partnering decisions made at the project level. These issues should be addressed comprehensively and deliberately as part of planning and decision making—by the project team, radical innovation hub, oversight boards, and senior management.

DEVELOP A PARTNERING COMPETENCY. Few radical innovation project team members have experience in forming and managing partnering relationships. The radical innovation hub can help nascent projects develop internal and external partnerships. In addition, the hub can provide training to help the radical innovation team develop the skill sets required for managing partnerships.

ESTABLISH PARTNERSHIP AGREEMENTS THAT ARE APPROPRIATE FOR RADICAL INNOVATION PROJECTS. Even though high uncertainty is a fact of life in radical innovation projects, the radical innovation team should strive to structure each partnership agreement as clearly as possible. This will establish a shared understanding of the roles, responsibilities, and expectations of each partner and make it easier to navigate together through the murkiness of the radical innovation development process. On the other hand, each agreement should also establish a mutual understanding that evolution of the relationship is likely, since the course of the project will change as a result of learning. If the agreement embodies the flexibility required for adaptation, then it will reinforce mutual trust and confidence.

Therefore, it should define how the relationship can be revised and additional partners brought into the project downstream, as necessary, to fill in unanticipated competency gaps. Both partners must be prepared to accept dilution of their rewards in order to bring in new resources and competencies that may be required to complete the project and to make their collaboration have market value.

At the end of the day, project teams that fall short don't fail. They just run out of resources before they have learned how to succeed and run out of the time needed to develop or acquire the competencies to complete their tasks. This chapter has focused on approaches to overcoming this challenge, which is encompassed by one of the four types of uncertainty—resource uncertainty. These insights can help ensure that promising projects have the opportunity to achieve the radical innovation success their firms want and need.

THE FINAL LEG OF THE JOURNEY

When the project approaches maturity and is ready to transition to operating status, it typically encounters other competency and resource gaps that must be bridged. The project must complete application development, educate customers, and develop the capacity for manufacturing in volume. Because of the residual uncertainties of radical innovation projects—even late in the game—these activities require special skills typically not found in project teams or in receiving business units. To prevent failure at the very end of the long journey, the project team or the receiving business unit must develop transition management capabilities, or a transition management team must be assembled to fill the gap. The challenges of completing the final tasks of the radical innovation life cycle are tackled in the next chapter.

CHAPTER 8

MAKING THE
TRANSITION
TO OPERATIONS

THE RADICAL INNOVATION PROJECT TEAM FACES A LAST SET
of hurdles at the end of its long and winding road. It must make it
through the metamorphosis from project to operating business. It
seems reasonable to expect that the momentum of a project would
propel it through this final transition. After confronting and con-
quering many technical, market, organizational, and resource
uncertainties, how difficult can this last hurdle be? At the start of
our study, we and our industrial partners assumed that once the
project was sufficiently mature, the receiving operating unit would
be able to employ tried and true project management techniques.
Contrary to expectations, this wasn't the case. It turned out that the
transition was difficult, because typically there were major residual
uncertainties and new uncertainties to be resolved. Dave Feretti, the
program manager in the receiving unit that took on the responsibility for Biomax, lamented: "I sure expected this to be further
along when it got shifted over to me."

During transition, market and technical issues continue to beset the project. Prototyping and applications development continue and often restart as a result of market entry. Additional challenges also arise. Although early adopters are often willing to accept a prototype and work with the innovating firm to define the form and function of the new product, customers who are buying a commercial product expect the development to be fully completed. A new product based on a radical innovation will be sufficiently different from current products that potential customers need to be educated. Technical specifications that were adequate for the prototype stage require substantial revision as the new product is customized for specific applications. Manufacturing ramp-up is challenging when significant changes from established approaches are required.

Organizational and resource issues also present problems during transition. Partners who were significant contributors during development may come up short during the final phase. The internal organizational destination of the innovation is an even greater concern, and each alternative has its various pros and cons. Should the project be spun off as a separate entity? Should it become the core of a new operating group? Or should it be ported directly into one of the corporation's existing business units?[1]

In chapter 3 we discussed the conversion gap between a radical innovation idea and the formation of a project. Here we see another conversion gap—this time between the project and the operating unit.[2] Often neither the receiving unit nor the project team is prepared to work through these transitional issues. The receiving unit, which is focused on generating revenues as soon as possible, expects the project to be mature enough that it can implement standard product launch and ramp-up management techniques. The project team is accustomed to the "probe-and-learn" approach to innovation development and prefers to continue trying to develop newer and better versions of the product rather than making firm and final design decisions.[3] The project team may also be uncomfortable with a firm budget and hard schedule imposed by managers trying to drive the conversion. In most cases neither the receiving operating unit nor the project team can be expected to develop the competencies that will accelerate the project through the transition. A transition team—formed and supported by the radical innovation hub—can be a more effective organizational approach. Although this will require two handoffs rather than one—from project to transition team and from transition team to operating unit—we believe the probability of successfully bridging two smaller gaps will turn out to be much higher than trying to bridge one substantial gap.

FINDING THE RIGHT HOME

Selecting the appropriate location for the new operating business is a critical decision. If the firm chooses to develop the new business internally, the most straightforward transition is to an existing business unit (Strategic Business Unit [SBU]). When there is not a good fit with an existing business unit, then it makes sense to establish a new business unit. However, the costs and risks for these start-up operations are likely to tempt corporate executives to have an SBU adopt the promising but homeless project, even if it requires a "force fit." This is "a round peg into a square hole" problem. There is typically a misfit between the needs of the radical innovation project and the business unit's current capabilities in manufacturing, sales and marketing, distribution, and so forth. The greater the misfit, the greater the investment required for retraining personnel and modifying the business unit's operating systems. Unless there is a corporate commitment to support this process—with financial resources and an adjustment in performance metrics, there will likely be resistance from the business unit.

Of the nine projects in our sample for which there was no clear SBU home at the outset, three were "force fitted" into an existing SBU with some resistance or concern on the part of the SBU. Of the remaining six, one was shopped to a welcoming SBU; four formed new receiving units—either new divisions or spin-out ventures; and one had not considered the issue before the project was shut down for technical reasons.

Force fitting a project into an existing SBU can have fatal consequences, as the existing SBU may either fail to give it full support or attempt to drive it through its inappropriate systems of distribution, financing, and performance review.[4] In one of our case studies, the new business development manager received the go-ahead from corporate management to initiate the handoff to a business unit. When he contacted the head of the business unit, she asked where he had manufactured the prototypes. She was surprised to find out that the prototypes had been manufactured on her production line.

The transition effort drifted along. The initial project manager was reassigned within the first year of the effort—never really getting engaged in the transition. The second product manager got off to a slow start because of the messy handoff from the original product manager. It didn't get a hard enough push from the business unit manager and, as a result, did not receive priority attention from the product manager. It was just one of several product management responsibilities for them, and they were being measured on their success in increasing revenues for their portfolio of products. The radical innovation was far from ready to generate revenues. The second project manager was dedicating his "spare time" to completing the transition process—obviously not a prescription for transition success. The lack of communication between the radical innovation project team and the receiving unit can cause unnecessary surprises, as in the case described above. Similarly, the absence of commitment from operating unit management, in the form of dedicated personnel and resources, can cause a project to fall off its priority list.

Accomplishing the transition for a radical innovation that fits within an existing business unit is difficult enough, but when the radical innovation doesn't have an obvious home, the transition is that much more difficult. When the innovation is divergent from the firm's existing strategic framework, the innovation is an *unrelated diversification*.[5] This situation is exemplified by Polaroid's development of a memory storage technology, an innovation that was far outside the corporation's strategic boundaries. Polaroid's vision was to transform the product structure of the company in order to encompass the new technology, so they established a new business unit and developed a strategic partnership with another firm.

If the fit is poor and if the firm is unwilling to leverage the innovation to stretch its competency base, then the business will most likely be spun off.[6] In this situation, the parent firm must determine its relationship with the spin-out firm. Are there competitive issues related to access to technology? Will the spin-out firm be a key supplier? How can the parent company maximize the return on its investment in the discovery and development of the radical innovation? This is important, not only with respect to financial returns but also because of the impact—positive or negative—on the firm's efforts to extend its technical capabilities and market experience.

A firm may decide that it will not under any circumstances pursue the development of a radical innovation that does not clearly fall within its strategic framework. However, if it chooses to spin out the technology into a new venture, the firm stands to gain the benefit of the competency stretching that will naturally occur from participating in the development that precedes the spin-out. While this is not the complete benefit of learning from the project, it is more than the firm would gain if it chose to ignore the opportunity altogether. And, the firm still benefits financially from its equity investment in the spin-out. This was certainly the case for Nortel Networks with respect to its spin-out of NetActive. If none of these options are feasible, then technology out-licensing or shelving is the usual course of action.

Let's look at the options in greater detail, using some of our case projects as examples.

The following case illustrates how a seemingly straightforward transition to an obvious business unit home can be surprisingly difficult. Project teams need to be aware that the operating unit will not always welcome the radical innovation with open arms, even if technical and market uncertainties have been resolved.

GE: TRANSITION TO AN EXISTING BUSINESS UNIT

GE's digital X-ray project had a natural home from the beginning. The GE Medical Systems (GEMS) division had initiated the project and had funded early development. GEMS was already serving the medical imaging market with its traditional X-ray, CT, MRI, ultrasound, and other products. The new technology would serve that same market and could be effectively marketed, distributed, and serviced by GEMS personnel. Clearly, when the project matured, it would transition into the GEMS business unit.

A funny thing happened on the way to successful development.

The GEMS division manager changed priorities and ceased being a supporter of the project. This manager was keen on the numbers and was highly regarded for achieving his financial performance targets in the current lines of business. He was alarmed by the project's technical uncertainties and by the potential negative impact that further development would have on the short-term financial performance of the division. Under the direction of project manager Bruce Griffing, the project continued with corporate and government funding, but with neither the support nor the involvement of the business unit that would be its logical future home.

The project team gradually solved most of its technical problems. Team members conducted successful prototype tests with key customers and eventually the project was ready to make the transition to the business unit. But the digital X-ray project would go nowhere without the support of the GEMS division manager.

In 1997, that executive unexpectedly left the company. As luck would have it, his successor recognized the potential of the innovation and engaged in a thorough assessment. Convinced of its promise, he became an enthusiastic backer. The digital X-ray project was now ready for the handoff to GEMS—or so it appeared.

One of the key concerns of the now-departed head of GEMS had been the need to partner with another firm capable of manufacturing key components with satisfactory quality and yield for the digital X-ray project. The project team had found a credible partner and worked with it throughout the development process. But at the time of transition, this manufacturing partner could not produce adequate yields. As a result, during the transition, the challenge of manufacturing scale-up was brought into central research and development. Under the close oversight of project manager Griffing, manufacturing of key components of the system took place in one of R&D's mothballed facilities.

In this case, one of the firm's business units had a long successful track record in the target market for the radical innovation. Marketing, distribution, and service systems were well established. At the project outset, the business unit was driving the project forward and providing the funding. There was no question that the radical innovation would eventually transition to the established business unit.

On the surface it seemed that market, organizational, and resource uncertainty were relatively low. The primary uncertainties were technical, in other words, proving the technology and developing manufacturing capability. Yet senior management turnover, problems with the manufacturing partner, and difficulties in obtaining funding became showstoppers at several points in the radical innovation life cycle. In addition, uncertainty about initial applications was higher than expected. It turned out that the technical challenges, though significant, were the easiest to overcome.

In the next case, it was clear that the project would transition to an entirely new business unit. Inevitably, this meant the firm would invest not only in the launch of the radical innovation product but also in the establishment of the new business entity. After the long period of investment in the development of the innovation, the firm was anxious to see positive cash flow and a return on that investment. But the transition uncovered new and attractive applications possibilities. The case revealed tremendous organizational and resource tensions, while technical and market uncertainty remained high.

ANALOG DEVICES: TRANSITION TO A NEW BUSINESS UNIT

From the outset, one of CEO Jerry Fishman's objectives in forming Analog Devices's accelerometer project was expansion into the white spaces between existing business units. Stata wanted Analog Devices to get into the automotive market with the advanced chips that would be part of the sophisticated electronics systems for next-generation automobiles. Hence, it made sense to establish a new business unit to address applications in this new market and to explore other markets for this technology.

The transition from project to operating business moved ahead, but not without significant problems: loss of key personnel, difficulties in reaching breakeven, and tension between ramping up the air bag sensor business and developing new applications for the accelerometer technology. Though Analog Devices tried to keep the project champion, Richie Payne, involved in the new business unit, Payne chose to leave Analog Devices for another entrepreneurial venture.

When the accelerometer project became a new operating unit, it created financial challenges for Analog. Ramp-up efforts required continuing investment to cover negative cash flow, a common problem in high growth ventures. Analog Devices applied increasing pressure on the new business unit to get to breakeven. The leadership of the new business unit believed that additional applications of the innovation should be pursued if Analog was going to maximize the long-term returns. Hence the accelerometer business unit leadership resisted that short-term pressure and continued to juggle ramp-up of the air bag sensor business and the simultaneous pursuit of other applications for the technology, for example, computer games and simulators. In a sense, the new operating unit was stuck in an extended transition mode—with the new application development efforts retaining the characteristics of radical innovation projects. At least in the short term, the transition team succeeded in sustaining senior management commitment. It continued to receive the financial support required to cover the negative cash flow associated with manufacturing ramp-up and with continuing application development.

This case highlights the tension between a parent company's desire to reach breakeven as soon as possible and the desire of its new venture to continue experimentation with new applications. The parent company risks stunting the growth of the venture by focusing on exploitation of existing applications—such as the air bag sensor in this case—in order to achieve near-term profitability. Alternatively, it can choose to support the growth of the venture via exploration of new application arenas—with all the accompanying uncertainty. This latter path requires continued senior management support, attention to renewing the team with the right kinds of skills, and continued investment to keep the transition going.

In the last of our three cases, the parent company decided to pursue a spin-out rather than give up on the potential return from its investment in a radical innovation that didn't fit within the firm's strategic framework. Although the firm expected to reduce its risk by attracting an outside investor and by creating an independent entity to complete commercialization, this strategy carried its own risks. The parent company would have limited direct control and influence over the development of the spin-out business and would rely on its independent partners to perform effectively. It also assumed that it could achieve what it considered fair compensation for its role.

NORTEL NETWORKS: TRANSITION TO A SPIN-OUT

The initial business plan developed by the NetActive team with the help of the Nortel Networks venture board experts called for spin-out in late 1997. Unanticipated but related problems delayed the transition. Identifying the appropriate target customers and distribution channels was more difficult than anticipated. Because of these difficulties, the potential venture capital investors targeted by Nortel Networks assigned a value to the venture that was unacceptably low. As a result, Nortel Networks decided to invest more heavily in the hope of creating a more favorable valuation for its innovative offspring.

The additional investment by Nortel Networks increased the pressure to complete NetActive's transition to a stand-alone company. The venture team was pushed to land its first outside investment between Thanksgiving and Christmas of 1998, when it was difficult to get the attention of the investment community because of the holiday season. However, after an all-consuming team effort and a difficult negotiation, the financing from an investment bank was secured. NetActive was spun out as an independent company during the summer of 1999, with Nortel Networks retaining a 45-percent equity stake.

As is so often the case in radical innovation projects, the firm's assumptions and expectations did not hold up. The challenges turned out to be more difficult than anticipated, and it took longer and cost more to reach an acceptable outcome. The VP of the New Ventures Division, Joanne Hyland, indicated that NetActive was an important step up the learning curve for her organization.

LINGERING UNCERTAINTIES

Everyone—especially the personnel in the receiving operating unit—wishes that the radical innovation project team would hand over a fully specified, tested, and ready-to-manufacture product, with a manufacturing line ready to go and a set of customers anxious to put in their orders. This would allow the operating unit to crank up manufacturing, significantly increase its revenues, and maintain or even improve its profitability. But in most cases, uncertainties related to changing technical requirements, market development, finalizing the business model, attracting customers, funding the transition, and organizational and human resource issues remain unresolved. On the other side, the project team—faced with resolving market uncertainties, finding a customer base, and demonstrating market acceptance—is in unfamiliar territory. The team would like the operating unit personnel to do this work, letting them move on to another technically challenging project. Failure to address these lingering uncertainties can kill the project—even in this final phase of the radical innovation life cycle. Let's take a look at the long list of troublesome and unanswered questions that confronted the project teams in our twelve case studies.

ARE TECHNICAL SPECIFICATIONS SET?

Lining up real customers willing to pay for the new product or service provides an impetus for the transition. Initial interactions with customers sometimes reveal the need for additional technical development, particularly as the new product is customized for specific applications. In the DuPont Biomax case, the marketing campaign funded through corporate resources uncovered extensive interest among potential customers. As a result, new applications emerged that required reformulation of the material and the development of new manufacturing processes. The decision was made to transfer the project to the business unit that would manufacture the material.

In addition, manufacturing issues in prototyping are very different from those that determine the success of ramp-up. In the GE digital X-ray case discussed earlier, manufacturing of prototypes was focused on getting a "klugey" but functional system into use by early adopters. As in many other cases, we saw the completion of the transition process delayed because of unforeseen complications in resolving residual technical uncertainties.

Do Market Expectations Match Reality?

In radical projects, the time and financial investment for market development is grossly underestimated. Indeed, we found that project teams understood the necessity for dedicating time and toil to deal with *technical* uncertainty in radical innovation. However, they were less aware of and prepared for the efforts required for *market development*. Identifying a few enthusiastic early adopters does not create a foundation from which the sales curve can rapidly take off. The path from first application partners to high-volume sales can be torturous and tricky, and requires concentrated attention and skills that are different from normal selling and account management skills.

What's the Best Initial Application?

Everyone would like to find a "killer application" capable of dominating a mass market. But killer apps often don't emerge in the early commercialization period of radical innovations.[7] The process of probe and learn continues through transition and even after the operating unit is up and running with new products. To encourage market development, several project teams we studied moved to a strategy of early niche-entry applications. IBM's silicon germanium chip project was transitioned to the operating unit on the strength of initial customer enthusiasm within a set of identified applications. But a year later it was still in the "project stage" within the operating unit. Mike Concannon, vice president of IBM Microelectronics/Wireless Business Line, was still blazing new trails to applications. The original killer market had not materialized as quickly as project champion Bernie Meyerson had expected. Concannon began pursuing the global positioning systems market. The silicon germanium chip was targeted for use in GPS handset receivers.

A similar situation beset Texas Instruments's DLP project. After a number of application iterations, TI's manufacturing partners came to market with large venue installed projection systems for auditoriums and board rooms. The initial price tag made it unlikely that this would be a mass market application. However, TI was confident that it would be able to grow the market based on this and several other applications with modest market potential.

As presented in chapter 5, the Biomax project found no killer application in the early years of commercialization. As a biodegradable material in a world choking in nonbiodegradable waste, Biomax has thousands of possible uses. DuPont's challenge was to make its product the material of choice in thousands of packaging and other applications. Placing ads in technical journals and trade magazines was one method DuPont used to learn about potential niche applications. That exercise resulted in the identification of over thirty applications. Eventually, the product manager in the business unit targeted the four that seemed most promising.

The ultimate killer app for a technology frequently *cannot* emerge first, since the infrastructure required to run and maintain it is not yet developed.[8] Take the case of the "personal digital assistant" (PDA), which was defined as a "highly portable, easy-to-use computing and communications device aimed at the mass market."[9] In 1993 the earliest entrants to this market (Amstrad's PenPad, Apple's Newton, and Tandy's Zoomer) were targeted at the broadest horizontal consumer mass market—and all failed. The next wave of entrants (IBM and BellSouth's Simon, Sony's Magic Link, and Motorola's Envoy) targeted more clearly specified niche applications (e.g., mobile professionals in health care, financial services, and schools) with somewhat greater success.[10] They made faster progress because entry did not require the development of a mass market infrastructure.

How Much Market Development Will We Have to Do?

Because a product based on a radical innovation represents a significant departure from current products, customers are naturally wary. They may be uncertain about reliability, getting locked into a proprietary technology, and/or the commitment of the innovating firm to provide customer support and to stay the course with the new product. Inevitably the sales and marketing process for a new product based on a radical innovation is more complex and time-consuming than would be typical for an incremental innovation. It requires application development, customer education, and user training.

As illustrated earlier in the NetActive case, initial assumptions about target customers can prove false. By educating lead users about the technology and probing potential applications, the project team learns from and about the market.[11] The NetActive team applied the learning from its false start to redirect its marketing efforts toward more promising potential customers. However, this delayed the financing it was seeking, and therefore lengthened the transition period.

How Will Applications and Markets Unfold?

The process of market development is one in which the firm not only learns about the market, but also helps the market learn about and understand the technology and its possibilities. This process occurred in the development of the PDA market. In October 1995, a survey of PDA owners reported that most owners used it for organizing schedules and that the communications functions so widely viewed as key benefits of the technology were not being utilized.[12]

These sorts of innovations experience "application migration," a term used by a senior scientist involved in DuPont's Biomax project to describe the cycle in which the firm learns about the market, chooses an initial entry application, and continues to learn and expand into other appications. Simultaneously, early adopters and lead users in other market domains become aware of the innovation and inquire about adapting it for different uses. For example, Analog Devices is now following up on inquiries from the entertainment industry for the use of its accelerometer in computer games. A proliferation of application prospects allows the team to migrate toward the most promising early market opportunities, as happened in the Biomax case, and may eventually lead to the discovery of the killer application that is not initially obvious. Even in the GE digital X-ray project, for which the overarching application was clearly medical imaging, initial target applications emerged through market learning—and were not those originally anticipated to be primary targets.

In fact some radical innovations have become major commercial successes even though no major customers or mass-market applications were identified initially.[13] Success in these cases resulted from serving many smaller markets. In effect, many apps can lead to a "killer business." We do not mean that the search for the killer application is unimportant. What we observe, though, is that the development of a market for a radical innovation may take many paths.

How Do Manufacturing Challenges Impact Market Entry Objectives?

Manufacturing issues may also influence the development of a market-entry strategy. In one case, early manufacturing yield problems required that the entry strategy focus on high margin applications first, leaving mass-market applications until later. In other cases, firms focused on large mass-market applications to impose a dominant standard early on in the game and paid the price in short-term financial performance. Analog Devices, for example, took orders and promised deliveries of its air bag sensors long before its manufacturing process provided reasonable yields. In the first several years of operation, the new operating unit was still losing money but was receiving great PR and growing sales. Its objective was to set a new standard for the industry by gaining market share and to allow the market to value the technology.

How Do We Deal with the SBU's Expectations during Transition?

Creating a killer business out of many applications follows a period of discovery in which the innovative firm educates the market even as the market educates the firm about possible applications.

Tensions are heightened, however, when early promises of big markets are not delivered immediately. Operating units are usually under pressure to show sales volume and market-share growth soon after new products are introduced.[14] Entry strategies are typically built around maximizing those objectives. By contrast, our projects presented a much broader set of objectives. These included creating new markets that did not yet exist; moving the firm into parts of the value chain in which it had no previous experience; and ultimately, building new strategic competencies. The entry strategies to accomplish these larger objectives may be in conflict with the SBU's shorter-term requirements. Even so, it may be wiser to seek a buildup of smaller application niches that, together, form a killer business than to promise delivery of a single mass market. Managing the SBU's expectations in this regard is critical. Since business unit managers have sales objectives to meet, the trial and error required to find the right market entry point or to build the business through many small niche applications may make them uncomfortable.

How Do We Finalize the Business Model?

The activities required to create new markets or educate existing ones will stimulate the market's evolving understanding of the innovation. Hence, the business model cannot remain static. Those responsible for accomplishing the transition must continue to develop and refine the model as the market grows and develops and as learning accumulates.

In some cases, the firm needs to provide the market with a more complete product than has been defined in the business model. The objective is to help the market begin to use the product quickly.[15] Texas Instruments's early decision to provide the entire display engine (the DMD chip, the lens, the housing, and the power source) was not directed at capturing more of the value chain. Instead the company determined that OEMs were not prepared to build the chip into their own devices. Although this was not TI's preference, the firm decided to provide the entire display engine, expecting that this would accelerate the adoption of the innovation. Once several applications were well established, TI unbundled its innovation and provided the core technology alone to customers who had superior capabilities for delivering other parts of the value chain. Suppliers of lenses, housings, and power sources emerged, and new applications demanded different specifications for those parts anyway. This resulted in a shift in the underlying business model.

How Do We Sustain Funding during Transition?

Just when it appears that revenue may be in sight, the firm needs to invest in ramping up a new business. Expecting the operating unit to invest its already stretched resources in getting a radical innovation to market has been the death knell to many a project. To benefit from the learning that comes from initial market entry, the project requires additional investment to accelerate ramp-up engineering and development, market development, and customer education. In addition, failing to invest at this critical juncture delays generating revenues. So the job is not finished—not by a long shot. It is unlikely that the transition team will be able to acquire the kinds of external funding (for example, government R&D funding) available for early development. Transition funding will most likely come from internal sources or from external partners.

How Do We Bridge the Organization Gap?

The project team builds the knowledge base on which the new business can be launched, but expects the operating entity to build the business. It announces: "We're done. It's your turn." But the operating business wants the venture only when it is ready to operate. According to the chief scientist on GM's hybrid vehicle project, operating business units are not opposed to new ideas, as long as they are new ideas that don't require the operating units to do much that is new. The receiving unit naturally wants the uncertainty and risk reduced to the minimum, so that it can focus on producing and selling the product, growing the market, and generating increasing revenues and profits.

In transition the venture is neither fish nor fowl—neither a radical innovation development project nor an up-and-running operating business. Even when some or all of the project team packs up its cumulative learning and migrates into the operating business, and even when the new or established business unit is ready to receive the project, the organizational transition is beset with difficulties. The transition team needs the knowledge and skill sets of people from both sides of the transition gap, but it also needs people who are expert at executing transition tasks based on repeated experience.

How Do We Handle Personnel during Transition?

Difficulties with team members and their expectations during project transition are typical.[16] In seven of the nine projects in our study that made it to transition, key personnel either left the team or were reassigned. The mismatch between the skills and interests of the champion and the needs of the project as it moves through the transition creates a human resource challenge. At Analog Devices, Richie Payne wasn't willing to play the corporate politics required to mainstream the accelerometer project. Often, individuals who play critical developmental roles in the project team don't have the skills or the sense of commitment required to be effective members of the transition team.

There is also significant danger of handing off responsibility for an innovative product to a product manager in a business unit whose training, skills, and expectations relate to growing revenues and market share for established product lines. Typically the manager has responsibility for multiple product lines. Both the product manager and the business unit are accustomed to basing performance evaluation on short-term results. For radical innovations, there is often a significant lag in market development. Hence in the short term, managing the transition activities is a distraction from the other activities that produce the kind of measurable results on which the product manager is judged.

In one of our case studies the initial transition manager did not dedicate sufficient energy and attention to getting the radical innovation into the market and the project languished. A second manager from the business unit was assigned, but progress was still so slow that, in frustration, the director of new business development—who was judged by the results of the projects he transferred to the business units—sought new approaches to bridging the transition gap.

Keys to Effective Transition Management

The lingering questions discussed in this chapter reveal that managing the transition from a radical innovation project to a real business is neither simple nor easy. Resolving residual uncertainties takes longer and requires greater investment than may be anticipated. But by defining a transition as a specific set of activities requiring special skills and resources, companies can accelerate the transition process, reduce the risk of failure, and improve the firm's transition management competency. We offer six keys to effective transition management that should be considered in all radical innovation transition efforts.

Create a Transition Team

To accomplish the job of bridging the difficult gap between project and operating business, a transition team should include three sets of individuals:

- personnel from the radical innovation project team;
- personnel from the receiving operating unit; and
- transition management experts.

Since a successful transition requires that the accumulated learning of the innovation project team be brought to bear, key project team members should be either placed on the transition team or made available to serve as advisers. If the project champion has been effective, he or she should play a key role, possibly as leader if he or she has the right skills. If the project manager doesn't have the skill set required to manage the transition, senior management and experts in the radical innovation hub need to manage the leadership succession process carefully. Many project managers are likely to have a problem with letting go, particularly since they were the prime movers in overcoming multiple hurdles to get the project to this point. Naturally, they feel attached to "their baby." A key challenge is retaining the project manager. If the firm manages the succession well, the project manager will serve in another project or become an expert in the radical innovation hub—and the transition team will get the leader it needs.

Members of the operating unit *and* members of the original radical innovation project team should both be on the transition team. The operating unit personnel will carry the knowledge base into the new business. Ideally, the transition team will be headed by a manager with specific transition management skills and capabilities. Finally, other people who have knowledge and experience in facilitating transitions should be recruited for the team. These "experts" may be drawn from the radical innovation hub. In some firms, people who have been engaged in turnaround efforts may also be attractive candidates.

The radical innovation hub, with its accumulated knowledge, should be called on to take the lead in assembling the transition team. Further, the hub group should construct the team to provide on-the-job training and mentoring of a new generation of transition managers.

The performance of the transition team should be measured by standards that are different from those of the operating unit and from those of the R&D-based radical innovation project team. Similarly, the transition team's budget should not be provided by either R&D or the operating unit. Each of these two constituencies has a stake in the success of the transition, but each has biases that may compromise the effectiveness of the transition team. The transition team needs to aggressively continue "probe-and-learn" activities to continue learning, but does not have the luxury of a long-time horizon before coming to closure. It will be expected to move into operating mode, and thus must finalize products, business models, and selection of applications in order to establish a foundation for generating operating revenues. The more success it can demonstrate in reaching closure in these decisions, the more likely it will be permitted to explore emerging application opportunities. These provide the foundation for maximizing the firm's ultimate return on investment. Transition management is an intense and demanding balancing act reflecting the need to accelerate to closure while simultaneously pursuing new opportunities.

Who should judge the performance of the transition team? Neither the receiving operating unit nor the R&D organization that spawned the project is appropriate. Instead, the radical innovation hub, in consultation with its senior management board, should create a separate oversight board for each transition effort.

Assess Transition Readiness

This involves information sharing and negotiation between the project team and the receiving operating unit. The two sides determine how much progress the project team has made and how much progress the receiving team will require. With this mutual understanding, the transition tasks can be identified, and the resources and competencies required for completing the transition can be defined.

If the project team resolves as many uncertainties as possible and the operating unit develops an effective "early receiving" capacity, then the gap will be minimized. However, to the extent that either side lacks the skills for or commitment to transition management, they may engage in activities ineffectively and increase the likelihood that the project will flounder. Assessment of transition readiness is likely to be more efficient and more accurate if a third party takes the lead in conducting the exercise. This is another task that is appropriate for the professional staff in the radical innovation hub. The hub, through experience, will develop a competency in expediting this process and ensuring the quality and usability of the outcome. Further, radical innovation hubs can be proactive at studying game changers within their industries. This will allow them to understand patterns of entry strategies and market buildup through historical tracking, and help set appropriate expectations for the innovation's progress in the market.

Develop a Detailed Transition Plan

This should be the first task of the transition team. Most of the information for the plan should be available in the project team's knowledge base and from the readiness assessment exercise. This plan should define the tasks, a timetable, and the roles and responsibilities of team members.

The transition plan should guide the efforts of the team and provide a yardstick for measuring progress. However, because transition management is significantly different from traditional project management, we caution against the assumption that tried-and-true project management practices can be applied. Since the transition will inevitably involve confronting residual uncertainties—some of which will emerge only during the transition—the plan needs to provide slack time and resources. Of course, it should also provide a mechanism to kill the project if progress is limited or unacceptably slow.

IDENTIFY TRANSITION
SENIOR MANAGEMENT CHAMPIONS

The leadership of the firm—senior corporate management, the chief technology officer, the R&D director, and the receiving business unit managers—need to give the transition process a high priority if it is to be successful. If business unit managers know that their performance evaluations will include an assessment of growth related to the adoption and commercialization of radical innovations, then they too will insist that their managers aggressively engage in the transition process.

Typically radical innovation projects do not reach the transition phase without a "push" from senior technical managers. The probability of transition success is enhanced if there is also "pull" from the receiving business unit. All the R&D managers we interviewed stressed the importance of having two champions: one at the SBU and another at a high corporate level. As exemplified by the General Electric case, in which the new GEMS chief enthusiastically supported Bruce Griffing's digital X-ray project, the transition is most likely to succeed when a champion is found within the receiving unit. This individual creates *SBU pull* by articulating the value of the project to the future of the unit. At the same time, an innovation also needs backing by someone at or near the top of corporate leadership. This person's authority safeguards the project against intentional or unintentional resistance. In the IBM silicon germanium case discussed earlier, John E. Kelley, who at that time ran a semiconductor fabrication facility, played a pivotal role in the early days of the transition of the project into the microelectronics division. He provided "under-the-table," discretionary resources required to keep the program alive. He was part of the informal network of executives crossing division boundaries who were critical to the success of the project.

Establish a Transition Team Oversight Board

A transition team oversight board can be a useful organizational mechanism for concentrating the power of senior management supporters. It also provides a natural mechanism for reviewing progress of the transition team and ensuring cooperation of the various stakeholders. As in all other situations, the oversight board will be effective only if it is composed of the right people—those with the organizational clout to make things happen and with the knowledge of the dynamics of the transition process to know what needs to happen.

Provide Transition Funding and Commitment

One of the big dangers to a radical project is the possibility that the receiving business unit will not commit the resources needed to realize the innovation's full potential. This is a real concern to people who have dedicated a decade or more of their professional lives to pushing an innovation over many obstacles. A demand for short-term returns is one of the best ways to suboptimize an innovation's potential. Recognizing this, some companies (e.g., Air Products, DuPont, and GE) continue to support the activity with R&D funds and/or personnel during the transition. In the digital X-ray case, GE corporate R&D supported the project with fifty people even *after* the project was officially handed over to the receiving operating unit, GE Medical Systems. We estimate that this support cost central R&D

some $12 million. Senior management must ensure that corporate funding, whether through the R&D unit or from general corporate funds, is available to complete the transition.

LAY THE GROUNDWORK FOR A BIG MARKET

The ultimate goal of any radical innovation project is a killer business. From a market development perspective, that goal can be reached through several alternative paths, ranging from pursuit of a killer application to building revenues through many niche applications.

Even where there is a single, large potential market—for example, as in the case of the telecommunications applications of IBM's silicon germanium technology—it may not be easy to break into it. As described in greater detail in chapter 5, the best strategy is often the pursuit of many small applications, at least initially. Taking this approach helps educate potential users about the innovative features of the technology and thereby helps create major new markets.

It is difficult, but critically important, to set realistic expectations about the likely evolution of the market. There will continue to be dead ends and unexpected opportunities, as well as applications that work out as expected. Unless there is flexibility in the ramp-up of the new business, there is a risk the firm will shelve the project rather than continue to invest in the market development activity required to reap the benefits that the innovation offers.

WE'VE NOW FOLLOWED PROJECTS ALONG THE ROUTE FROM inception through transition to operating status. A variety of people at different levels within the organizations we studied were instrumental in initiating, supporting, and protecting the project, and keeping it moving forward. We've pointed out instances where the intervention of key personnel at critical junctures saved projects from being killed. Since the initiative and capabilities of individuals are so critical to the success of radical innovations, we devote the next chapter to exploring their roles in more depth.

CHAPTER 9

DRIVING RADICAL INNOVATION

THE IMPORTANCE OF INDIVIDUALS

THE FIRMS PARTICIPATING IN OUR STUDY EARNESTLY WANTED radical innovation to follow a systematic, organization-driven process. However, we found just the opposite: radical innovation was primarily driven by individual initiative. We were surprised by the lack of corporate attention to the critical roles played by creative technologists, entrepreneurial managers, and visionary champions in the success of radical innovation projects. Because of the nature of the radical innovation life cycle, and the uncertainties and resistance these projects engender, the established and accepted managerial processes and systems of the mainstream organization proved to be inconsequential or, worse, counterproductive. These processes and systems often had to be overcome if radical innovation hoped to succeed. Against this backdrop, experimentation with new managerial approaches for grappling with the uncertainties of radical innovation projects was ad hoc and usually not sustained.

Though there is no cookbook process for radical innovation,

our research indicates that new roles, organizational structures, and mechanisms can support the drive, energy, intensity, and persistence of creative people. Effective organizations use leadership and management structures to leverage the high energy and drive we observe in radical innovators.

IBM: A RADICAL INNOVATION CHAMPION AT WORK

For most of the months and years that Bernie Meyerson worked on the development of silicon germanium chips, he and his ad hoc team of collaborators operated as a band of mavericks—tolerated but not officially sanctioned by the IBM R&D establishment. However, his relationship with Paul Horn, the senior vice president of R&D, was one of mutual trust and respect. Horn allowed Meyerson to continue with his project, though without his official approval.

Like many radical projects, Meyerson's was viewed as an irritating virus within the R&D host. The usual organizational antibodies were applied in an attempt to neutralize it: withholding of funding, general nay-saying, and subtle signals that it might not be "career smart" to associate with the project. As an IBM Fellow, Meyerson was immune to the implication of these signals. His project continued.

Meyerson understood the power of data in winning over the minds of scientifically trained people. So he went to great lengths in preparing his presentations, showing his experimental data and contrasting it to performance data for pure silicon and for gallium arsenide, leading contenders for higher-performance, next-generation chips. He also began writing scholarly articles and took his data on the road, making presentations at a variety of professional conferences. Though the project was essentially off the radar screen of his own company, conference attendees representing Northern Telecom, Analog Devices, Hughes Electronics, and other leading companies recognized the potential of SiGe research. These potential users were natural targets for Meyerson and helped him fill in the details of what had initially been a fuzzy vision of important applications of SiGe technology in their businesses, particularly in telecommunications.

As indicated in chapter 4, the testimonials of "brand name" potential lead users with high credibility in the eyes of senior management could only enhance the legitimacy of the project. Meyerson wisely cultivated his associations with these scientists and encouraged them to provide feedback to senior IBM executives about the value of his work. "[Our own people were telling us,] 'You are not funded. You are not real. Go away. You're a pain in the ass.' Then, in comes the CEO of a very large company that IBM is trying to work with who says: 'This stuff is awesome!' That got their attention."

Meyerson's data also stimulated the interest of other IBM researchers. As they began to share his sense of SiGe's market potential, they became members of his small but modestly funded team. Others volunteered part of their time to the project. The first was Dave Harame, a scientist with expertise in manufacturing silicon wafers. Together, they experimented with growing wafers from SiGe and estimating the commercial costs of production. Others followed—mostly people who had worked with Meyerson on other projects and with whom he shared a high level of mutual respect and trust. Among them was Paul Cunningham, a long-time trusted friend who had worked in sales, forecasting, and market development in the mainframe systems group. Cunningham helped explore applications and develop partnership relationships outside IBM. He was persistent, clever, and respected for his technical and business capabilities.

Meyerson's work was not pursued in a vacuum. When it began in the early 1980s, IBM ruled the world of computing. That domination would fade over the next ten years—partly due to declining demand for the company's mainframes and partly because of a loss of customer focus. A new CEO—an industry outsider—was brought in to guide the hamstrung giant of computing back to greatness.

Lou Gerstner took the reins of IBM in April 1993. He quickly concluded that Big Blue had to stop pushing hardware and get back to its tradition of being the customer's great information problem solver. Suddenly, the hunt was on for new and profitable businesses. Furthermore, Gerstner dictated that IBM would begin selling chips to the outside world—something it had long resisted.

Barry Seidner, a business development manager assigned the task of uncovering promising new businesses within IBM's microelectronics unit, soon heard about Meyerson's project. Seidner,

Meyerson, Cunningham, and the rest of the project team developed a business plan that communicated the opportunity in a way the management review board could understand. In August 1994, IBM's innovation funding board did a complete review of Meyerson's project and made it fully funded (although Meyerson claimed he remained underfunded). The SiGe project was tracked to transition to Microelectronics Research and given greater priority.

The story of Meyerson and the development of the SiGe chip highlight three key issues related to engaging individuals in radical innovation:

- senior management plays a critical leadership role in fostering radical innovation;
- radical innovation individuals take on multiple roles; and
- radical innovation teams are composed of people with special capabilities and characteristics.

Senior managers were involved to a lesser or greater extent in every one of the projects in our study. Their actions dramatically accelerated or retarded the progress of the project team. In fact, in five of the twelve projects, the CEO had a direct, major impact on the success of the project. In two of the three projects that were discontinued, the CEO made the decision to pull the plug. Other senior managers—CTOs, central lab directors, heads of business units, VPs—also played pivotal roles in the projects. Given the general dearth of established managerial systems developed specifically for radical innovation efforts, the leadership of senior management is a critical factor in the success or failure of such projects.

The Critical Importance of Leadership

While innovation can start anywhere in a company, it can't succeed without evangelism and a lot of push from the executive suite. The chairman and CEO of 3M, Livio D. DeSimone, continually pushes his company's commitment to innovation. 3M invests more than $1 billion annually, almost 7 percent of its annual revenues, in R&D. A long-standing goal of the company is to produce 30 percent of its annual sales from products that are less than four years old. Ten percent of sales is expected from products less than one year old. DeSimone writes: "Today the grace period of market dominance for new products and technologies is short—and getting shorter."[1] These goals and this attitude, driven from the top, support an orientation toward sustained innovation.

A top-level commitment to innovation is equally compelling at Nokia. Until ten years ago, this 134-year-old Finnish company manufactured a broad range of products, from paper to chemicals to rubber goods, and some mobile telephones. Today, mobile phones account for more than 60 percent of Nokia's net sales, making it the global leader in digital communications technologies. To support this strategy, Nokia invests 9 percent of its sales in R&D, which employs 13,000 people in forty-four R&D centers in twelve countries.

Support for radical innovation demands real courage from senior management. Its costs are high, its outcomes are unknown, and it threatens to undermine the existing business.[2] The current situation of retail brokerage houses is emblematic of the hard choice that corporate leaders face as they consider innovation. These firms are caught between the need to invest in new e-trading systems and the imperative to support their traditional businesses. The first threatens to savage the second, but standing still is not an option.

We found four distinct kinds of senior manager involvement. They act in the following roles:

- champions;
- protectors of pet projects (patrons);
- initiators and supporters of radical innovation activity (provocateurs); and
- shapers of culture.

EXECUTIVE AS CHAMPION

In three of the ten companies in our study, the senior executive was not only a supporter of radical innovation projects, but also a hands-on champion.[3] In two of those cases (TI and Nortel Networks), the leader initiated the formation of a radical innovation hub organization, and in the third case (Analog Devices), the CEO personally established and funded the radical innovation project we studied. Jerry Junkins, TI's former CEO, stimulated radical innovation in his firm with his call to find new opportunities in the white spaces between the company's established business units. He personally drove the formation of a new venture development organization—TI's radical innovation hub—and supported the adoption of the Digital Light Processor project by the hub. Similarly, Gedas Sakus, president of Advanced Technology at Nortel Networks, was the prime mover behind the establishment of Nortel Networks's Business Ventures Group and the Ventures Program headed by Joanne Hyland, discussed in earlier chapters. The intense commitment of senior executives can play a powerful role in energizing their firms to engage in radical innovation.

EXECUTIVE AS PATRON

Throughout history, kings, princes, the powerful, and the rich have supported and protected artists, composers, sculptors, musicians, and philosophers. These "patrons" used their positions and resources to identify and nurture the development of people who could not be supported in other ways. While patrons were critical to the artists' success, there was no system for connecting patrons and artists. The search for a patron was not a well-defined process, and there were no clear standards for convincing the patron to fund the artist.[4]

We observe a similar system of patronage at work in corporate innovation. In all ten firms in our study, one or more senior executives played the role of enlightened patron, variously providing organizational protection, resources, and encouragement. Bernie Meyerson's project, for example, would not likely have survived without the implicit protection of Paul Horn. Likewise, in the early transition of this program to the IBM Microelectronics division, another executive, John E. Kelly, also played a pivotal role in providing the "under the table" resources required to keep the program alive. The same can be said of Bruce Griffing's digital X-ray project, which gained a new lease on life under the sponsorship of CTO Lonnie

Edelheit, who promoted the project to GE's CEO Jack Welch, prompting both an infusion of funds and the support of twenty technical researchers. The network of informal executive supporters crossing division boundaries is critical in any such enterprise.

We found across most projects that the patron had faith in the champion because of the champion's personal characteristics, a lengthy historical relationship between the two, and the champion's track record in bringing other important projects to fruition.

The importance of supportive senior managers is underscored by remarks made to us in our interviews with innovators:

> "A new technological idea was developed and the president and chairman wanted it proven."

> "We put on a show for the senior corporate guys. The CEO saw it and liked it. So now it's in the product plan."

> "We made our pitch to the chairperson who recognized it would be an excellent technology. It turned out to be a $10 billion market."

> "This project is his [senior corporate manager's] pet project, so he protects it."

> "If the CEO hadn't supported it, it never would have happened."

> "I reviewed the project with the CEO every two weeks, so it was his program."

The patronage model has three major problems. First, to be an effective patron, the CEO or senior manager must be accessible; otherwise the project will not appear on his or her radar screen. Bernie Meyerson had access to Paul Horn, who supported and protected his silicon germanium project in its early phases. But how many others never surfaced for lack of a patron?

Second, to be an effective patron, the senior executive must have a passion or personal liking for the project. Because of his belief in the promise of the digital X-ray technology Lonnie Edelheit, GE's CTO, was able to successfully pitch the project to Jack Welch. Edelheit's years of experience as a senior GE Medical Systems manager helped him recognize the potential in the project. He developed a belief in and passion for the project, which he communicated to the CEO, the ultimate patron.

Third, CEOs and senior executives come and go. Like the princes of Florence, Rome, Vienna, London, and elsewhere, who supported the artists of their times, corporate executives die, abdicate, and are sometimes overthrown, leaving innovators high and dry. For patronage to be effective, the senior executive must sustain support for the project or pass on the role to another executive. In half of the companies we studied, the senior executive who followed the project's departed patron either slowed or killed the project.

EXECUTIVE AS PROVOCATEUR

In 90 percent of our sample companies, senior managers played active roles in driving radical innovation. Air Products's CEO voiced his concern that the company had missed the previous game-changing innovation in its field and stated: "By God, we're not going to miss the next one." At a Friday afternoon meeting with his trusted managers, Otis Elevator's J. P. van Rooy challenged his team to return on Monday with ideas for solving the mile-high building "Holy Grail." The bidirectional elevator emerged from that challenge.

In actively provoking movement on the innovation front and engaging their organizations broadly, these executives probably had more impact than they would have had as patrons of individual projects. Supporting radical innovation in a general sense—by setting standards and raising expectations—is a powerful, efficient mechanism for stimulating and maintaining innovative capability in the organization.

EXECUTIVE AS SHAPER OF CULTURE

One of the executive's greatest contributions to innovation is to shape the organizational culture in ways that make radical innovation a more natural, accepted, and valued activity. Dick Drew, one of the most innovative researchers in 3M history, had that impact on 3M, and though many of that corporation's employees are too young to have any personal recollection of him, his influence on 3M's innovation culture remains profound and his principles are cited regularly in company literature. One of those principles is that management cannot order creativity or an investigative spirit, but it can create an environment in which those qualities flourish.[5] 3M's senior management realizes that principle in programs that set goals for innovators, encourage their work, and provide recognition and rewards.

Founder and retired CEO Ray Stata put a similar stamp on the culture of Analog Devices. Current employees remain familiar with Stata's approach to innovation and risk-taking and feel empowered to follow his example. One story, in particular, continues to be told and retold by company personnel and is used to justify breaking the rules when rules stand between an employee and an attractive business opportunity. Early in the history of Analog Devices, Stata identified a new and attractive opportunity through a small engineering company to expand into a new technology. He felt Analog Devices should acquire the company because he believed that the nascent technology would become important in the years to come. The company's directors disagreed, feeling that the target company was operating in technologies and markets too far afield from the firm's area of competence. Undeterred, Stata used his founder's stock to acquire the company. Before long, Analog Devices's directors saw the merit in Stata's new company, bought it, and integrated it into their operations. It has since become a cornerstone of Analog Devices's success.

Employees of Analog Devices have nothing approaching Ray Stata's personal resources, and none have his level of personal clout with the powers that be. Still, his example has entered the company lore and encourages employees at every level to do what they see as the right thing, even when others say "that will never work" or "that's not the business we're in." The solid-state accelerometer project we followed in our work with Analog Devices was a maverick project outside the strategic context of the firm's traditional business. Nevertheless, the project found the support it needed. Stata took an active interest in the project and continued to support it even in retirement.

Analog Devices's management is concerned about the firm's willingness to take similar risks now that Stata has retired. We heard the same concern echoed by Hewlett-Packard executives who had known and worked with the founders, William Hewlett and David Packard.

If corporate culture can be a positive force for innovation, it can also inhibit it. Even though senior managers in the companies we studied articulated the importance of innovation for their firms' futures, some did not walk the talk in the eyes of the project teams, as indicated in these comments:

> "The culture at this company allows radical innovations, but it doesn't foster them."

> "We aren't exactly enthusiastic about any change other than incremental change."

> "We are extremely controlled and controlling in relationships."

> "We are very poor at innovating concepts."

> "There are some things about the management structure of this organization that inhibit people from coming out with ideas. Only certain people are allowed to have ideas, and they have to be the right ideas."

> "We don't do anything in an organized, systematic, or consistent way to stimulate ideas."

> "Radical innovation happens rarely here. We have a very good record of living off incremental innovation."

> "We are very cautious when it comes to stepping out technically."

There is an obvious disconnect between the cultures of these companies, and the cultures that their leaders intend to create. Our field studies indicate that this problem is widespread. If high-sounding statements by themselves do not create innovative cultures, what can? Executive intentions must be reflected in organizational mechanisms that support innovative behavior, for example, radical innovation hubs, project oversight boards, and the deployment of hunters and gatherers. Executives need to institutionalize capabilities for radical innovation.[6]

THE MULTIPLE ROLES OF RADICAL INNOVATORS

Few radical innovation projects are glamorous at the outset (if ever). Our research found few instances in which companies took a "we-will-put-a-man-on-the-moon-in-ten-years" approach to creating breakthroughs. Most radical projects we studied were driven by inspired and determined individuals—people who would not take "no" for an answer and who often had to swim against a current of corporate indifference, if not outright resistance.

Project champions, team members, affiliated researchers, radical innovation hub supporters and advisers, even project participants from external partners—all the individuals engaged in radical innovation projects—brought enormous passion and intensity to their roles and tasks. They were not simply showing up for work each morning to put in their hours.[7] They came with a mission that carried them through lean times when resources dried up and gave them the courage and stamina to overcome barriers thrown in their way. In some cases—such as IBM's silicon germanium chip project—the team was composed of a band of mavericks, working against the mainstream. It was their own passion and the support of well-placed patrons or champions that kept them going. In other cases, the firm had implemented some supportive systems to counter organizational resistance, but individual initiative and intensity were still essential in keeping the projects moving ahead.

Few of the organizations we studied had a clear, proactive, and planned approach to engaging individuals in innovation. In many cases radical innovation did not have a clear organizational mandate. The importance of the roles individuals played was often not fully understood or appreciated by at least some of the executives who could have a significant impact on radical innovation efforts. The prevailing attitude seemed to be fatalistic: "Somehow at least a few of those radical innovation types will find their way into our organization. Their creativity will shine through. They will inevitably think and act outside the box the firm tries to impose on them. Somehow or other they'll come up with breakthrough innovations and their passion and persistence will force the firm to take notice." The reality of individual contributions to radical innovation and of interaction between the individual and the organization is much more complex. Individual initiative can and should be engaged in a proactive, deliberate, and systematic way.

Some radical innovators, such as IBM's Meyerson, are irrepressible and will fight the good fight until they take their last breaths. But others in our projects were eventually worn down, discouraged, and demotivated by the responses of others in the firm.

We heard frequent (and predictable) lamentations about how progress was slowed by the demands of the corporate bureaucracy: filling out forms for purchasing new equipment; negotiating with a facilities manager for work space; concocting reports to soothe nervous managers in which today's "facts" are instantaneously out of date; putting on "dog and pony" shows for review boards; complying with human resource policies designed for mainstream organizations but inappropriate for radical innovation projects; and dealing with business unit managers who fear the cannibalization of their current product lines.

Meyerson is a prototypical innovator and entrepreneur—technically competent, competitive, persistent, energetic, internally driven, and creative in his efforts to find resources. He built his team by drawing on his network of friends. "I called in my chits with them," he said. He found ways to get support when conventional methods failed.[8] He worked quickly, negotiating his own contracts, and built bridges to potential users—behaviors associated with small, nimble start-up firms. We observed these same skills in Meyerson's counterparts at other organizations. All were good at the following tasks:

- asking questions;
- listening and probing;
- recognizing problems;
- generating alternative development paths;
- scrounging resources;
- communicating the potential benefits of their innovations; and
- maintaining an open and fluid culture within their project teams.

THE CHALLENGE OF RETENTION

If big companies have trouble recruiting entrepreneurial, innovative people, they also have trouble retaining them.[9] "These people are going to leave us after two or three years, unless they have an attractive alternative," according to Nortel Networks's Joanne

Hyland. Joining a radical innovation venture is a career option for those who might otherwise leave.

In other cases, many of the innovators we interviewed in our research told us that they considered quitting due to frustration. Of twelve project champions in our study, two threatened to quit, four actually quit, and two were fired. Keeping these individuals requires much more than a big paycheck.

So, why do some innovators stay? The technical and financial resources of their corporations are the primary reason. These resources may be difficult to access, but at least they are available to the clever and persistent project leader. According to Meyerson: "I have had job offers for many times my present salary. I must be out of my mind for being here, but I am here anyway. The reason I am here is that IBM is a world-class organization. I believe that, at its core, the premise of the company is fabulous. We are still technologically unequaled. There is no venture in the world that has the breadth of technology IBM has." Reservoirs of technical know-how, fabrication facilities, testing labs, and so forth, all exist within the corporate tent, which can rarely be said of small firms. These organizational assets are, of course, burdened with a number of drawbacks, but most of our project leaders stayed because they believed that the advantages outweighed the disadvantages.

Meyerson reflected the feelings of many radical innovators we interviewed when he stated:

> IBM's great attraction to a hard-core entrepreneur is its mix of enormous technical horsepower, the ability to drive innovation into the broad marketplace, and its unrivaled depth and breadth of technical talent. Great things do not happen in a vacuum, they are enabled through this balance of physical and intellectual assets. What makes this career "sticky" is faith that data will ultimately win out over corporate and personal bias. It is when that trust is violated that good companies come apart at their seams.

RISKS AND REWARDS

Individuals at several of our study companies and in our workshops pointed to the fear factor associated with being part of these risky projects. "The origin of a successful breakthrough project is often forgotten," one person told us, "but an R&D effort that fails is never forgotten." Thus there is a perceived career risk in getting off track and associating with a project that may be in conflict with the mainstream organization and, in addition, has a significant probability of failure.

It seems logical that individual performance in radical innovation efforts would be measured with sensitivity to the risks those individuals take for the organization. Yet we seldom saw this. Instead, we heard repeatedly about the substantial career risks faced by people involved in radical projects. We observed several instances of people being punished through demotion for their past sins (not meeting projections in project plans) once their projects were mainstreamed. Even though in most cases the reward systems are attuned to performance in the mainstream, and not with radical innovation activities, radical innovators push ahead relying on intrinsic motivation.[10] Their rewards came from their own sense of accomplishment tied to making progress in bringing something new, exciting, and valuable to the world.

Procter & Gamble is experimenting with a system to help reduce career risk for individuals working in radical innovation projects within the Corporate New Ventures Group. Radical projects are approved by a review board that includes the CEO and the chief technical officer (CTO). Senior management explicitly promises project members that their careers will not be at risk. The rotation of team members back into line management positions in the mainstream organization is part of the package. In the few years the Corporate New Ventures Group has been existence, management has indeed fulfilled its promise. This demonstrates to other project members and to people in the larger organization that it is safe to work on radical innovation projects.

Entrepreneurs expect to benefit financially from the success of their ventures. Likewise, large companies can use financial incentives to motivate innovators. Lucent Technologies and Nortel Networks, for example, explicitly allowed project teams to participate in the financial success of their ventures.[11] As a way of retaining innovators, however, the evidence that this reward mechanism is effective has yet to be documented.

AN ABUNDANCE OF CHAMPIONS

The project champion is often the most indispensable individual contributor to a project. Successful projects usually have many champions.[12] In most of the projects we studied, project participants didn't identify a single project champion; rather, they identified a host of them. We categorize these as technical champions, project champions, business unit champions, and executive champions. An earlier section in this chapter on the roles of executives included a discussion of executive champions. In the following sections, we focus on the other three types.

TECHNICAL CHAMPIONS. Technical champions are usually the inventors or discoverers of the innovation—the idea generators we described in chapter 3. Their role is to bring the technical idea to the attention of opportunity recognizers (hunters and gatherers) who can see the implications of the technology in the marketplace. Technical champions often fight an uphill battle to get and keep their ideas on the radar screen of R&D managers and to secure sufficient funding to continue technical development in the fuzzy front end.

Technical champions are also known as "hero scientists." Every one we identified in the early phases of our projects enjoyed a high degree of organizational credibility because of past performance in solving technical problems. A number of them had received prestigious Fellow designations from their companies, which signified their worth to the company and provided them with recognition, job security, independence, and access to senior management that few other employees enjoyed. (In four of our cases, company Fellows were associated with a project.) In many cases technical champions are also project champions, at least early in the radical innovation life cycle.

PROJECT CHAMPIONS. Project champions manage the interface with the rest of the organization and with external partners, deflect organizational resistance, lobby for resources, and take on all the other project management tasks described in chapter 4. They focus efforts and keep people moving forward, particularly early on, when everybody is guessing at what the technology's benefits might be and struggling with what appear to be unsolvable problems.

Project champions have the confidence and skill to reach up through the hierarchy of the firm and grab the attention of people with the authority to legitimize their work and funnel resources to their projects. Successful project champions understand intimately how the organization works and what they must do to accomplish their ends. They are great game players and are willing to put their careers on the line to keep their projects moving ahead.

In the most successful projects we studied, individual project champions were surprisingly similar. Like IBM's Meyerson, they were animated and extroverted and came from the technical side of the business. They were extremely skilled at building connections to people both inside and outside the firm and at evangelizing their projects throughout the organization. They were excellent at lobbying, at bootlegging resources, and at inspiring strong loyalty in team members. In short, they were highly entrepreneurial people within their organizations. People we interviewed described them variously as creative, mercurial, hating boredom, colorful, credible, and passionate in their commitments. The champions we interviewed described their own relationship to their projects as follows:

> "You fight for the ones you believe in, not because they're yours, but because you believe in them. Your experience and your guts tell you to pursue [certain projects]."

> "If you have conviction, you're going to make a strong case, and you're going to fight for it. And it makes a difference."

> "I like living on the edge, and that's the way we run this project. We live on the edge of disaster all the time."

> "[The champion] has a deep understanding of technology, but he's not just a technologist. He understands and makes it his business to talk to customers, to work in the larger community, to understand what's going on in the world."

> "I am finally getting to drive forward a project that they killed so many times I've lost count."

> "After two years there was a good deal of progress on the project. Then I went on special assignment for roughly two years,

and during those years the project stalled. I don't think the project would have stalled if I'd been there."

BUSINESS UNIT CHAMPIONS. These champions provide the "pull" that every radical project needs to make a successful transition to a business unit. In our study, three of the twelve projects were clearly destined for an identified operating unit from the very beginning. In two of those cases, the business unit champions moved on to new jobs before the project matured to the transition point; each of these projects stalled as a result.

GENERATIONS OF CHAMPIONS AND NETWORKS OF SUPPORTERS

Given the long lives of most radical projects and the fact that researchers cycle in and out over the years, a series of committed leaders is often necessary. The DuPont Biomax case described in chapter 2 is typical. In that case, the cast of champions changed several times. At General Motors, Analog Devices, Air Products, IBM (electronic book project), Texas Instruments (DLP business operations), DuPont (Biomax project), Polaroid, and Otis Elevator, we witnessed turnover at the champion levels.

Turnover can actually strengthen a project's support base if project members move on to other parts of the organization and become allies. These supporters can open doors, supply resources, and endorse the project for key executives. The radical innovation hub can enhance this effect by developing and maintaining an "alumni network." Otherwise, when people move on, they may become consumed by their new assignments and may not have time to play active roles as supporters.

Generational turnover of champions can also hinder progress to the extent that it reduces consistency of purpose. In several instances, the projects we observed stalled or were shelved when their champions retired or moved on. In some instances, these projects resurfaced, but only after the loss of precious time. In one case, the project languished when the champion was temporarily transferred to another assignment but picked up again when he returned.

Because of the dependence of project survival on individual champions and the negative effects of champion turnover, a project oversight board can be useful in maintaining motivation, legitimacy, and continuity of support for radical projects. It can also be a source of future champions. This organizational mechanism is discussed more fully in chapter 10.

THE COMPOSITION OF RADICAL INNOVATION TEAMS

Much has been written about project teams in the past half dozen years—probably more than enough. Dozens of books and hundreds of articles have told us about the "wisdom" of teams, how teams members should be selected, how their work can be effectively coordinated, and how they should be led.[13] Unfortunately for radical innovation projects, most of this advice is either irrelevant or inappropriate, particularly in the early stages of the project.

The cross-functional team composition advocated for incremental innovation product development projects typically includes a technical guru, engineer, designer, manufacturing expert, marketing specialist, and even a bean counter. All the skills needed to develop the technology, iron out the final manufacturing wrinkles, and launch the new product into the market are onboard and working in a coordinated manner. This is the right recipe for a project of incremental innovation, but it is wrong for the radical project in its early phases.

We found that manufacturing people were particularly unwelcome in the early stages of radical projects involving fabricated or assembled products. The reasons are twofold: First, the physical characteristics of the product are undetermined. Second, any change in the status quo means headaches for manufacturing, whose people try to minimize changes and lobby strenuously to have the innovative product fit existing manufacturing capabilities. This is like the tail wagging the dog. Early in the course of a radical project, it is better to have a team member with a scientific interest in manufacturing processes rather than an active member of the manufacturing function from a plant or business unit environment. This may have motivated Bernie Meyerson's choice of Dave Harame as a team member, a physicist who could see many alternative manufacturing possibilities, but who was not part of the IBM chip manufacturing establishment. Similarly, traditional marketing personnel were neither found nor welcomed on these teams. As we argued in chapter 5, traditional marketing approaches such as surveys and focus groups don't work and are inappropriate when potential customers have no experience with the developing product or service.

Instead of cross-functional teams, radical innovation requires a core group of multifunctional individuals, particularly in its early phases. These individuals may be technical people first and foremost, but their value to the team is enhanced if they have had exposure to marketing (i.e., can think broadly about application possibilities for novel technologies); are interested in the financial impacts of alternative courses of development; or appreciate the consequences of development choices on manufacturing. The core group can bring in individuals with specialized knowledge as needed, but it is the core group that keeps the project on target.

People who say, "I'm a scientist. It's not my job to think about those things," do not fit the needs of a radical innovation project team. They may make a critically important contribution to the discovery and early exploration of the technology, but lack the interest or motivation to push toward commercialization of the radical innovation. In fact, one of the interesting observations made by our workshop participants is that radical innovation is like basic research with an immediate commercialization interest. As a result, we find that the best core team members have multifunctional skills; are curious about the impact of their ideas on the marketplace; are able to think outside of their narrow technical specialties; and flourish in a highly dynamic, uncertain, and ambiguous environment.[14]

The senior R&D managers who participated in our workshops recommended starting with people who have superior technical capabilities. But the following must also be included in a description of individuals who are likely to excel in a radical innovation project:

Inquisitive	Passionate
Not afraid to be different	Broadly educated
Extremely bright	Integrative
Aggressive	Flexible
Able to take risks	Goal-oriented
Entrepreneurial	Eager to learn the business

And what types of people are not wanted on research teams, according to our workshop participants? Their conclusions are as follows:

- people who can't communicate;
- people who want to pursue a lifetime career in one thing;
- people who are too oriented toward "group process";
- politicians (as opposed to network builders); and
- those who are overly risk averse.

Unfortunately, very few R&D scientists have been trained to be multifunctional and they are unprepared to take on the non-technical tasks that confront them in the project.[15] When they do, they do it out of necessity.

In several of the cases we studied, a person with a commercial development background was added in the early stage to help guide the development of the business concepts arising from technical work.[16] These individuals, too, were multifunctional generalists. Every one of them had many years of experience in the company, had held positions in at least one business unit, and had been involved in marketing, sales, and operations in one way or another. In the vast majority of cases that we studied, however, no business development personnel were involved with the project. In their absence, team members had to either bungle their way through or draw on the help of allies from a business unit. Neither of these approaches worked satisfactorily.

ADDING SPECIALIZED HELP

At some point, the core team must begin to enlist the help of specialized individuals. For example, once IBM decided it wanted to do more than manufacture silicon germanium chips at the foundry level, it needed to hire chip designers. The challenge of finding and enlisting designers who understood telecommunications applications was daunting and took much more time than expected. Ultimately, the need for these specific skills drove IBM's decision to build a new facility close to a university that was well known for expertise in this area, simply to be able to recruit graduates from that program. Also, in order to enhance its capacity to support application-specific integrated circuit design, Bernie Meyerson spent several months identifying and assessing potential acquisition candidates. Ultimately, IBM acquired CommQuest for its complementary capabilities in chip design.

New Skills Required for the Project's Transition

The skills needed for project management change as a project matures, yet some core team members are reluctant to move on when their particular skills could be better used on other projects. People who are very capable at operating under conditions of exploration and ambiguity and who are helpful in defining directions and strategies are not necessarily good at implementation under short time constraints.[17] In one case, a manager of a project in transition was pushed to present development plans and sales forecasts that were impossible to meet. Sure enough, the team was unable to meet the forecast, and the project manager was demoted and demotivated.

Core team members don't always manage later processes well. Yet, rather than being rewarded for the enormous strides they make in a domain fraught with high uncertainty, they are allowed to set themselves up to fail. Firms need to consider how to better handle these issues. Core team members may want to stay in touch with a maturing project, but it may be better for them and for the project if they disengage at some point and are reassigned to another project that is in its early stages. The project oversight board, in conjunction with the radical innovation hub, needs to take on this responsibility and manage team composition and leadership during the transition.

Keys to Effectively Engaging Individual Initiative

We have looked at the traits of successful radical innovators, the characteristics of the people they work with, and the role that the firm's leadership plays in setting the context for radical innovation.

In this final section, we offer suggestions for improving the firm's attention to its people, the most important ingredient in successful radical innovation.

Motivated, entrepreneurial individuals are critically important to radical innovation, and firms unwittingly throw obstacles in their paths. Organizations could do much to improve the recruiting, training, rewarding, and retaining of individuals who drive radical innovation and, by extension, increase the yield on radical innovation efforts.

Promote an Entrepreneurial Mind-set

Technical innovators and business people generally operate in different worlds of education, experience, and language. The result is that few technical people are equipped to formulate and express their ideas in ways that have an impact on the business people who hold the purse strings. They can talk for hours about the technical aspects of their experiments, but very little of this talk answers the key questions in the mind of the businessperson: "What is the product? Who will think it's valuable? Can we create a profitable business from it?" Reward systems can be structured to encourage this sort of skill development as well.

Senior management needs to promote an organizational mind-set for recruiting and developing entrepreneurial people. New career paths and reward systems need to be put in place. We have identified idea "hunters" and "gatherers" in earlier chapters as new roles. Similarly, firms need to recognize the importance of an entrepreneurial dimension for key technical, project, and business unit champions.

Establish and Cultivate Internal Networks

Encourage scientists and project champions to build and nourish the informal networks of supporters that can provide quick, easy, and inexpensive access to information and resources. Large companies have many intellectual and physical resources that could be used by the radical innovation project if only they could be accessed. When these efforts have succeeded, it is because the project champion knows people in the organizational networks who can help. For these reasons, deliberately finding people to manage and champion projects who are nodes in large organizational networks is important to pave the road to project success. Likewise, deliberately encouraging radical innovation team members to build and maintain informal networks is an inexpensive investment that will yield high return.

Establish Project Oversight Boards

Oversight boards can maintain continuity of energy and purpose in the face of senior management turnover. When a new case must be built to defend the project every time there is turnover among senior or key middle management, time and momentum are lost, and the project risks stalling or being killed. A project oversight board, composed of supportive senior managers, representatives from the radical innovation hub, technical and market experts from the business units or corporate staff, and strategically critical external partners can help maintain continuity of purpose at critical times in the life of the project. In addition to serving in an advisory capacity to the team, the oversight board sets corporate management's expectations and helps manage the interfaces with the rest of the organization, two equally important roles.

Recruit the "Right" People to Radical Teams

Firms must recognize the key importance of multifunctional individuals as core team members and work to recruit and train more of them. Every scientist doesn't have to become a business development person. Indeed, we have defined roles for individuals in the radical innovation hub who provide business development resources and expertise to complement technical expertise. Still, the development of multifunctional individuals requires an emphasis on expanding the learning horizon of some R&D scientists.

Companies should also actively recruit technical employees who are not simply competent in their specialties, but visibly energetic, highly committed, multitalented, and self-confident—people disposed to push back against uncertainty and resistance in support of their ideas. The traits that experienced R&D managers look for were noted earlier. People with business or marketing sense should be among those recruited to project teams, and the earlier the better.

It is also important to recognize when to replace or reassign current team members and to recruit new ones. Typically this responsibility will fall to the project manager and the oversight board. This admonition applies as well to the project champion and/or manager. As the project matures and different types of skills are required, project leaders may need to assume alternative roles within the project team or graduate to other roles in the organization. They may become key players in other radical innovation projects or in the radical innovation hub. Alternatively, if they move into a position in the mainstream organization, they should be cultivated as new members in the network of supporters. Even though they may prefer to retain leadership responsibility in the project and resist moving on, finding appropriate follow-on roles will counter the possibility that they will see themselves as cast aside. This approach recognizes their value to the project and their continuing value in the firm's radical innovation efforts.

Provide Career Development and Rewards for Potential Radical Innovators

Research managers should identify high-potential technical individuals, who are open to nontraditional work opportunities. They should seek out ways to actively broaden the experience, expand the knowledge, and build the personal networks of the individuals. This can be accomplished through periodic reassignments, work on special task forces, and other opportunities to rub shoulders with customers and sales people.

The firm needs to confront the issue of rewards. If firms hope to retain entrepreneurial individuals, they need to find ways to reward them. In several of our cases, firms were unable to deal with this issue effectively and lost key champions to more entrepreneurial environments. Also, rewards for success are often fairly clear, but rewards for attempting and persevering are usually less obvious. This is a complex and difficult issue for which we see no clear answer from our data. It needs further study in order to provide appropriate solutions for radical innovators.

ESTABLISH A CULTURE THAT VALUES AND PROMOTES RADICAL INNOVATION

Senior management must create an innovation-friendly culture—for both senior executives and radical innovators—buttressed by the right organizational structures. The culture of the corporation, like the culture of science itself, should be skeptical of innovation. Being otherwise risks dissipating scarce resources on low-value, high-risk projects. However, there is a big difference between being skeptical and being indifferent or hostile.

Radical innovators may have to swim against the current in most large corporations, but management can take steps to encourage the effort and to eliminate unnecessary obstacles. Some companies, such as 3M, have long histories of success in establishing a corporate culture that encourages and supports innovation. During the past five years, we have witnessed aggressive experimentation with new approaches at other firms. Some have so far proven positive (for example, at Lucent and Procter & Gamble) while others have been a disappointment.

Senior managers have played critical roles in each of the projects in our study. It takes courage and commitment to serve as champions, patrons, and provocateurs, but it is even more challenging to serve as shapers of culture. Radical innovation presents the firm and the project team with the most difficult test of managerial skills and processes.[18] Senior executives need to establish a culture of leadership that challenges them to push the envelope of management excellence in both the mainstream and radical innovation domains.

The ultimate challenge for senior management is to find the balance between focusing on the excellent performance of ongoing mainstream operations in the short term and creating the future of the company by sustaining the search for new avenues of long-term growth through radical innovation. Senior management can build and maintain radical innovation hubs; sponsor project oversight boards; recruit and develop radical idea hunters and gatherers; and implement appropriate evaluation criteria for radical innovation projects. These steps relieve senior managers of the burdens of being patrons and allows them to leverage their commitment to radical innovation. They go far beyond protecting individual projects and ultimately help firms build a radical innovation competency.

RADICAL INNOVATION IS DIFFICULT AND REQUIRES COURAGE. It requires great people and supportive organizational systems. The final chapter summarizes our key recommendations for how organizations can develop systems that foster, rather than discourage, radical innovation.

CHAPTER 10

A RADICAL
NEW PARADIGM

THE AMERICAN ECONOMIC SYSTEM LEADS THE WORLD IN innovation and entrepreneurship. That leadership stems from an abundance of three resources: innovative technologies, entrepreneurial talent, and risk capital. Where radical innovation and technological entrepreneurship flourish, the three types of resources flow freely and coalesce around market opportunities. It is almost as if the entire environment were supercharged, superfluid, and superconductive. New ventures created by entrepreneurs and venture capitalists have been remarkably successful in capitalizing on opportunities in this environment. In spite of their economic power, most large established firms, however, are unable to generate a sustained flow of radical innovations that lead to new economic value. They are bound up by their assets, their infrastructures, and their current business models. These rigidities constrain them from pursuing radical innovations and business opportunities with creativity, flexibility, and speed.[1]

Today, large firms are under tremendous pressure to sustain growth. As a consequence, senior management challenges the firm's technical organization to convert its knowledge base into radical innovations—even while expecting it to continue serving the development needs of mainstream businesses. Operating units themselves are challenged to develop entirely new lines of business—even as they are pressured to achieve short-term financial targets.

The organizational stress in the scenario just described is huge. The antidote is not to transform the mainstream environment into an entrepreneurial hotbed, nor to impose mainstream management disciplines on the radical innovation process. The challenge—and the opportunity—is to simultaneously excel in both operating modes and manage the interfaces to ensure complementarity rather than mutual destruction.

So, how can mature firms outsmart the upstarts in the radical innovation game? *Impermanence* is the Achilles' heel of the entrepreneur/venture capitalist model, and that weak point provides an opening for established firms. Many entrepreneurs pursue an opportunity to build a venture only once. Either they fail and don't try again, or they succeed, take their winnings, and find less stressful ways to spend their time. Though venture capitalists accumulate experience over many investments, the entrepreneurial teams with whom they work are generally composed of rookies who must climb a steep learning curve. That learning ends when the venture is harvested via IPO or acquisition. Thus, the entrepreneurial team is not around long enough to accumulate a deep reservoir of experience and expertise.

By comparison, established firms have opportunities to form structures and systems capable of accumulating learning from an ongoing stream of radical innovation projects. They can create a discipline of radical innovation and a cadre of people who excel in it. They can provide attractive, continuing opportunities for innovation veterans, thereby retaining their resources, skills, and wisdom. Established firms can develop and embed in their structure a radical innovation capability that sustains a flow of radical innovations and the growth of the company.

BUILDING THE CAPACITY FOR RADICAL INNOVATION

Radical innovations have traditionally been incubated within corporate R&D (CRD). Project teams—sometimes assisted by a business development staff person—are expected to develop the technologies needed to create an innovative product and prepare it for adoption by a business unit. The incubation idea is to protect young radical projects from the short-term financial and political pressures of the mainstream organization and to give them time to mature. The idea is on target, but its implementation often falls short.

The three sections that follow build on our observations of how firms are trying to enhance their capacity for radical innovation. The first section focuses on approaches for reducing organizational and resource uncertainty. The second section provides an evolutionary perspective of radical innovation competency development. Finally, the most effective support systems, organizational structures, and management disciplines are useless without a cadre of people who excel in radical innovation. Because excellence in radical innovation starts at the top, the final section returns to the critical issue of leadership.

REDUCING ORGANIZATIONAL AND RESOURCE UNCERTAINTIES

Throughout this book, we have made a big deal of the many uncertainties and discontinuities that plague radical projects. If some of these could be diminished from the start, radical projects would have a much higher probability of success. There are mechanisms that firms can put in place to reduce the resource and organizational uncertainties that often swamp technical and market development challenges.

ESTABLISHING A RADICAL INNOVATION HUB

A radical innovation hub—or even better, a distributed network of small, nimble hubs—can serve as the repository for the cumulative learning about managing radical innovation. In addition, a hub is a natural "home base" for all those who play pivotal organizational roles in making radical innovation happen—radical innovators, idea hunters and gatherers, internal venture capitalists, members of evaluation and oversight boards, and corporate entrepreneurs. Most important, hubs help manage the interfaces between radical innovation projects and the mainstream organization, enhancing the flow of positive resources and diminishing the flow of negative elements. Radical innovation hubs can serve a variety of functions for the firm and for individual radical innovation projects, as discussed in the following sections.

ENGAGE IN BENCHMARKING. The hub can provide senior management with performance standards for radical innovation activities. Though those standards will look very different from those applied to mainstream and incremental innovation activities, they can provide a means to assess progress and to aid in decision making. The hub can benchmark against radical innovation activities in other firms and in the entrepreneur–venture capital world. It can also benchmark internal radical innovation projects against each other. The hub can assemble and continually update a database that shows how long radical innovations take to develop, how long their markets take to develop, how much they cost, and so forth. Even though there will be issues of comparability, benchmarking can help set management's expectations regarding reasonable timing and expenditures for breakthroughs in their industry/technology domain.

IMPLEMENT A HIGHLY DEVELOPED SYSTEM FOR CAPTURING RADICAL INNOVATIONS. In chapter 3, we discussed the key roles of radical innovation idea hunters and gatherers, as well as the role of the hub in serving the idea receiving function. The hub can recruit and train hunters and gatherers, be a ready receiver for radical innovation proposals, and establish and facilitate an assessment and decision-making process that is appropriate for radical innovation projects. When it performs this function well, the flow rate of radical innovation ideas and the conversion rate of ideas into projects should increase dramatically. The hub serves as a supporting knowledge management system and repository tracking the history and experience of the organization's radical innovation activities.

CREATE A RADICAL INNOVATION CADRE. One member of a radical innovation team that had been recruited from an entrepreneurial start-up asked: "Why would people with the capability for and interest in radical innovation be attracted to an established firm?" As we have been urging, firms need to learn how to attract, develop, reward, and retain radical innovation people. The first step is to discover and encourage the radical innovation types who already work within the firm. The hub can serve as a magnet to draw these people out of the corporate woodwork and can also actively search through the organization for radical innovation talent. Working with the firm's senior executives, hubs can take a leadership role in establishing an environment and a corporate culture that is attractive to radical innovation types. Dynamic leadership, an effective innovation support infrastructure, and deep reservoirs of technology, capabilities, knowledge, and talent can create a culture and environment that are appealing to innovators and entrepreneurs.

The radical innovation hub can work closely with the firm's HR group in the selection, development, retaining, and rewarding of radical innovation project managers and team members. Training can extend to individuals engaged in hub activities, including opportunity recognition, radical innovation assessment, project intervention, mentoring, and so forth. Hub personnel can also help train those who serve on project-oversight and venture-investment decision-making boards.

PROACTIVELY ENGAGE PROJECT TEAMS AND SERVE AS EXPERTS AND MENTORS. The radical innovation hub can establish project management systems, refine them through cumulative experience, and help radical innovation teams implement them. It can guide teams in utilizing new market-learning approaches, converting technology into early prototypes, and implementing resource acquisition strategies. Further it can engage its own networks to help the radical innovation project teams gain access to internal and external partners and to structure appropriate partnerships. It can use these intervention mechanisms to help projects through key activities, crises, and critical transitions. Hubs can serve as organizational collection points for radical innovation personnel who don't remain with projects after they transition to operating status. This talent pool can be a source of team members for nascent radical innovation projects and also for "loaned experts" to engage in resolving specific issues facing multiple projects.

ORGANIZE AND RECRUIT RADICAL INNOVATION PROJECT ADVISORY BOARDS. One of the most widely used mechanisms for helping standalone entrepreneurial ventures is the advisory board or board of directors. These boards perform both advisory and progress-monitoring functions for the ventures. Typically they meet on a quarterly basis to review progress, to help management set strategic direction, and to provide a liaison to key external stakeholders. Yet we seldom saw this applied to corporate radical innovation projects. Radical innovation hubs can establish project advisory boards to perform functions similar to those just described, drawing on their own talent pool and their informal network within the larger organization for board members. They should also be prepared to go outside the organization to staff these boards. The further removed the innovation is from current capabilities/markets of the organization, the more the need exists for external board members.

ASSESSING HUB PERFORMANCE

Measuring the performance of a radical innovation hub is a challenge, given the long time frames and risks associated with radical innovation projects. The hub should report to a senior manager—probably to the CEO or CTO—through a carefully constructed, stable, competent, and powerful oversight board. The combination of long-term performance, a powerful hub oversight board, and sustained commitment from senior management will go a long way toward ensuring organizational legitimacy for the hub organization and for radical innovation activities.

UNDERSTANDING THE CHANGING ROLE OF R&D

The traditional roles of R&D are being stretched considerably by the organizational demands of radical innovation. R&D is still expected to conduct basic research, although in many firms that role is increasingly being proscribed or downsized. R&D is still expected to support the technical development needs of the business units on an ongoing basis, including the development of incremental innovations for existing products. In addition, today in many firms R&D organizations are under tremendous pressure to come up with radical innovations and to develop them to the point that they are ready for business units to take them to the marketplace.

R&D personnel are primarily good at dealing with technical uncertainty. That's why they went into R&D in the first place. However, radical innovation projects require that they also confront market, organizational, and resource uncertainties. The R&D radical innovation project team is expected to take responsibility not only for reducing technical uncertainties, but also for reducing market uncertainties and for developing the business model. Team members and team managers have to negotiate with the larger organizational environment, manage organizational interfaces, and acquire adequate resources. Clearly, this requires a redefinition of the traditional roles for R&D personnel. They need to stretch their capabilities to respond to this challenge, while still retaining their capabilities for traditional R&D. R&D leadership needs to ensure that radical innovation projects have appropriate project management and business development capabilities to complement technical capabilities. The radical innovation hub can fulfill an important role in enabling the R&D organization to meet its new challenges.

DEVELOPING A RECEIVING CAPACITY WITHIN OPERATING UNITS

Business unit personnel continue to be driven by senior management to achieve short-term financial performance targets. But they can't avoid the new pressure from management for growth through the creation of new products and new lines of business. The last thing they want is to be stuck in no-man's-land between R&D and full production—with resources being squandered on projects limping along, full of promise but producing no significant revenues. Thus they need to develop a receiving organizational capacity for radical innovation projects. Rather than resist, they need to figure out how to engage the radical innovation team and the hub most efficiently.

DEPLOYING RADICAL INNOVATION TRANSITION TEAMS

Even if the R&D organization and the business units expand their capabilities to fully respond to the challenges of their changing roles, the handoff of the radical innovation from the project team to the operating unit will still be extremely difficult. After the hard work and investment in getting the radical innovation ready, there are still major uncertainties related to target applications, production, technical development for unanticipated applications, and so forth.

There is great risk of failing to convert the radical innovation into a substantial business. A transition team should be established with high expectations for bridging the gap. It should include personnel from both R&D and the receiving business unit *plus* transition management experts. The radical innovation hub can and should play a central role in forming the transition team, assembling a new board of directors, and implementing transition management systems. Senior management needs to remain visibly committed to making sure the transition process comes to fruition. As in the case of the radical innovation hub, senior corporate management or the transition team oversight board should evaluate the performance of the transition team. Corporate funding should be provided so that the financial burden does not negatively affect the business unit results.

CREATING AN INTERNAL VENTURE CAPITAL ORGANIZATION

As indicated in the discussion about resources in chapter 7, firms are experimenting with a variety of venture capital approaches. They all start with three fundamental activities: creating a pool of risk capital that can be invested in radical innovation projects, establishing an approach for soliciting and receiving proposals, and engaging a screening and decision-making board that makes funding decisions. The objective is to enhance the firm's ability to fuel the growth of radical innovation activity, but to do so judiciously. The firm needs to invest the right amounts of capital at the right times in the right projects to ensure their success. Easy to say. Hard to do. Here are four approaches to making internal venture capital organizations successful:

ESTABLISH MULTIPLE FUNDING SOURCES. A distributed but interconnected set of funding sources will often be more effective than a single, centralized investment pool administered by one powerful venture board. The distributed approach allows radical innovation teams the opportunity to sell their story to a variety of potential investors. It also permits the firm to compare the performance of one internal venture capital group against others. That doesn't mean that one of the funding sources can't be at the corporate level or centered on the R&D operation. The single, centralized fund can be effective when the decision makers are really committed and really capable. But this single, central fund approach is weak when the "good guys" leave or retire and a less committed individual inherits the program. (We've seen this happen in several companies.) Also, when times get tough, the central venture capital fund is an easy target for cutbacks. It's more difficult to kill it or compromise it when the system is distributed.

Besides establishing a corporate-level venture fund, there are other options for funding radical innovation projects. Managers throughout the organization, even business unit managers, should have discretionary funds that are restricted to seed funding of game-changer activities. Assessing how they use these funds should be part of their performance evaluations. Likewise, the radical innovation hub or hubs should have discretionary funds for seed investing—as at Nortel Networks. The firm should explore opportunities to partner with external venture capital funds (as TI and Intel have recently done). Finally, the firm should have a government-contracting function that excels at identifying sources of R&D funding within government agencies and helping innovators write funding proposals. This function may be handled by the hub organization or may be done in collaboration with it.

PROMOTE AN ACQUISITION MENTALITY. Radical innovation relies on resource acquisition. (For example, even with his substantial success to date in GE's digital X-ray project, Bruce Griffing is still scrambling for resources to continue technology development and to build the business. Currently he is operating with funding from four sources: the GE Medical Systems business unit, the Central Research and Development budget, government research and development grants, and the discretionary funds of CEO Jack Welch.) The radical innovation hub should provide training and information to assist radical innovation teams in resource acquisition. Radical innovation project teams should see the resource acquisition process as a vehicle for qualifying and developing their ideas and for accumulating internal and external support.

ATTRACT AND/OR DEVELOP INTERNAL VENTURE CAPITALISTS. All the money and risk capital management systems in the world won't compensate for managers who aren't skilled venture capitalists. Partnering with external venture capital funds may provide an opportunity to "apprentice" employees who have been identified as potential internal venture capitalists. The company may also opt to hire consultants or retired venture capitalists to implement a training program.

LINK VENTURE CAPITAL FUNDING ACTIVITY TO RADICAL INNOVATION HUBS. The synergies are obvious. The business development capabilities resident in the hub can improve the performance of the radical innovation teams and enhance the return on investment of the venture capital funds.

THE RADICAL INNOVATION LEARNING CURVE

In any book such as this, there is a tendency to suggest solutions that are idealistic—and perhaps even unrealistic in the eyes of some readers, at least in the short term. Many of our recommendations require substantial changes in leadership approaches, organizational culture and systems, and human resource practices. Implementing these changes fully may take a long time, requiring persistence and consistency over a number of years.

Depending on the degree to which an organization is "radical innovation mature," there are different approaches to solving the major challenges we've identified. Radical innovation *maturity* is defined as the degree to which the organization has systematically implemented organizational processes for initiating, supporting, and rewarding radical innovation activities. Table 10-1 contrasts approaches for tackling the challenges identified in earlier chapters for organizations with nascent radical innovation competency versus those with mature radical innovation competency.

Moving from lower to higher maturity is not easy. However, failing to make this happen means the firm must rely on the combination of serendipity and the extraordinary efforts of heroic individuals. In firms with a mature radical innovation capability, radical innovation hubs—the repositories of the firm's expertise in radical innovation—can play a supporting role in some tasks and in others take the lead. Leadership and sustained commitment of the firm's senior executives are critically important in establishing a mature radical innovation capability.

THE IMPORTANCE OF LEADERSHIP

When the firm feels increasing pressure to improve short-term financial performance, often new management is installed that focuses on controlling costs and enhancing profitability. "There is no long term without the short term" becomes the mantra, and non-revenue-generating activities such as radical innovation projects get squeezed. This reduces the motivation to engage in radical idea generation. It increases the uncertainty associated with radical innovation projects, extends the time to commercialization, increases project costs, and increases the risk of failure—if it doesn't kill the projects outright. Radical innovators disappear into the corporate woodwork or flee the company. During the anti-radical-innovation periods, the firm's capacity in radical innovation diminishes or disappears. Lack of persistence and continuity works against developing a radical innovation capacity.[2]

In nine of the ten companies in our study, strategic priorities—and the senior corporate and business unit managers that set

TABLE 10-1

LEVEL OF RADICAL INNOVATION MATURITY AND ASSOCIATED MANAGEMENT MECHANISMS

	INVOLVING SENIOR MANAGEMENT	CAPTURING RADICAL INNOVATIONS	ACQUIRING RESOURCES	ENGAGING INDIVIDUAL INITIATIVE	MANAGING INTERNAL/ EXTERNAL PARTNERS	MANAGING TRANSITIONS
Early Radical Innovation Capability	Executives act as provocateurs, patrons, and champions to compensate for lack of supportive culture.	Mavericks try to catch the attention of patrons. There is a lack of infrastructure and systematic approach.	Acquisition of resources is ad hoc. Project teams often expect a budget allocation to fund their work.	Completing radical innovation tasks, staffing the project team, and engaging champions rely on individual initiative.	Relationships with internal and external partners are developed on an ad hoc, project-by-project basis by each project team.	Communication is poor between the radical innovation project and the business unit. Project often transitions too early and radical innovation flounders. Project relies on intervention of senior management for transition.

| Mature Radical Innovation Capability | The firm's leadership sets expectations, develops radical innovation culture, establishes facilitating organizational mechanisms, and develops goals and reward systems. | Radical innovation idea hunters seek opportunities. Radical innovation hubs help establish effective evaluation boards that use appropriate criteria. Non-traditional marketing and business development personnel work with radical innovation technical teams to develop the business model. | Individual managers with authority to provide seed funding and internal venture capital provide multiple sources of capital for radical innovation. The firm adopts a portfolio approach to funding radical innovation projects. | Radical innovation hubs work with HR to develop a strategy for identifying, selecting, rewarding, and retaining radical innovation champions, experts, and team members. | Relationships between radical innovation activity and internal and external partners are developed at a strategic level—relying on the collaboration of the project team, the radical innovation hub, and the oversight board. | Transition team is established to continue application and market development until uncertainty is reduced sufficiently to ensure a successful transition to the operating unit. |

them—changed dramatically, often more than once, during the project lifetimes. A senior technical manager in one of our participant companies has documented a recurring seventeen-year cycle during which strategic attention to the development of radical innovations rose and declined. The start-up of the radical innovation project in his company occurred early in the supportive phase, when the articulation of strategic intent by senior management focused on growth. Eight and a half years later, right on schedule, R&D personnel were informed that their promotions and raises would be based solely on their contributions to current business operations.

Implementing a change process for achieving a mature radical innovation capacity demands deliberate intention, strong and sustained commitment, and courage from the firm's leadership. The steps are well known but tough to follow. First, the firm's leadership must convince key players of the necessity for the change. Second, the leadership must articulate and sell the radical innovation vision and strategic intent to the entire firm: "Engage in radical innovation; build our capacity for radical innovation; and stay the course." Third, the leadership, along with the implementation team, needs to develop a plan for implementing the change process and for countering the roadblocks and resistance. The rewards for the individual behaviors and actions required for achieving a mature radical innovation capacity need to be spelled out. Finally the plan must be executed.

For firms just getting started in developing a radical innovation capability, senior management will need to take an active operational role—as a patron and promoter of individual projects and as the driving and sustaining force behind the development of the firm's radical innovation capacity. As the firm develops a supporting infrastructure and accumulates learning, senior management can take on a more strategic and less hands-on role.

It can be done. In all ten companies in our study—and in many of the others connected to this project through the Industrial Research Institute, the Rensselaer Key Executives Program, and our think tanks and workshops—the individual and organizational initiatives aimed at promoting radical innovation are bearing fruit. The development of this capacity is itself a radical organizational innovation. It will not become a commodity. Those firms that excel in developing and implementing a radical innovation capacity will have a tremendous source of long-term competitive advantage.

EPILOGUE

As this book went to press, the firms that participated in our research provided updates on the various projects described herein. Following is the status of each initiative as of late spring 2000. We want once again to express our appreciation to the firms and project team members for their openness with us and for allowing us to observe the progress of each of these projects as they take their natural course.

AIR PRODUCTS

Air Products moved the SEOS oxygen generator project to a development program manager from the Gases and Equipment Group operating unit, who is now leading the effort to develop a replicable manufacturing process for a commercially viable generator. Several breadboard SEOS oxygen generators have been made and initial entry application efforts are focusing on medical use and metal fabrication. The large scale MEOS ITM Oxygen Project remains in the research stage and is being advanced by a multicompany development team under a U.S. Department of Energy (DOE) cost-shared cooperative program. The ITM Syngas application for converting natural gas to hydrogen and synthesis gas for liquid transportation fuels is moving into Phase 2 of a three-phase, eight-year $85 million development program, undertaken in cooperation with the DOE and led by a team of twelve companies and other entities, including future commercial end-users. This program will culminate with the demonstration of the technology, which will subsequently be ready for commercial deployment.

ANALOG DEVICES

The technology of micromachining has made a successful transition into a stand-alone business division of Analog Devices. Over 50 percent of the air bag crash sensors used worldwide are produced by the Micromachined Products Division (MPD) of Analog Devices. In addition, sensors that have applications in video games, health and sports, and a wide range of other motion-sensing functions are being created by Analog Devices. Five hundred thousand accelerometers per week are manufactured and shipped with a workforce of over 400 people. The development of a gyro using the same process technology has also been demonstrated and is being sampled to potential customers in navigation and automotive safety. MPD is the only division of Analog Devices that has a dedicated manufacturing facility integrated with engineering and business functions. This allows MPD to focus on both the manufacturing and business aspects of their division.

Ray Stata continues to maintain close ties and interests in MPD. He served as the general manager for three years, taking the division to profitability and stable production in the new Cambridge facility by the end of 1999. The technology is finding new disruptive innovation opportunities in optical networks as the Internet creates market opportunities for micromachining and tremendous demand for a stable manufacturing capability ready to achieve high levels of reliability and volume immediately. For additional information on integrated micromachining at Analog Devices, see www.analog.com/imems.

DUPONT

ELECTRON EMITTER

In mid-April 2000, DuPont formally announced the formation of the Displays Business Unit. This unit is directing attention toward finding materials for use in the Flat Panel Display industry. In addition, the Electron Emitter Project—the work described in this book that began in 1994—is housed in this new unit and continues to move forward, with the structuring of key manufacturing alliances and further development work.

BIOMAX

DuPont's biodegradable polyester remains in the operating unit under the guidance of an experienced product manager. Markets have not emerged in agricultural applications as quickly as expected, and DuPont has returned its attention to packaging applications, which was one of the first application ideas for the material. However, DuPont remains committed to the technology, and continues to seek other markets. Most recently, Japan and other geographic markets have appeared more appropriate as commercial opportunities for a degradable material, and are being pursued.

GENERAL ELECTRIC

By the end of the first quarter of 2000, GE announced that its earnings, at 20 percent, were higher than expected. One of the quarter's highlights was the GE Medical Systems's (GEMS) unveiling of the GE Senographe 2000D, the world's first fully digital and FDA-approved mammography system, and the Innova 2000, the first digital cardiovascular X-ray system. Their combined sales were more than $50 million for the quarter.

Currently, detector manufacturing remains within GE for the mammography and cardiac applications. The mammography system is manufactured at GE's factory outside of Paris, France. (The vast majority of the mammography product's initial sales were in Europe because FDA approval took longer than expected.) EG&G (now called Perkin-Elmer) is manufacturing the chest-sized detector in California, which has been on the market since last year in a wall stand product. In addition, a table-based product was introduced last year.

Within GEMS, 400 product engineers are dedicated to this platform of products. Bruce Griffing and the R&D team are focusing on expanding each platform to offer numerous other features enabled by the digital technology. Bruce is also continuing to explore and respond to queries regarding other applications, including one for screening and early detection of lung cancers.

GENERAL MOTORS

The level of interest in alternative propulsion systems has remained high at General Motors. GM's hybrid vehicles symbolize automobile development that meets the goals of the Partnership for a New Generation of Vehicles (PNGV). The goals of PNGV include attainment of fuel efficiency triple that of the base (1993) family sedans. The GM effort on this count is showcased in the Precept, a new model for North America. To achieve performance targets of 80 mpg fuel economy and Tier II emissions, Precept features a four-wheel-drive parallel hybrid propulsion system that pairs an advanced diesel engine with GM's Generation III electric drive. In addition to this novel power train, Precept has many other innovations designed to help with fuel economy. In total, their PNGV vehicle features 132 technology innovations and holds 44 Records of Invention. And even though this is a concept vehicle, they are already spinning off many of these new technologies for use on their conventional products. In fact, they believe that 75 percent of Precept's technology has application to their mainstream product lineup.

Another General Motors alternative propulsion vehicle is a fuel cell version of the Precept that evolved from the merger of three technology arenas: their EV1 and hybrid electric propulsion projects; the Precept PNGV vehicle, the world's most efficient platform; and their fuel cell development program, which involves GM researchers and engineers working in Germany, Rochester, New York, and Warren, Michigan, and researchers in Japan who work for Toyota, their alliance partner on advanced vehicle technology.

IBM

ELECTRONIC BOOK

IBM's Display Business Unit has grown significantly since this study began and now manufactures and sells over a million flat panel displays per year. The output goes into ThinkPad notebooks and IBM monitors, but a significant fraction is now sold through OEM channels to other notebook and monitor manufacturers. High-resolution technology for more readable displays, higher image quality, and greater information content has proceeded, but at an evolutionary pace. IBM has demonstrated prototype displays with resolutions over 200 dots per inch and content over 5 million (2560 x 2048) color pixels. Meanwhile, several other companies have demonstrated their own high-resolution prototypes, such as Toshiba with their polysilicon 6.3" display, which also has over 200 dots per inch. These prototypes are gradually finding their way into limited production for special applications and new product development.

However, the move toward high-resolution has been slowed by both the flat panel shortage in the last few years (which made the delivery of the current products much more urgent than introducing new products) and the lack of complete software support for high-resolution. Nevertheless, each year brings higher resolution products to the mainstream, such as the 15" SXGA+ (1400 x 1050) notebook displays, which IBM was first to manufacture, and IBM's recently announced 20.8" QXGA (2048 x 1536) panel. Furthermore, there is new interest in high-resolution displays for platforms such as next generation PDAs, and new electronic document software is emerging, such as Microsoft's ClearType, which can make high-resolution color displays much more readable. The expectation is that these trends will continue and high-resolution displays will become an increasingly important share of the market.

SILICON GERMANIUM

IBM's silicon germanium (SiGe) technology program is now fully integrated into the product and technology roadmaps of the IBM Microelectronics Division. Of more significance, and providing the highest level of validation, the great majority of commercial semiconductor organizations in the communications sector have been forced to follow IBM's lead into this technology. Recent announcements of future competitive offerings by Lucent, Motorola, Infineon, Texas Instruments, Conexant, and many smaller companies have accelerated market acceptance of this new technology, as have the numerous IBM product announcements. Perhaps the most remarkable product announcement thus far has been Alcatel's use of IBM's SiGe technology for its leading edge telecom products, shipping data at rates of 10 to 40 billion bits per second in systems fielded in 1998. At the consumer end of the spectrum, SiGe technology is now found broadly in cellular phone handsets and numerous other wireless applications.

IBM Microelectronics has leveraged this leadership by broadening its product design capabilities, creating world-class R-F and mixed signal design organizations in Boston, Massachusetts, and Encinitas, California. Providing a focus for these expanded efforts, the Communications Research and Development Center has been formed, bridging the IBM research and microelectronics divisions, and coordinating work across these organizations. Dr. Meyerson now heads the Center, and remains focused on maintaining IBM's leadership in what has evolved into a mainstream technology.

Nortel Networks and NetActive

Since NetActive's spin-off from Nortel Networks on June 30, 1999, the business has evolved on its own to become a major player in its sector.

NetActive has undertaken massive programs for its clients, which now include major industry players such as Blockbuster, Disney, General Mills, Rogers Video, Electronic Arts, Electra, and Time Warner. More than 10 million copies of NetActive PC games, software, and music videos are currently helping these companies create online relationships with consumers, making NetActive the largest manager of rights-managed digital content in the world. Examples of NetActive's programs include: an ongoing monthly contract to supply full-version entertainment for the country's most popular computer gaming magazine, *incite*; shrink-wrapping millions of CDs with NetActive content to cereal boxes as part of a major motion picture promotion; and, in the online arena, becoming the largest broadband deliverer of full-version computer games, working with many of Time Warner's Road Runner franchises. NetActive is also a member of the steering committee of the Broadband Content Distribution Forum (BCDF), an industry association dedicated to improving the delivery of broadband content. Other BCDF members include Nortel Networks, AT&T, NBCi, and Sun Microsystems. The company has just completed a second round of financing led by Upstart Capital, a Silicon Valley–based venture capital group headed by Michael Spindler, ex-CEO of Apple.

From a Nortel Networks internal corporate venturing program perspective, a repeatable commercialization process has been developed to take early-stage ideas through to commercialization both efficiently and effectively. By using a venture capital model, a results-oriented approach was created to capture first-mover advantage and, ultimately, improve the success rate of the investments. The program has been the source of study by academics, is being considered a leading benchmark for other companies creating internal corporate venturing programs, and by its third year of operation was considered by many to be one of the top three programs in North America. During that time, it reviewed close to 300 ideas from employees, took 28 concepts to the seed funding stage, and incubated a total of 11 ventures. Five of these were spun off from the company and are currently valued at over $200 million, one completed a successful technology licensing arrangement, and five were spun back into the company.

In the late fall of 1999, it was Nortel Networks's decision to wind down its internal corporate venturing program. The decision, in part, reflects the strategic evolution of a company and its continual need to focus on its core activities, combined with an increasing trend to outsource noncore activities. In the same way that Nortel Networks only three years ago chose to pursue an internal corporate venturing program as a way to deal with radical innovation, a gradual shift from internal to external incubation as a way to foster this process is taking place. Industry-specific, value-added external incubators did not exist when the Nortel Networks Ventures Program was initiated. As it happens, Nortel Networks is currently in the throes of assessing external incubator relationships as the next logical step in working with radical innovation. What it now knows is that external incubators are emerging quickly as the next progressive way of dealing with creative new business concepts and technology.

By way of a final evaluation, it is former Nortel Networks employees, such as those at NetActive, that have gone on to form their own companies through the corporate venturing program who have pointed to the program's greatest asset. They have spoken positively of the benefits of having a formalized program in place to help them build their businesses.

OTIS ELEVATOR

The Otis Odyssey system was a product ahead of its time. Although it was a revolutionary elevator system, strongly grounded in existing elevator technology, the company's timing was poor. Odyssey, ideally suited for super-tall buildings, was announced just months before Asian economies collapsed, wiping out in just a few weeks the world's largest and most dynamic market for new skyscrapers. Otis quietly mothballed Odyssey system development, but is ready to rekindle it when market conditions become more favorable.

Interestingly, the process by which Odyssey came into being was also responsible for creating an equally innovative, and ultimately far more lucrative, elevator system. Otis became interested in developing an elevator system that would require no separate machine room. This would reduce construction costs, improve architectural lines, and increase rentable building space. To achieve this feat, two dozen Otis employees representing a broad cross-section of skills—engineering, sales, purchasing, and field installation and maintenance— spent a week locked away in a formal, facilitated innovation session.

Their unique idea, an elevator system that uses thin, flat, coated steel belts to lift the elevator, was whisked through the formal product development process in only eighteen months, and was introduced to the market as the GeN2™ elevator system in February, 2000. The product has since become the fastest-selling new product in Otis history. The company expects GeN2™ elevators to represent half of the company's new equipment sales worldwide in less than three years.

POLAROID

The computer memory storage device project matured to the point where Polaroid and its strategic partner confronted the need to ramp up funding by an order of magnitude. Polaroid's partner was going through its own difficult period, and was unprepared to make the necessary investment. Rather than seeking alternative financing partners, Polaroid chose to close down the project and refocus on its core technologies and markets. With the demise of the computer memory project, the New Business Division was disbanded in late 1999.

TEXAS INSTRUMENTS

Texas Instruments's Digital Imaging Business, based on MEMs technology, is now part of the Semiconductor Business Group. There are four product platforms currently in the marketplace. The first, conference room and mobile systems projection products, currently supplies approximately twenty Original Equipment Manufacturers (OEMs) with Digital Light Processing technology. An example of a product in this arena is the ultra-portable projector, which weighs less than five pounds. TI commands 70 percent market share of this product category. The second platform is large venue installed projection systems for theaters, auditoriums, and concert halls. TI holds 90 percent market share in this market space. Third are video walls, which are large display boards that are stacked to form large screen-like displays. The NASDAQ's new display board is one example. Finally, a newly introduced platform is DLP-based photofinishing equipment, which is just being deployed.

There are numerous other applications of the DLP technology under various stages of development. DLP home entertainment systems are expected to be introduced in late 2000, and DLP-based cinema projectors are being deployed worldwide from Tokyo to Cleveland for strategic showings of movies from *The Phantom Menace* to Disney's *Tarzan* and *Toy Story 2*. Other DLP proof-of-concept–nondisplay activities include automotive displays, optical telecommunications, and biomedical applications. TI is working furiously on incremental innovations to improve brightness levels and to condense the weight and size of current system configurations. Finally, the Digital Imaging business model has evolved from providing complete display engine turnkey solutions to providing DMD component sets to OEMs for OEM development of complete, integrated, application-specific systems.

For up-to-date information on Digital Imaging's DLP technology, products, and markets, see www.ti.com/dlp.

Appendix

CORPORATE VENTURE CAPITAL MODELS

Presented here is a comparison of the venture capital models at 3M, Lucent Technologies, Nortel Networks, and Procter & Gamble.[1] The information describing the mechanisms for managing and funding internal corporate ventures is organized by category: structure of the VC organization, venture board composition, source of venture funding, opportunity pipeline, project evaluation and management, funding decision criteria, length of funding, harvesting, and firm's assessment of effectiveness.

Organizational Structure

3M. The internal venturing operation is loosely structured, even ad hoc. Every one of the thirty-five business units—each a distinct business, operating in a distinct market and industry, with different products—has the impetus and the ability to spawn new units. In other words, every opportunity is a potential new division. The driver is a corporate-wide requirement that every unit produce 30 percent of its sales each year from products that have been introduced in the preceding four years. In recent years, the Corporate Enterprises Development (CED) organization has been structured to capture and nurture new business ideas that are in the "white spaces." The CED was established to augment the division-sponsored venture development activities.

LUCENT. A new division, the New Ventures Group, started to handle the venture operation, incubates internal technologies and opportunities. It is staffed by twenty people who specialize in early business development. The group complements its funding role by providing advice and incubating services; it does so by drawing on the expertise of corporate-level staff in areas such as human resources, finance, and legal.

NORTEL NETWORKS. Primary responsibility lies with a senior vice president who oversees corporate strategy, alliances, and venturing—including the company's Business Ventures Group (BVG). An executive investment committee, which is the overall governing body, deals with these ventures along with other strategic investment decisions for the corporation. The BVG is accountable for managing its portfolio and leveraging expertise within the company.

PROCTER & GAMBLE. Procter & Gamble's Innovation Leadership Team (ILT) serves as the company's venture capital board. It has a $200 million annual budget to invest in ideas that come up from existing business groups and corporate R&D through one of two "upstream" groups—one focused on marketing (the Corporate New Business Development Group, or CNBD), the other on technology (the Global Technology Council, or GTC). The ILT's responsibilities include providing counsel to improve the potential of ideas submitted for funding, and authorizing financial support and incubating services for those ideas with promise.

VENTURE BOARD COMPOSITION

3M. Other than the nascent CED leadership, there is no corporate-wide venture board.

LUCENT. The president of this VC division and three vice presidents act as the partnership for the internal venture capital firm.

NORTEL NETWORKS. The BVG puts in place boards of directors and advisers for its ventures composed of a BVG representative, executives from the lines of business, and appropriate outside experts.

PROCTER & GAMBLE. The ILT is comprised of the company's chief executive officer, the chief technology officer, and one of Procter & Gamble's seven global business unit presidents.

SOURCE OF VENTURE FUNDING

3M. Each business unit is responsible for providing funding and expertise to potential ventures. Advanced technology is funded by corporate-level funding, which supports staff laboratories and technology centers spread throughout 3M's divisions. High-visibility and high-priority programs receive disproportionate levels of such funds, to supplement divisional funding. Division management secures this funding through links to senior corporate management.

LUCENT. Lucent's New Ventures Group is allocated a fund each year from the corporate budget for investment purposes. Additional funding is sought from outside investors.

NORTEL NETWORKS. A pool of funds is set aside each year at the corporate level to fund investments. External investors are brought in as the businesses grow and are spun off.

PROCTER & GAMBLE. Funds come from the business units through an imposed tariff that promotes competition among business units to win back resources, in other words, to become the home to some of the ventures that are approved by the ILT and incubated by the CNBD or within R&D.

OPPORTUNITY PIPELINE

3M. Projects start—and stay—in their home business unit. Each business unit is responsible for providing expertise to potential ventures. As the opportunity gradually takes shape, it acquires dedicated resources.

LUCENT. Radical projects migrate to the company's New Ventures Group both proactively and reactively. The new venture staff goes out looking for opportunities, and Lucent employees (especially from Bell Labs) bring ideas to the group for consideration. Once the new venture group takes on an idea, it owns it.

NORTEL NETWORKS. Company employees submit proposals through an intranet Web site. The BVG also uses its network to surface more radical investment opportunities within the company. Initial screening eliminates incremental innovations such as extensions to existing products or market expansions. These are directed to the appropriate lines of business with the BVG's assistance.

PROCTER & GAMBLE. Original proposals from existing business units go first to either the CNBD or GTC (each of which has a budget to provide early seed funding for the exploration of radically new product ideas). For example, an idea might originate from a research team, which would apply for seed funding from the GTC to explore the application of a new technology. Promising results would lead to exploration of the business opportunity by the CNBD, and the results would then be presented to the ILT.

PROJECT EVALUATION AND MANAGEMENT

3M. 3M's model is evolutionary. Ventures start as programs within existing business units, then progress to become projects, then departments, and ultimately stand-alone divisions if the project evolves into something that does not fit neatly within the current business unit. A champion is key to acquiring resources for the nascent opportunity.

LUCENT. Lucent employs a four-stage process: opportunity identification (OI), market qualification, new business commercialization, and value realization. At the first stage, the ventures group assesses potential opportunities. Stage two is comparable to a seed stage in the venture capital world. Next is actually forming the venture. The final phase is the planned exit, when Lucent reaps the return for its investment.

NORTEL NETWORKS. Nortel Networks has adopted a two-phase creation and commercialization approach to its four stages of new venture development. The venture opportunity team creates compelling investments by seeding business concepts based on the first two stages: conceptualization and market qualification. The venture commercialization team places venture investments and follows the next two stages: value development and final placement. Truly radical business concepts become ventures, receiving funding and incubation services.

PROCTER & GAMBLE. Project management proceeds along the phases identified for funding: seed funding, first-phase funding to develop a testable prototype, and last, additional funding to take the idea to a learning market. Project teams report periodically to the CTO and business unit president to identify critical issues and ensure their resolution. These are informal meetings, used to insulate fledgling projects.

FUNDING DECISION CRITERIA

3M. Loosely defined criteria such as critical mass levels of sales are part of the decision to transition an opportunity from one level to the next.

LUCENT. Extensive due diligence is conducted and then various levels of funding appropriate to the risk are provided tied to milestone performance. General criteria include market opportunity, evidence of a sustainable value proposition, strong team capabilities, promise of financial reward, and appropriateness of the venture model for commercialization.

NORTEL NETWORKS. For Nortel Networks to adopt an idea as a venture, it must have the potential to become a sustainable standalone business, not an extension to current products. Due diligence is conducted to identify investment merits and risks based on proven venture capital criteria (including evidence of a strong team, a large potential market, and a differentiated value proposition). A milestone-based investment model is followed to build business value and mitigate risks.

PROCTER & GAMBLE. The innovation focus at Procter & Gamble is on marketing, rather than technology. Successful venture ideas must show "good consumer insight" and meet some particular market thresholds. The Innovation Leadership Team (ILT) works hard to drive "exacting financial analysis" from its evaluation criteria for funding. It looks primarily at the "plausible market size" and pricing (i.e., could this be a $2 billion market?). Many innovation projects align with one of the current business units. ILT portfolio analysts compare potential projects on the relative level of risk—from a technical as well as a marketing point of view—and require higher levels of market promise for the higher technological risks. Each proposal is also considered in the context of the current portfolio, which typically stands at thirty to forty projects. Those with lowest potential could be dropped in favor of a new venture with the possibility of better returns.

LENGTH OF FUNDING

3M. Ideas progressing through the stages of venture development at 3M draw on the resources of the parent business unit from the seed funding stage through to the point at which they become stand-alone business units.

LUCENT. Lucent ventures receive funding support from the seed stage to harvest.

NORTEL NETWORKS. Nortel Networks funds its internal ventures throughout the incubation time frame from seed stage through to spin off. Driven by critical time-to-market factors, average incubation time frames have been reduced considerably over the last three years from approximately two to three years, to six to twelve months.

PROCTER & GAMBLE. The CNBD and GTC provide seed money; first- and second-stage funding comes from the ILT. In the second stage (what Procter & Gamble calls the "learning market"), the value proposition is demonstrated through market trials of a prototype. Following that, the venture is assimilated into an existing business unit.

HARVESTING

3M. 3M harvests opportunities once they progress from dependence (surviving on resources provided by the host business unit) to independence as new divisions under the corporate umbrella. The process draws full circle when new business units are then expected to nurture a new generation of ideas that have potential to become new business units.

LUCENT. Some Lucent ventures are spun out into legal entities; others stay under the corporate umbrella. Joint ventures are also an option. The trend is for Lucent to spin out companies early in the incubation process.

NORTEL NETWORKS. Opportunities that move through Nortel Networks's new venture development process are on track to become separate, independent businesses. Nortel Networks remains a shareholder, retaining an equity stake in the business. Divestitures, joint ventures, and technology licensing are also externalization options. Some ventures are spun back into a line of business.

PROCTER & GAMBLE. Most of Procter & Gamble's venture projects align quickly with an existing business group. Procter & Gamble has structured a Corporate Enterprise Group to take ideas that do not fit into a current business group directly to market. Procter & Gamble is also considering partnering with external venture companies for radically different projects.

ASSESSMENT OF EFFECTIVENESS

Each of the four firms provided an assessment of their venture capital model, as described below:

3M. 3M has successfully used its venture capital strategy to add divisions. The strategy works because it allows for entrepreneurial spirit. The team knows they have the potential to run their own division someday.

LUCENT. Lucent's corporate venture capital model creates an urgency that pushes people to do their best work. Its design involves senior executives and attracts industry experts as venture board members. This would not happen if the projects remained the purview of the business groups. The structure allows for more creativity in deploying functional expertise (e.g., human resources, legal) than if under business groups. Lucent seeks to become more disciplined in selecting leadership teams.

NORTEL NETWORKS. Nortel Networks has been effective in reaching the grassroots of the organization where creativity and entrepreneurship flourish and ideas are often lost. The "funneling effect" has been used to create a great deal of flow while at the same time transferring business acumen to more technical employees. Targets for improvement center on building businesses not only around technology but also around "inklings of ideas," leveraging external resources more effectively, and moving ventures out the door more quickly.

PROCTER & GAMBLE. Involvement at the highest level of the corporation and support from the global business units are essential to the Procter & Gamble model. The CEO's involvement in the ILT is key. The company wants to develop more opportunities through the CNBD and through business unit engineering and manufacturing planning groups. The company is currently making changes to ensure that it can mobilize resources more quickly for any given opportunity.

SUMMARY

A comparison of the four models shows some interesting contrasts:

THE ORIENTATION TOWARD KEEPING THE BUSINESS WITHIN THE COMPANY VERSUS SPINNING IT OUT. While both 3M and Procter & Gamble are oriented toward retaining the businesses, either through finding a fit within a division or starting up a new division, Nortel Networks and Lucent are oriented toward spinning off companies that do not easily fit within the current core business focus. Recognizing that Nortel Networks and Lucent are looking to benefit primarily from the financial rewards, there is also considerable value derived from fostering entrepreneurship and collecting the associated learning for other parts of the business.

THE FORMALITY OF THE NEW VENTURE PROCESS. 3M's structure evolves from within the business units. It is relatively unformalized and proceeds incrementally as the business shows promise, following a growth pattern from the team through the basic program, through the business project, through the business department, to the business division. There are no formal boards. The other three programs have formal boards and processes that are operating at the highest levels of the corporation.

THE ORIENTATION TOWARD RETAINING VERSUS ALTERING THE CURRENT CORPORATE STRUCTURE. 3M's success hinges on the firm's willingness to spawn new business units without much resistance. This allows entrepreneurial drive to flourish, since the team itself knows they have the potential to run their own division someday. Yet 3M keeps the business within the company and does not offer the opportunity to "spin it out." In contrast, Nortel Networks and Lucent are much more focused on spinning out the new businesses. In fact, if an idea looks like it really belongs in the business unit, both Nortel Networks and Lucent are willing to help the idea generator "articulate it as a business concept," but then spin it back into the business unit as quickly as possible. Procter & Gamble, on the other hand, is experimenting with both models. Its tax system causes business units to compete for the business opportunities that emerge from the process. Procter & Gamble is just beginning to develop "enterprise groups," each of which will spin into one of the business units designated to incubate opportunities for which there is currently no clear home.

THE WILLINGNESS TO BRING IN OUTSIDE EXPERTISE IN THE EVALUATION AND MANAGEMENT OF VENTURES. Lucent builds external expertise into the venture's evaluation and management boards. Nortel Networks also brings in outside advisers to leverage the right expertise. Movement into unfamiliar terrain requires that they seek specific experts. The other two have not built this into their programs.

CONCENTRATION OF THE NEW VENTURES SYSTEM. 3M has a system that is widely diffused throughout the corporation and is not dependent on any single senior manager or board. New ventures in each of the other companies are dependent on the commitment of a governance body composed of senior managers.

NEW PRODUCTS VERSUS NEW BUSINESSES. At Procter & Gamble, the ILT approves projects when they are ready for the prototype stage. The orientation is very much toward a new product or a new application of a known technology. The evolutionary model at 3M allows it to think in terms of new platforms that could lead to new businesses. Lucent's and Nortel Networks's spin in/spin out structures allow them to consider either possibility.

EVALUATION OF THE NEW VENTURES PROGRAM. Since 3M's new ventures program is not so much a program as a culture, it is not subject to evaluation per se. Nortel Networks's and Lucent's programs are subject to evaluation criteria similar to those used in most independent venture capital funds—return on equity. The problem is their vulnerability to the company's economic state or strategic mind-set. Both programs have only been in existence since 1996. The Nortel Networks program in its current form was wound down in early 2000, although the company's commitment to venturing in general continues to evolve. The ability of any firm to persevere in radical innovation development and corporate venturing for the long term, which such investments require, is very difficult, given its many constituents. Procter & Gamble's program was founded in 1994 and continues to evolve.

NOTES

CHAPTER 1

1. Joseph Schumpeter is credited with initiating the argument that small, entrepreneurial firms are most likely to be the source of most innovation (The Theory of Economic Development [Cambridge, MA: Harvard University Press, 1934]). Subsequent research in the field, in fact, has been inconclusive on this point. Schumpeter himself later claimed that large, established firms that possess some degree of monopoly power are the stronger agents of technical progress because of their superior access to capital and skilled labor, as well as their ability to appropriate innovations from the smaller start-ups (Capitalism, Socialism, and Democracy, 3rd ed. [New York: Harper, 1950]).

Other studies that examine the relationship between firm size, market power, and innovative activity have, in general, found no systematic relationship (see W. L. Baldwin and J. T. Scott, *Market Structure and Technological Change* [New York: Harwood Publishers, 1987]; and W. M. Cohen and R. C. Levin, "Empirical Studies of Innovation and Market Structure," in R. Schmalensee and R. D. Willig, eds., *Handbook of Industrial Organization* [New York: North-Holland, 1989]), meaning that there is no clear-cut answer to the question across industries. However, the more recent work of Rebecca Henderson, "Underinvestment and Incompetence as Responses to Radical Innovation: Evidence from the Photolithographic Alignment Equipment Industry," *Rand Journal of Economics* 24, no. 2 (Summer 1993): 248–270, showed that, in fact, established firms invest more resources in incremental innovation than do start-ups and that the research efforts of incumbents seeking to exploit radical innovations are significantly less productive than those of new entrants. Thus, we begin with the thesis that managing radical innovation in established organizations is a severe challenge.

2. Recognition of the challenge of converting new technologies into business growth is pervasive. The Industrial Research Institute, a professional association of the senior technology managers of large, established companies committed to R&D, conducts an annual survey of its members. In 1998 "making innovation happen" was rated the top challenge facing technology leaders. Five years earlier it didn't even make the list of top challenges. The IRI report of the annual survey also indicated that IRI counterparts in Australia, Brazil, Korea, Europe, and Japan also rated "making innovation happen" at either the top or near the top of the list of the biggest problems facing their technology leaders.

3. See in particular Richard Foster, *Innovation: The Attacker's Advantage* (New York: Summit Books, 1986); James M. Utterback, *Mastering the Dynamics of Innovation* (Boston: Harvard Business School Press, 1994); and Clayton Christensen, *The Innovator's Dilemma* (Boston: Harvard Business School Press, 1997).

4. Numerous other writers have recognized the difficulty of managing radical innovation in large, established firms. Clayton Christensen's *Innovator's Dilemma* indicates that it is highly uncommon for firms that manage established lines of business well to anticipate and respond effectively to a disruptive technology coming from an external agent, much less to commercialize one themselves. Dorothy Leonard-Barton's description of the core rigidities of the organization in *Wellsprings of Knowledge: Building and Sustaining the Sources of Innovation* (Boston: Harvard Business Press, 1995) mirrors Christensen's observations, though she provides the reader with some new tools for managing against rigidity. Robert Katz and Thomas Allen describe the opposing forces in the organization that compete for organizational attention and resources, and stress the need for balance and dualism in "Organizational Issues in the Introduction of New Technologies" (in *The Management of Productivity and Technology in Manufacturing*, P. R. Kleindorfer, ed. [New York: Plenum Press, 1985], 275–300), much as Rosabeth Moss Kanter calls for large firms to manage both mainstreams and "newstreams" ("Swimming in Newstreams: Mastering Innovation Dilemmas," *California Management Review* [Summer 1989]: 45–69).

Michael Tushman and Charles O'Reilly's call for ambidextrous organizations in *Winning through Innovation: A Practical Guide to Leading Organizational Change and Renewal* (Boston: Harvard Business School Press, 1997) repeats the same cry. They point out that internally developed innovation is often squandered in large, established firms because of senior management's inability to lead dramatic organizational change. Deborah Dougherty's "Interpretive Barriers to Successful Product Innovation in Large Firms"(*Organization Science* 3, no. 2, [1992] 179–202) describes organizational resistance to innovation as a function of differing lenses or "thought worlds" that cause factions in the organization to interpret information differently. While every one of these writers has described the problem in a robust and enlightening manner, few, aside from Zenas Block and Ian MacMillan (*Corporate Venturing: Creating New Businesses within the Firm* [Boston: Harvard Business School Press, 1993]), have provided practical prescriptions to enhance an organization's readiness to commercialize radical innovation.

5. Joseph G. Morone, *Winning in High-Tech Markets* (Boston: Harvard Business School Press, 1993).

6. See, for example, Frederick Betz, *Strategic Technology Management* (New York: McGraw-Hill, 1993). See also Morone, *Winning in High-Tech Markets*, and Gary Hamel and C. K. Prahalad, *Competing for the Future* (Boston: Harvard Business School Press, 1994).

7. Utterback, *Mastering the Dynamics of Innovation*; Christensen, *The Innovator's Dilemma*.

8. See Morone, *Winning in High-Tech Markets*, and Tushman and O'Reilly, *Winning through Innovation*.

9. James G. March, "Exploration and Exploitation in Organizational Learning," *Organization Science* 2, no. 1 (February 1991): 71–87.

10. The exploration process has commonly been described as inherently uncertain, dynamic, and seemingly random. See the following: Rosabeth Moss Kanter, "When a Thousand Flowers Bloom: Structural, Collective, and Social Conditions for Innovation in Organizations," in B. Staw and L. Cummings, eds., *Research in Organizational Behavior,* vol. 10 (Greenwich, CT: JAI Press, 1988); J. J. Jelinek and C. B. Schoonhoven, *The Innovation Marathon* (Cambridge, U.K.: Basil Blackwell, 1990); and James Brian, "Managing Innovation: Controlled Chaos," *Harvard Business Review* 63 (May–June 1985): 73–84. On closer examination, though, Yu-Ting Cheng and Andrew H. Van de Ven find that it is not a random process, but rather a chaotic one (see "Learning the Innovation Journey: Order Out of Chaos?" *Organization Science* 7, no. 6 [November–December 1996]: 593–614). Chaos is a nonlinear, dynamic system, which is neither orderly and predictable nor stochastic and random. Learning in chaotic conditions calls for an expanding and diverging process of discovery, and learning under more stable conditions (incremental innovation) requires a narrowing and converging process of testing. The point the researchers make is that chaos is not randomness, and a chaotic environment is a manageable one, albeit in a very different way from an orderly environment. We agree with this point and work throughout the book to provide insight into appropriate management tools for such "chaotic" environments.

11. Morone, *Winning in High-Tech Markets.*

12. We see the beginnings of the descriptions of exploration competencies in various writings including Dorothy Leonard-Barton's *Wellsprings of Knowledge*, and Gary Lynn, Joseph Morone, and Albert Paulson's "Marketing and Discontinuous Innovation: The Probe and Learn Process" (*California Management Review* 38, no. 3 [Spring 1996]: 8–37), among others.

13. Our definition is generally in line with definitions used by other researchers. See for example Abdul Ali "Pioneering versus Incremental Innovation: Review and Research Propositions," *Journal of Product Innovation Management* 11 (1994): 56–61; M. Lee and D. Na, "Determinants of Technical Success in Product Development when Innovation Radicalness Is Considered," *Journal of Product Innovation Management* 11 (1994): 62–68; Rebecca Henderson, "Underinvestment and Incompetence as Responses to Radical Innovation," 248–270; J. E. Ettlie, W. P. Bridges, and R. D. O'Keefe, "Organization Strategy and Structural Differences for Radical versus Incremental Innovation," *Management Science* 30, no. 6 (1984): 682–695; and J. Stopford and C. W. F. Baden-Fuller, "Creating Corporate Entrepreneurship," *Strategic Management Journal* 15 (1994): 521–536. These authors variously use the following terminology:

- radical technological development;
- radical innovation within the firm (first-time use in a firm); and
- radical process (cost) or product (features) that transform an industry.

14. Previous authors have also noted that managing organizational change depends on dimensions similar to those we identify. Of particular note is Rumelt's work on types of organizational diversification (see Richard Rumelt, *Strategy, Structure and Economic Performance* [Ph.D. diss., Harvard University, 1974]). He notes that organizational performance varies depending on how related or unrelated the diversification effort is to the core business. He and many others have documented higher performance for firms that diversify into related fields. Clearly, there are major challenges associated with moving into unfamiliar product or market domains. Other researchers, however, observe that unrelated diversification offers a hedge against technological surprise, especially for firms in R&D intensive industries and, thus, in the long run, is a necessity for organizational health. See Yegman Chang and Howard Thomas, "The Impact of Diversification on Risk-Return Performance," *Strategic Management Journal* 19 (1989): 271–284; and Craig Galbraith, Bruce Samuelson, Curt Stiles, and Greg Merrill, "Diversification, Industry Research and Development, and Market Performance," *Academy of Management Proceedings* (1986): 17–20.

15. Robert Burgelman and L. R. Sayles describe this process as "retroactive rationalization" in *Inside Corporate Innovation* (New York: The Free Press, 1986).

16. Digital Light Processing, DLP, Digital Micromirror Device, DMD, and DLP Cinema are trademarks of Texas Instruments.

CHAPTER 2

1. Biomax is a registered trademark of E. I. DuPont de Nemours and Company. Only DuPont makes Biomax.

2. Lycra is a registered trademark of E. I. DuPont de Nemours and Company. Only DuPont makes Lycra.

3. All unattributed quotes in this book are from interviews conducted by the authors.

4. We know of no other empirical research that documents the time lines of radical innovations with the exception of Andrew Van de Ven and his colleagues at the University of Minnesota, who studied a number of innovations, some radical and others not (see Harold L. Angle and Andrew H. Van de Ven, "Suggestions for Managing the Innovation Journey," in *Research on the Management of Innovation: The Minnesota Studies*, Andrew H. Van de Ven, Harold L. Angle, and Marshall Scott Poole, eds. [New York: Harper and Row, 1989]). Those authors note that the more "highly innovative" of these projects were characterized by a number of the dimensions we've identified here, including setbacks and mistakes because of unanticipated environmental events, time line jolts, and inability to incorporate information that was counter to expectations—a concept they labelled "learning disabilities."

Rosabeth Moss Kanter characterizes the "newstream" development process in established organizations with descriptors similar to ours ("Swimming in Newstreams: Mastering Innovation Dilemmas," 45–69). She describes the process as being fraught with high uncertainty and high levels of intensity, which she characterizes as bursts of activity and attention followed by lulls.

5. For an excellent discussion of stage-gates, see Robert G. Cooper, "Stage-Gate Systems: A New Tool for Managing New Products," *Business Horizons* (May–June 1990): 44–54. See also Robert G. Cooper, *Winning at New Products: Accelerating the Process from Idea to Launch*, 2nd ed. (Reading, MA: Addison-Wesley, 1993).

6. The original source of this definition is Ansoff's matrix of growth opportunities (H. Ansoff, "Strategies for Diversification," *Harvard Business Review* 35 [September–October 1957]: 113–124). According to this typology, market growth opportunities determine appropriate product development responses. Growth strategies that target existing markets with existing products and technologies result in incremental products. Growth strategies that pursue new markets with new products and technologies (and concomitantly high levels of uncertainty) produce really new innovations. Innovativeness has also been defined in terms of the product's newness relative to the firm and to the outside world, where "newness" refers to the degree of familiarity the firm has with the underlying technologies and application markets. (See Booz•Allen & Hamilton, *New Product Management for the 1980s* [New York: Booz•Allen & Hamilton, 1982]; E. J. Kleinschmidt and Robert J. Cooper, "The Impact of Product Innovativeness on Performance," *Journal of Product Innovation Management* 8, no. 4 (1991): 240–251; and Eric M. Olson, Orville C. Walker, Jr., and Robert W. Ruekert, "Organizing for Effective New Product Development: The Moderating Role of Product Innovativeness," *Journal of Marketing* 59, no. 1 (January 1995): 48–62.

7. Other researchers have recognized the importance of organizational and resource uncertainty. In particular, see Deborah Dougherty and Cynthia Hardy, "Sustained Product Innovation in Large, Mature Organizations: Overcoming Innovation-to-Organization Problems," *Academy of Management Journal* 39, no. 5 (1996): 1120–1153; Robert Burgelman and L. R. Sayles, *Inside Corporate Innovation* (New York: The Free Press, 1986); Rosabeth Moss Kanter, *When Giants Learn to Dance* (New York: Simon and Schuster, 1989); and Clayton Christensen, *The Innovator's Dilemma*. Building on their work, our research recognizes the impact of all four uncertainties in the established corporate environment, as well as the impact of their interactions with one another on the project's managerial agenda.

8. For an interesting discussion of strategic decision making under various types and degrees of uncertainty, see Hugh Courtney, Jane Kirkland, and Patrick Viguerie, "Strategy under Uncertainty," *Harvard Business Review* 75 (November–December 1997): 66–79. Although their context is corporate-level strategic choices, and the "levels of uncertainty" differ from ours, the authors offer an interesting perspective and range of analytical tools for managing differently under these different conditions, echoing the point we are making throughout this book.

9. Venkataraman and Van de Ven use a similar concept to our "showstoppers" in discussing the impact of "environmental jolts" on the evolution of new ventures, although they refer exclusively to jolts from the external environment (see S. Venkataraman and Andrew H. Van de Ven, "Hostile Environments, Environmental Jolts, Transaction Set, and New Business," *Journal of Business Venturing* [May 1998]: 231–255). We are expanding this concept to recognize that jolts to the project can come from within the corporation as well as from outside its boundaries.

CHAPTER 3

1. See also Vijay K. Jolly, *Commercializing New Technologies: Getting from Mind to Market* (Boston: Harvard Business School Press, 1997); and Block and MacMillan, *Corporate Venturing.*

2. At the start of our research project, our industrial partners were forthright in describing the initiating activities of radical innovation projects as the "fuzzy front end." Academic scholars have picked up on this term as well. See, for example, Albert L. Page and John S. Stovall, "Importance of the Early Stages in the New Product Development Process," in *Bridging the Gap from Concept to Commercialization* and Edward F. McDonough III and Chuck Tomkovick, eds., 1994 Proceedings of the Product Development and Management Association, 46–50. See also Peter A. Koen, "Corporate Entrepreneuring: Securing Funding for 'Initiative from Below' Fuzzy Front End Projects," *Achieving Excellence in New Product Development and Management*, Chuck Tomkovick, ed., 1998 Proceedings of the Product Development and Management Association, 12–24.

3. Greg A. Stevens and James Burley, "3,000 Raw Ideas = 1 Commercial Success," *Research Technology Management* (May–June 1997): 16–27.

4. Edward Roberts and Alan R. Fusfeld provide a description of the informal roles necessary for leading the early phases of innovation in "Critical Functions: Needed Roles in the Innovation Process," in *Career Issues in Human Resource Management*, R. Katz, ed., (Englewood Cliffs, NJ: Prentice-Hall, 1982), 182–207. They note that idea generators—people who have the personal and technical qualifications for scientific inventiveness and the prolific generation of ideas—are rare finds. They state that these individuals must be singled out, cultivated, and managed in a special way. We address these issues in chapter 9. Andrew Van de Ven believes that "firms wear blinders that limit the inventory of ideas" and attributes this to managers' lack of attention to individuals. In these cases, attention is so scant that "many innovative ideas cannot be judged effectively" (see "Central Problems in the Management of Innovation," *Management Science* 32, no. 5 [1986]: 590–607).

5. We thank Dr. Nick J. Colarelli for drawing this insight to our attention. J. P. Guilford defines "associative fluency" as a dimension of thinking activity that calls for "the production of a variety of things related in a specified way to a given thing." (J. P. Guilford, "Three Faces of Intellect," *The American Psychologist* 14, no. 8 [1959]: 473).

6. Gary Hamel and C. K. Prahalad, *Competing for the Future* (Boston: Harvard Business School Press, 1994), 129–135.

7. Gary Hamel and C. K. Prahalad, "Corporate Imagination and Expeditionary Marketing," *Harvard Business Review* 69 (July–August 1991): 81–92. The authors explicitly describe the need to consider new opportunity horizons that stretch beyond the boundaries of the firm's current businesses, through the use of imagination and a "benefits view" of an emerging core competence.

8. Theresa Amabile has shown that creativity is most productive if it's directed. One tool that she recommends to help increase a researcher's intrinsic motivation (and thereby his or her creativity) is for senior management to grant more freedom to individuals. We note that it is a very different type of freedom from what researchers conventionally understand as "slack time." The freedom that Amabile describes is autonomy over the *means*, but not the *ends* of the project. People will be more creative, she states, if the strategic goals they're called to work on are clearly specified, but they are expected to decide the methods used to pursue the goal. She notes that one way firms mismanage freedom is by changing the goals too frequently. Thus, the staying power of senior management's strategic intent is critical to building and maintaining a radical innovation capacity in an organization. See Teresa M. Amabile, "How to Kill Creativity," *Harvard Business Review* 76 (September–October 1998): 77–87.

9. As Vijay Jolly points out, everything, even technology, is politics. Imagining the breakthrough may be the first part of innovation, but taking the next few steps, including considering robust uses for it and mobilizing enough support to convert the insight into a project worth pursuing, is where many researchers run into trouble (see *Commercializing New Technologies*). While Jolly recommends techniques for the researchers to follow, we believe there is a serious opportunity here for the organization to build in a structural support mechanism at this crucial juncture: the "radical innovation hub."

10. Similar terms have been used by others, but they describe slightly different sets of activities. Rosabeth Moss Kanter's concepts are most similar to ours. She refers to "scouts" and "coaches," where a scout is the receiver of new ideas and has corporate money to allocate to them, while the coach has the more active role, helping refine the idea and create the "sales pitch" to help senior management understand its importance and eventually find a funding sponsor. See *When Giants Learn to Dance*. The "information gatekeeper" identified by Roberts and Fusfeld ("Critical Functions: Needed Roles in the Innovation Process") scans the internal and external environment. However, they identify separate roles for individuals who scan the technical literature and those who scan the marketplace for customer trends. We do not define hunters and gatherers quite so narrowly. In fact, we believe that, in order to be effective opportunity recognizers, hunters and gatherers must have some acumen in both the world of market learning and the world of technological possibilities.

11. In *When Giants Learn to Dance*, Rosabeth Moss Kanter describes several internal venture funds (Teleflex, Ohio Bell, and Eastman Kodak) and their early evaluation processes. In all cases, evaluation involved connecting the idea generator with internal experts to help evaluate the robustness of the opportunity, and other mechanisms for avoiding the firms' conventional evaluation processes and metrics.

12. Block and MacMillan, *Corporate Venturing*, 103.

13. Jolly provides details on case comparisons of projects that were able to gain internal support and those that were not (see *Commercializing New Technologies*). He attributes the successes (i.e., those that passed initial evaluation) to an ability to demonstrate the scientific promise of the innovation early on. Much of that ability he attributes to early networking with peers in the scientific community to help problem solve and come up with a number of technical development paths should any single one not bear fruit.

14. We need to distinguish this question from what Christensen observes and describes in *The Innovator's Dilemma*. His principal point is that firms that are managing with their fiduciary responsibility to their stakeholders in mind pass up early "inferior" technologies because the market is too small. He is referring to *current* markets and *current* loyal customers. We, on the other hand, along with a host of others, including Hamel and Prahalad and Leonard-Barton, observed teams asking about *future* markets. That is why stringent financial justifications are nearly impossible, and the robustness of the technology and its ability to be deployed in many application domains are the more oft-used mechanisms for building confidence in the technology's value.

15. See, for example, Deborah Dougherty and Cynthia Hardy, "Sustained Product Innovation in Large, Mature Organizations," 1120–1153. See also Kanter, *When Giants Learn to Dance*.

CHAPTER 4

1. See, for example, *The Project Management Book of Knowledge, 1996* (Project Management Institute, 1996).

2. Ibid., chapter 11.

3. Rita G. McGrath and Ian MacMillan, "Discovery Driven Planning," *Harvard Business Review* 73 (July–August 1995): 4–12.

4. See J. David Bernard's *Milestone Planning for Successful Ventures* (New York: Boyd and Fraser, 1994), chapter 1, "A Framework for Milestone Planning," by Zenas Block.

5. The learning plan is one of several approaches that have been described by others for managing innovation projects under conditions of high uncertainty. See, for example, Hollister B. Sykes and David Dunham, "Critical Assumption Planning: A Practical Tool for Managing Business Development Risk," *Journal of Business Venturing* 10, no. 6 (November 1995): 413–424; Block and MacMillan, *Corporate Venturing*; and McGrath and MacMillan, "Discovery Driven Planning." Each of these writings defines a disciplined approach to innovation development, allowing for mistakes, discovery of false assumptions, and unexpected outcomes through actions described as "recycle" or "redirect." Similarly, Leonard-Barton's concept of "failing forward" and Lynn, Morone, and Paulson's concept of "probing and learning" are tools that require flexible, trial-and-error approaches to managing projects with high levels of uncertainty. See, respectively, Dorothy Leonard-Barton, *Wellsprings of Knowledge*; and Lynn, Morone, and Paulson, "Marketing and Discontinuous Innovation: The Probe and Learn Process," 8–37.

6. In "Central Problems in the Management of Innovation" (*Management Science* 32, no. 5 [1986]: 590–607), Andrew Van de Ven notes the *necessity* of retaining a degree of uncertainty and not seeking premature closure in highly innovative projects. He refers to the concept of *double loop learning* (Argyris and Schon, 1978), which is something we observed throughout our cases. Argyris and Schon describe *single loop learning*, which represents conventional monitoring activity, with actions taken based on the findings of the monitoring system. Double loop learning, in contrast, involves a change in the *criteria of evaluation*. Past practices are called into question, new assumptions about the project are raised, and significant changes in strategy are allowed. Double loop learning can cast doubt on what the appropriate evaluative criteria should be to determine a project's progress. Van de Ven offers no canned procedures for systematic management of uncertainty. Rather, he offers a different paradigm, one that reflects his concept of radical innovation as a chaotic rather than a random process, which we see reflected in our cases as well. (See Yu-Ting Cheng and Andrew H. Van de Ven, "Learning the Innovation Journey: Order Out of Chaos?" *Organization Science* 7, no. 6 [November–December 1996]: 593–614; also Chris Argyris and Donald A. Schon, *Organizational Learning: A Theory of Action Perspective* [Reading, MA: Addison-Wesley, 1978]).

7. In "Sustained Product Innovation in Large, Mature Organizations: Overcoming Innovation-to-Organization Problems" (1120–1153),

Deborah Dougherty and Cynthia Hardy report that managers of unsuccessful projects differed from those of successful projects in their ability to acquire resources. The authors note that relying solely on an individual's capabilities for this critical activity makes sustaining innovation very difficult in established organizations. It follows that some type of organizational mechanism for aiding project managers in seeking and obtaining funding from a variety of sources is critically important. Angle and Van de Ven similarly found that innovation projects more often closed down because of resources drying up rather than for any other reason. (See Angle and Van de Ven, "Suggestions for Managing the Innovation Journey," chapter 21.)

8. See Clayton Christensen, *The Innovator's Dilemma*. See also Tom Peters, "The Mythology of Innovation, or a Skunkwork's Tale, Part II," *The Stanford Magazine* (Palo Alto: Stanford Alumni Association, 1983).

9. Skunk works have suffered criticism from a number of writers recently, because of the difficulties associated with folding the results of their work back into the company. Xerox PARC's struggle with this is well known. (See John Seely Brown, "Research That Reinvents the Corporation," *Harvard Business Review* 69 [January–February 1991].) Michael Schrage notes that the message sent to the main organization when a skunk works is funded is one of "innovation apartheid," which creates an elite group of innovators. He notes that this action may easily be interpreted not as management championing innovation, but rather as management giving up on the capability of the mainstream organization to innovate. (See "What's That Bad Odor at Innovation Skunkworks," *Fortune*, 20 December 1999, 338.)

10. Tom Allen ("Communication Networks in R&D Laboratories," *R&D Management* 1 [1971]: 14–21) discovered and publicized the importance of encouraging informal communication networks within the R&D lab. He notes the importance of "gatekeepers" in the lab, who develop ties to external technical information and then communicate it to the rest of the R&D organization. We found evidence of the same activity beginning to occur with market-related information and with organizational resources as well. Further, we observed that "communities of practice" transcended laboratory boundaries. Technical experts found one another across organizational divisions, though this happened in an ad hoc manner. As the communities-of-practice idea takes hold, we expect that the benefits of these networking ties will be enhanced even further.

11. Deborah Dougherty and T. Heller, "The Illegitimacy of Successful Product Innovations in Established Firms," *Organizational Science* 5, no. 2 (1994): 200–218.

12. Boundary-spanning activities, which contribute to establishing legitimacy of the radical innovation project team, have been found to vary extensively across types of teams. For a detailed discussion of this range of activities and its impact on team performance in highly innovative projects, see Deborah Ancona, "Outward Bound: Strategies for Team Survival in an Organization," *Academy of Management Journal* 33, no. 2 (1990): 334–365; and Deborah Ancona and David F. Caldwell, "Bridging the Boundary: External Activity and Performance in Organizational Teams," *Administrative Science Quarterly* 37 (1992): 634–665. Those researchers' results indicate that some teams simply inform the firm of their activities, others passively observe their external environment, and still others actively engage outsiders. This third group was found to have the highest project performance ultimately, although team cohesiveness was not high throughout the project.

13. Digital Light Processing, DLP, Digital Micromirror Device, DMD, and DLP Cinema are trademarks of Texas Instruments.

CHAPTER 5

1. In *Wellsprings of Knowledge*, Dorothy Leonard-Barton calls these "developer-driven development projects." Customers may not articulate a need, because they take for granted that the current solutions are the frontiers of technology. She advocates immersion in the user's environment to enable the insights into connections between novel technologies and known or unknown needs. Our first two types of innovation (outside the current strategic boundaries or in the white spaces) are characterized in her vocabulary as technology/market co-evolution, which, in themselves, require dramatically different market learning techniques.

2. Robert G. Cooper and Elko J. Kleinschmidt, "An Investigation into the New Product Process: Steps, Deficiencies and Impact," *Journal of Product Innovation Management* 3, no. 2 (1986): 71–85.

3. For more discussion of prototypes, see Lynn, Morone, and Paulson, "Marketing and Discontinuous Innovation: The Probe and Learn Process," 8–37; Robert J. Dolan, "Industrial Market Research: Beta Test Site Management," Case # 9-592-010 (Boston: Harvard Business School, 1992); and Michael Schrage, *Serious Play: How the World's Best Companies Simulate to Innovate* (Boston: Harvard Business School Press, 2000).

4. Leonard-Barton, *Wellsprings of Knowledge*, 124–125.

5. Morone, *Winning in High-Tech Markets*.

6. See Lynn et al., "Marketing and Discontinuous Innovation," and Leonard-Barton, *Wellsprings of Knowledge* for more examples of this technique of trial and error in the marketplace. When both the market and the technology are highly uncertain, focusing technology development requires a market application choice, and the two coevolve.

7. See Clayton Christensen, *The Innovator's Dilemma*; Geoffrey Moore, *Crossing the Chasm* (New York: HarperBusiness, 1991); and Barry Bayus, Sanjay Jain, and Ambar G. Rao, "Too Little, Too Early: Introduction Timing and New Product Performance in the Personal Digital Assistant Industry," *Journal of Marketing Research* 34 (February 1997).

8. "Iridium, Great Technology, Poor Marketing," *Washington Post*, 24 May 1999, E01. Also see "Why Cell Phones Succeeded Where Iridium Failed," *Wall Street Journal*, 23 August 1999, B1.

9. Eric Von Hippel, who coined the term "lead user," describes techniques and methods for identifying appropriate first experimenters with a novel concept or prototype. To be identified as a lead user, a firm or individual must face needs that will be general in the marketplace at some point in the future and be likely to benefit significantly from the technology. The term "lead user," we find, is often used quite loosely to indicate anyone that the project team chooses to work with early on as a potential customer-partner. Von Hippel found that they developed crude solutions to problems on their own, which, once discovered by the innovating firm, served as ideas for product development projects. See Eric Von Hippel, "Lead Users: A Source of Novel Product Concepts," *Management Science* 32 (July 1986): 791–805.

10. See chapter 4 of Jolly, *Commercializing New Technologies*. He points out that a thorough job of generating ideas about potential applications is as important to gaining internal buy-in for the project as is technical progress, and he offers his own thoughts about the biases that prevent that from happening.

11. See Edward F. McQuarrie, *Customer Visits: Building a Better Market Focus* (Newbury Park, CA: Sage Publications, 1993). McQuarrie argues that, in technology-driven industries and business-to-business markets in particular, a planned program of customer visits by every member of the team is important to achieving breakthrough new products.

12. Lynn et al., "Marketing and Discontinuous Innovation."

13. Gifford Pinchot III, "Innovation through Intrapreneurship," *Research-Technology Management* 30 (March-April 1987).

CHAPTER 6

1. David Rotman, "The Next Biotech Harvest," *Technology Review* (September–October 1998): 34–41; Richard Koenig, "Tricky Roll-Out: Rich in New Products, Monsanto Must Only Get Them on Market," *Wall Street Journal*, 1 May 1990, A1.

2. NetActive Web site, http://www.netactive.com, March 1999.

3. Chapter 7 provides a thorough description of the many partners required to effectively bring a technology with long-term profit potential to market. Jolly admonishes readers to think in a systems perspective during this part of the commercialization process (see *Commercializing New Technologies*).

4. Indeed, Roberts and Berry describe a host of entry strategies that ought to be followed, depending on the familiarity of the market and technology to the firm's base business (see Edward B. Roberts and Charles A. Berry, "Entering New Businesses: Selecting Strategies for Success," *Sloan Management Review* [Spring 1985]: 3–17). The further removed the application market and the technology are from the firm's current business, they suggest, the more appropriate it would be to acquire an expert firm or enter into a joint venture. While this seems a rational approach, we have been struck by the dependency of the technology's development path on very early business model assumptions, and so we suggest that the radical innovation team consider this material very carefully early on in the project.

5. Chandry and Tellis show that a firm's willingness to cannibalize its current investments in products, assets, and organizational routines is more important than its size in determining the likelihood of successfully commercializing a radical innovation. In other words, small firms don't get there more often because they're small, but because there is a vacuum left open by large firms that are unwilling to cannibalize their specialized investments until it's too late. The authors suggest that this is attitudinal in nature and, therefore, can be modified. See Rajesh K. Chandy and Gerard J. Tellis, "Organizing for Radical Product Innovation: The Overlooked Role of Willingness to Cannibalize," *Journal of Marketing Research* 35 (November 1998): 474–487.

6. The NetActive team found that e-commerce software and music distributors had developed the necessary capabilities to handle many small payment transactions. The problem of disk distribution was knottier. Eventually, it was decided to distribute them through Blockbuster Video. A charge of several dollars was placed on the initial purchase of the disks. At the time of this writing, NetActive management was aware of the probability that disks would be purchased once and passed along from friend to friend.

7. McIntyre points out that the building of the value chain and infrastructure takes time and is itself fraught with discontinuities. "Figuratively speaking, the infrastructure ratchets forward—it modifies and advances, stabilizes for a time—and then advances again" (p. 146). The implications are that (a) failure to take this market adaptation process into account can lead to overestimation of short-term sales and underestimation of long-term potential; (b) since the necessary infrastructure is not in place early on, it may be beneficial to provide a version of the innovation that is somewhat consistent with the current infrastructure, recognizing that such a product form may not leverage all aspects of the innovation; and (c) there is a distinct need to proactively stimulate the development of the infrastructure through alliances or through providing it for a time. See Shelby H. McIntyre, "Market Adaptation as a Process in the Product Life Cycle of Radical Innovations and High Technology Products," *Journal of Product Innovation Management* 5 (1988): 140–149.

8. See David Glen Mick and Susan Fournier, "Paradoxes of Technology: Consumer Cognizance, Emotions, and Coping Strategies," Marketing Sciences Institute working paper no. 98-112, Cambridge, MA, July 1998. The authors describe coping strategies that consumers use to avoid the time and angst required to learn and assimilate novel technologies, one of which is to simply avoid trying them.

CHAPTER 7

1. See also Dougherty and Hardy, "Sustained Product Innovation in Large, Mature Organizations," 1120–1153; and Angle and Van de Ven, "Suggestions for Managing the Innovation Journey," chapter 21.

2. Teresa Amabile finds that adding more resources above a "threshold of sufficiency" does not boost creativity among team members. Beyond this, we observe the organizational rigidity that sets in as management seeks to throw good money after bad. See Teresa M. Amabile, "How to Kill Creativity," and *Creativity in Context: Update to the Social Psychology of Creativity* (Boulder, CO: Westview Press, 1996). See also Jeffrey B. Schmidt and Roger J. Calantone, "Are Really New Product Development Projects Harder to Shut Down?" *Journal of Product Innovation Management* 15 (1998): 111–123, who find, through a controlled lab experiment, that managers are less likely to shut down radical innovation development projects than incremental innovation projects given the same set of inferior performance criteria, because the nature of the opportunity seems so exciting. While we recognize and advocate that different evaluative criteria are required for radical innovations, this experiment provides evidence that any tendency to overfund these projects in their early stages may lead to biased decision making later on.

3. Dougherty and Hardy, "Sustained Product Innovation."

4. Rosabeth Moss Kanter has led extensive research efforts in examining and describing various internal corporate venturing programs, including Raytheon's New Products Center, Teleflex's New Venture Fund, and Eastman Kodak's New Opportunities Program. See all previous Kanter references.

5. Information about the funding decision-making process at Nortel Networks was provided through an in-depth interview of Joanne Hyland, VP New Venture Development, and through her presentation during the Senior Management Briefing on Radical Innovation at Rensselaer on June 15, 1999.

6. Modesto A. Maidique, "Entrepreneurs, Champions, and Technological Innovation," *Sloan Management Review* (Winter 1980): 59–76.

7. See Leonard-Barton, *Wellsprings of Knowledge* for a discussion of building an "absorptive capacity" within the organization: the ability to identify, access and use technologies from a wide variety of sources outside the organization.

8. See Thomas Robertson and S. Hubert Gatignon, "Technology Development Mode: A Transaction Cost Conceptualization," *Strategic Management Journal* 6 (June 1998): 515–531.

9. See Peter Lorange and Johan Roos, *Strategic Alliances: Formation, Implementation and Evolution* (Cambridge, MA: Blackwell Publishers, 1992).

10. Leonard-Barton, *Wellsprings of Knowledge.*

11. Benjamin Gomes-Casseres, "Computers: Alliances and Industry Evolution," in *Beyond Free Trade*, David Yoffie, ed., (Boston: Harvard Business School Press, 1993), 79–128.

12. Lynn, Morone, and Paulson, "Marketing and Discontinuous Innovation: The Probe and Learn Process," 8–37.

13. Gene Slowinski, Gerard Seelig, and Frank Hull, "Managing Technology-Based Strategic Alliance between Large and Small Firms," *S.A.M. Advanced Management Journal* 61, no. 2 (Spring 1996): 14ff. Slowinski, Seelig, and Hull provide useful insights into the difficulties of managing partnering relationships and some practical mechanisms for dealing with these difficulties.

14. Gary Hamel and Yves L. Doz, *Alliance Advantage* (Boston: Harvard Business School Press, 1998), 5.

15. See Jolly, *Commercializing New Technologies,* chapters 5 and 9, for his discussion of factors that impact on the decision to share technological knowledge with partners, as well as on how to decide which pieces of the value chain to retain and which to manage through partnerships.

CHAPTER 8

1. Block and MacMillan, in *Corporate Venturing*, chapter 6, offer a thorough treatment of the alternative locations for a venture and offer thoughts about the trade-offs associated with each option.

2. Others have noted and discussed this transition difficulty as well. Ralph Katz and Thomas J. Allen, for example, prescribe the movement of people to build "human bridges" for transferring technology into the business unit. They suggest adding SBU development engineers to the team while it is still in R&D, and moving R&D people into the SBU for a while once the transfer has taken place. They also prescribe the building of specialized "transfer groups," but describe these mainly as useful for ensuring that the technology is well understood by members of the business unit, for conducting training in the technology, etc. Finally, they offer the concept of "integrator groups," which have the responsibility for straddling the various parts of the R&D and engineering organizations. They note the political difficulty of this job, since that group does not have the responsibility for either the sending or the receiving organization. The authors observe that such a team would require astute political sensitivity and informal influence and credibility within the organization. While we agree, and indeed prescribe a transfer team, we are calling for a richer agenda for that team, as we note in this chapter. Not only are they transferring the technology, but they have new work to do, in terms of defining and developing new applications, and creating a business plan and sales forecast on the basis of that application development. Because we call for its constitution to be of members of the hub as well as of the sending and receiving units, who will, in effect, carry out the plan, and because the team will be monitored and rewarded through the corporate structure of the radical innovation hub, we believe that the mechanism should overcome some of the informal political problems that Katz and Allen identify.

3. See Andrew Van de Ven and Douglas Polley, "Learning While Innovating," *Organization Science* 3, no. 1 (February 1992): 92–116, which empirically demonstrates the trial-and-error approach to learning throughout the market introduction process in one case of a biomedical innovation.

4. Block and MacMillan, *Corporate Venturing*.

5. Richard Rumelt, "Diversification Strategy and Profitability," *Strategic Management Journal* 3 (1982): 359–369; Raphael Amit and Joshua Livnat, "Diversification and the Risk-Return Trade-Off," *Academy of Management Journal* 31, no.1 (1988): 154–166; Charles H. Berry, *Corporate Growth and Diversification* (Princeton, NJ: Princeton University Press, 1975); Richard A. Bettis, "Performance Differences in Related and Unrelated Diversified Firms," *Strategic Management Journal* 2 (1981): 379–393; Ralph Biggadike, "The Risky Business of Diversification," *Harvard Business Review* 57 (May–June 1979): 103–111; Cynthia Montgomery and Harbir Singh, "Diversification Strategy and Systematic Risk," *Strategic Management Journal* 5 (1984): 181–191; C. K. Prahalad and Richard A. Bettis, "The Dominant Logic: A New Linkage between Diversity and Performance," *Strategic Management Journal* 7 (1986): 485–501; Clayton G. Smith and Arnold C. Cooper, "Established Companies Diversifying into Young Industries: A Comparison of Firms with Different Levels of Performance," *Strategic Management Journal* 9 (1988): 111–121.

6. See Roberts and Berry, "Entering New Businesses: Selecting Strategies for Success," 3–17, for a conceptual framework that helps analyze the variety of approaches for entering a new product market domain. They recognize that internal development is only one approach and provide suggestions for others depending on the level of familiarity the firm already has with the technology and market in question.

7. Jolly notes that "unlike the tradition of most diffusion-of-innovation studies, technology-based products should not be seen as a 'given,' which then have to be somehow made to be 'adopted' by different categories of individuals. Rather, it is more appropriate to see the 'product' itself as a variable" (in *Commercializing New Technologies*, p. 215). He notes that there are three types of product adaptations needed: (1) making the project conform to existing patterns of use; (2) making the technology invisible when targeting a certain category of customers; and (3) emphasizing the facet of the technology that is perceived as most valuable to the market/application domain at that point in time. We witnessed an even larger discrepancy: the application market originally envisaged was not going to develop quickly enough for the operating unit's needs, and, therefore, the search for application domains was once again renewed after the transfer was made to the business unit.

8. Shelby H. McIntyre, "Market Adaptation as a Process in the Product Life Cycle of Radical Innovations and High Technology Products," 140–149.

9. T. Halfhill, "PDAs Arrive But Aren't Quite Here Yet," *Byte*, October 1993, 66–86.

10. Bayus, Jain, and Rao, "Too Little, Too Early: Introduction Timing and New Product Performance in the Personal Digital Assistant Industry," 50–63.

11. Richard S. Rosenbloom and Michael A. Cusumano, in "Technological Pioneering and Competitive Advantage: The Birth of the VCR

Industry," *California Management Review* 29, no. 4 (1987), describe the long period of market experimentation required to develop the VCR into a mass-market product, and the long, winding course it took through specialized niche applications that allowed the market pioneers to learn enough to accomplish their ultimate objective. The period of experimentation and market development took twelve years.

12. Bayus, Jain, and Rao, "Too Little, Too Early," 50–63.

13. Rosabeth Moss Kanter, Jeffrey North, Lisa Richardson, Cynthia Ingols, and Joseph Zolner ("Engines of Progress: Designing and Running Entrepreneurial Vehicles in Established Companies: Raytheon's New Product Center, 1969–1989" *Journal of Business Venturing* 6 [1991]: 145–163) document the application migration path of the microwave oven, which grew out of Raytheon's New Product Center (NPC) and was based on microwave technology developed for military applications in the 1940s and 1950s. The military applications were for powering helicopters and trains, for linear accelerators, and for platforms in space that would convert solar energy to a usable form for earth. But an NPC researcher visiting a Hormel meat-processing plant recognized the need to quickly defrost 100-pound boxes of frozen meat for delivery to restaurants in a cleaner and healthier manner. Later, industrial microwave ovens were used in restaurants for pre-cooking bacon and then for curing rubber products such as large tires for earth-moving machines. None of these early applications, obviously, was the "killer app," but together they accounted for $10 million in annual sales by 1988, and the microwave business was set up as its own operating group, separate from the New Products Center. Another example is DuPont's Surlyn, which was used initially as a coating for golf balls to give them the right amount of bounce and as a replacement for the rubber tips of women's high heels. Subsequently, it grew into a multimillion-dollar business with myriads of applications, the primary one being as a food packaging material (Parry Norling and Robert J. Statz, "How Discontinuous Innovation Really Happens," *Research-Technology Management* 41, no. 3 [May 1998]: 41–44). Finally, Richard N. Foster ("Timing Technological Transitions," in Mel Horwitch, ed., *Technology in the Modern Corporation: A Strategic Perspective* [New York: Pergamon Press, 1986]) provides several examples of technological discontinuities that began as small niche inroads to established markets, only to become ultimately immense business platforms. For example, radial tires were considered "niche fillers" in the bias-ply tire market, and yet within four years, radials had taken an 80 percent share of the total tire market.

14. According to Christensen and Utterback, among many others, these are the primary reasons that incumbent firms cannot see the threat of invading technologies early on. They spend more time defending their established turf because of the severe and constant pressure to provide short-term results. Therefore, even if firms are able to generate break-through technologies, the willingness of operating units to take on the work of commercializing them is low. Rosenbloom and Cusumano indicate that radical innovations come from outsiders, not incumbents, and that, therefore, a broader-scoped effort is required for recognizing and building new markets early on.

15. McIntyre, "Market Adaptation as a Process in the Product Life Cycle of Radical Innovations and High Technology Products," 140–149.

16. See Block and MacMillan, *Corporate Venturing*, chapters 9 and 10.

CHAPTER 9

1. *CIO*, 15 August 1999, 114.

2. Joseph G. Morone describes the courage exhibited by a number of senior managers in four large, well-known industrial companies that have managed to successfully commercialize radical innovations. See *Winning in High-Tech Markets*. Also see Utterback, *Mastering the Dynamics of Innovation*, and Christensen, *The Innovator's Dilemma*, both of which describe the fear and risk perception that prevents most managers from making these important decisions.

3. Diana Day observed certain conditions under which senior managers, of necessity, must become hands-on champions. She notes that when the ventures are costly and high-profile, or when they represent decisive strategic reorientation of the firm, the level of risk involved warrants direct involvement by senior management. See Diana Day, "Raising Radicals: Different Processes for Championing Innovative Corporate Ventures," *Organization Science* 5, no. 2 (1994): 149–172. Similarly, ventures that have no clear home within the organization, or those that require crossing into the white space boundaries will need senior manager involvement at the tactical level. On this problem, see I. C. MacMillan and M. L. McCaffery, "Strategy for Financial Services: Cashing in on Competitive Inertia," *Journal of Business Strategy* (1983): 58–65; and Rebecca Henderson and Kim B. Clark, "Architectural Innovation: The Reconfiguration of Existing Product Technologies and the Failure of Established Firms," *Administrative Science Quarterly* 35 (1990): 9–30.

4. For a detailed description of the patronage model used during the Renaissance, see Irving Stone, *The Agony and the Ecstasy: A Novel of Michaelangelo* (New York: Doubleday, 1961).

5. E. Schein, *Organizational Culture and Leadership: A Dynamic View* (San Francisco, CA: Jossey-Bass, 1985). See also Amabile, "How to Kill Creativity," 77–87; Amabile, "A Model of Creativity and Innovation in Organizations," in B. M. Staw and L. L. Cummings, eds., *Research in Organizational Behavior*, vol. 10 (Greenwich, CT: JAI Press, 1988), 123–167; and T. M. Amabile, R. Conti, H. Coon, J. Lazenby, and M. Herron, "Assessing the Work Environment for Creativity," *Academy of Management Journal* 39, no. 5 (1996): 1154–1184.

6. The role of a senior manager in installing mechanisms for encouraging and supporting radical innovation, such as the formation of a new venture department, has been otherwise labeled as "orchestrator." See J. R. Galbraith, "Designing the Innovative Organization," *Organizational Dynamics* (Winter 1982): 5–25. In this role, senior managers have only an indirect influence on specific radical innovation projects, through the creation and financial support of the right structures via substantive and symbolic actions, which then allow the "invisible hand" of entrepreneurship to operate. See S. Venkataraman, R. G. McGrath and I. C. MacMillan, "Progress in Research on Corporate Venturing," in Donald L. Sexton and John D. Kasarda, eds., *The State of the Art of Entrepreneurship* (Boston: PWS Kent, 1992).

7. The strength of passion that we observed has been discussed by others as well. Indeed, as many note who write on the reward structures that are in place for radical innovators in corporations, it is *intrinsic rewards* rather than money that motivate those individuals who are currently coming forward in organizations. More than anything, they are anxious to know that they are having a big impact on the company and on others' lives, and, to the extent that they are publicly praised by management, they are happy. However, we recognize that this is short-term happiness and that, over the long haul, these highly effective people need the appropriate reward structures in order for the firm to expect to retain them. For a discussion of intrinsic versus extrinsic rewards, see T. M. Amabile, "Motivational Synergy: Toward New Conceptualizations of Intrinsic and Extrinsic Motivation in the Workplace," *Human Resource Management Review* 3 (1993): 185–201; also Edward L. Deci, *Intrinsic Motivation* (New York: Plenum Press, 1975).

8. In an article that is very rich with description regarding champions, their personalities, and their skills, Howell and Higgins note that successful champions are not simply renegades in their organization but that, like Bernie Meyerson, they are very adept at maneuvering through the "rational processes" that the organization requires. The authors indicate that this means presenting a solid business case, gaining the buy-in of top management, and then selling users on the idea. See Jane M. Howell and Christopher A. Higgins, "Champions of Change: Identifying,

Understanding and Supporting Champions of Technological Innovations," *Organizational Dynamics* (1991): 40–55.

9. Charles Fishman, "The War for Talent," *Fast Company*, August 1998, 104–107.

10. See Howell and Higgins, "Champions of Change," 40–55, in which the authors document that, in fact, champions believed so heartily in their ideas that they perceived no risk at all to their personal careers, so long as they could achieve the commercialization of the innovation.

11. See Kanter, *When Giants Learn to Dance*, especially chapter 9, in which she describes various methods of reward through different pay systems. Also see the appendix, which indicates that at 3M, Lucent, and Nortel Networks, at least, champions and team members live with the promise that they may get to run and become part owner of the new business that develops out of their hard work.

12. Venkataraman et al.; Souder; Madique; and Chakrabarti and Hauschildt all describe the need for multiple types of champions. Day, however, finds that the division of championing roles is risky in and of itself because having multiple champions does not promote the organizational legitimacy of the project. We did not find this to be the central issue, however. Because of the length of time required for these projects and their movement back and forth from R&D to the business units, we found that, in fact, organizational legitimacy was built through the use of multiple champions. See S. Venkataraman, R. G. McGrath and I. C. MacMillan, "Progress in Research on Corporate Venturing"; William E. Souder, "Encouraging Entrepreneurship in the Large Corporation," *Research Management* (May 1984): 18–22; Modesto Madique, "Entrepreneurs, Champions, and Technological Innovation," *Sloan Management Review* (1980): 59–76; A. K. Chakrabarti and J. Hauschildt, "The Division of Labour in Innovation Management," *R&D Management* 19, no. 2 (1989): 161–171; and Diana Day, "Raising Radicals: Different Processes for Championing Innovative Corporate Ventures," *Organization Science* 5, no. 2 (1994): 149–172.

13. See, for example, Deborah Ancona and David F. Caldwell, "Bridging the Boundary: External Activity and Performance in Organizational Teams," *Administrative Science Quarterly* 37 (1992): 634–665; Deborah Ancona, "Outward Bound: Strategies for Team Survival in an Organization," *Academy of Management Journal* 33, no. 2 (1990): 334–365; Steven C. Wheelwright and Kim B. Clark, *Revolutionizing Product Development: Quantum Leaps to Speed, Efficiency and Quality* (New York: The Free Press, 1992); and Patricia Holahan and Stephen K. Markham, "Factors Affecting Multifunctional Team Effectiveness," in *The PDMA Handbook of New Product Development*, Milton D. Rosenau, Jr., ed. (New York: Wiley, 1996), 119–135.

14. There are two emerging streams of literature that we find somewhat, though not entirely, appropriate to what we observed in our cases. One is the concept of "hot groups," described by Harold Leavitt and Jean Lipman-Blumen in "Hot Groups," *Harvard Business Review* 73 (July–August 1995): 109–116. These are "lively, high-achieving, dedicated groups, usually small, whose members are turned on to an exciting and challenging task. . . . They do great things fast" (109). While the intensity and excitement are observable in radical innovation teams, so are discouragement in the face of discontinuity and turnover, given the long process of maturity that the project requires. The second stream of literature is described in the article "Communities of Practice: The Organizational Frontier" by Etienne C. Wenger and William M. Snyder, *Harvard Business Review* 78 (January–February 2000): 139–145. These are described as "groups of people informally bound together by shared expertise and passion for a joint enterprise" (p. 139). These groups are not necessarily assigned tasks with any particular project objective. Members volunteer, and they find one another throughout the organization and share knowledge about the topic of interest. We find that, at least in the early stages of our cases, the project groups behaved in some respects like communities of practice.

15. See "Why Managers Fail," in Michael K. Badawy, *Developing Managerial Skills in Engineers and Scientists: Succeeding as a Technical Manager* (New York: Van Nostrand Reinhold, 1982).

16. See Edward B. Roberts and Alan R. Fusfeld, "Critical Functions: Needed Roles in the Innovation Process," in *Career Issues in Human Resource Management*, R. Katz, ed. (Englewood Cliffs, NJ: Prentice-Hall, 1982), 182–207.

17. See Edward B. Roberts and Alan R. Fusfeld, "Staffing the Innovative Technology-Based Organization," *Sloan Management Review* (Spring 1981): 19–26. Also see Ralph Katz, "Managing Creative Performance in R&D Teams," in *The Human Side of Managing Technological Innovation: A Collection of Readings*, Ralph Katz, ed. (New York: Oxford University Press, 1997), 177–186.

18. Robert Burgelman and Leonard Sayles, *Inside Corporate Innovation* (New York: The Free Press, 1986), 7.

CHAPTER 10

1. Gary Hamel, "Bringing Silicon Valley Inside," *Harvard Business Review* 77 (September–October 1999): 71–84.

2. N. D. Fast has observed the precarious position of the "new ventures division" (NVD) in many firms. He ascribes the short tenure of these divisions to shifts in senior management priorities or the political position of the NVD. For these reasons, we strongly urge that both the radical innovation hub and each venture's oversight board be staffed from multiple venues. In addition, firms should establish multiple radical innovation hubs. By embedding multiple organizational mechanisms deeply within the organization and by distributing them throughout the organization, the firm's radical innovation capacity has a greater likelihood of surviving turnover in senior management and the accompanying adjustments to the priority list than if a single department or division is responsible for all radical innovation activity. See N. D. Fast, " The Future of Industrial New Venture Departments," *Industrial Marketing Management* 8 (1979): 264–279. See also H. B. Sykes and Zenas Block, "Corporate Venturing Obstacles: Sources and Solutions," *Journal of Business Venturing* 4, no. 3 (1989): 159–167.

APPENDIX

1. This information was compiled through interviews with Andy Wong, General Manager at 3M; Bill James, Manager of Research and Development Coordination of Procter & Gamble Corporation; Steve Socolof, New Ventures VP of Lucent Technologies; and Joanne Hyland, VP, New Ventures Division of Nortel Networks.

BIBLIOGRAPHY

Ali, Abdul. "Pioneering versus Incremental Innovation: Review and Research Propositions." *Journal of Product Innovation Management* 11 (1994): 56–61.

Allen, Thomas J. "Communication Networks in R&D Laboratories." *R&D Management* 1 (1971): 14–21.

Amabile, Teresa M. *Creativity in Context: Update to the Social Psychology of Creativity.* Boulder, CO: Westview Press, 1996.

———. "How to Kill Creativity." *Harvard Business Review* 76 (September–October 1998): 77–87.

———. "A Model of Creativity and Innovation in Organizations." In *Research in Organizational Behavior*, vol. 10, edited by B. M. Staw and L. L. Cummings. Greenwich, CT: JAI Press, 1988.

———. "Motivational Synergy: Toward New Conceptualizations of Intrinsic and Extrinsic Motivation in the Workplace." *Human Resource Management Review* 3 (1993): 185–201.

Amabile, T. M., R. Conti, H. Coon, J. Lazenby, and M. Herron. "Assessing the Work Environment for Creativity." *Academy of Management Journal* 39, no. 5 (1996): 1154–1184.

Amit, Raphael, and Joshua Livnat. "Diversification and the Risk-Return Trade-Off." *Academy of Management Journal* 31, no. 1 (1988): 154–166.

Ancona, Deborah G. "Outward Bound: Strategies for Team Survival in an Organization." *Academy of Management Journal* 33, no. 2 (1990): 334–365.

Ancona, Deborah G., and David F. Caldwell. "Bridging the Boundary: External Activity and Performance in Organizational Teams." *Administrative Science Quarterly* 37 (1992): 634–665.

Angle, Harold L., and Andrew H. Van de Ven. "Suggestions for Managing the Innovation Journey." In *Research on the Management of*

Innovation: The Minnesota Studies, edited by Andrew H. Van de Ven, Harold Angle, and Marshall Scott Poole. New York: Harper and Row, 1989.

Ansoff, H. *Corporate Strategy*. New York: McGraw-Hill, 1965.

———. "Strategies for Diversification." *Harvard Business Review* 35 (September–October 1957): 113–124.

Argyris, Chris, and Donald A. Schon. *Organizational Learning: A Theory of Action Perspective*. Reading, MA: Addison-Wesley, 1978.

Badawy, Michael K. *Developing Managerial Skills in Engineers and Scientists: Succeeding as a Technical Manager*. New York: Van Nostrand Reinhold, 1982.

Baldwin, W. L., and J. T. Scott. *Market Structure and Technological Change*. New York: Harwood Publishers, 1987.

Bayus, Barry L., Sanjay Jain, and Ambar G. Rao. "Too Little, Too Early: Introduction Timing and New Product Performance in the Personal Digital Assistant Industry." *Journal of Marketing Research* 34 (February 1997): 50–63.

Bernard, J. David. *Milestone Planning for Successful Ventures*. New York: Boyd and Fraser, 1994.

Berry, Charles H. *Corporate Growth and Diversification*. Princeton, NJ: Princeton University Press, 1975.

Bettis, Richard A. "Performance Differences in Related and Unrelated Diversified Firms." *Strategic Management Journal* (1981): 379–393.

Betz, Frederick. *Strategic Technology Management*. New York: McGraw-Hill, 1993.

Biggadike, Ralph. "The Risky Business of Diversification." *Harvard Business Review* 57 (May–June 1979): 103–111.

Block, Zenas, and Ian C. MacMillan. *Corporate Venturing: Creating New Businesses within the Firm*. Boston: Harvard Business School Press, 1993.

Booz•Allen & Hamilton, Inc. *New Product Management for the 1980s*. New York: Booz•Allen & Hamilton, 1982.

Brown, John Seely. "Research That Reinvents the Corporation." *Harvard Business Review* 69 (January–February 1991): 102–111.

Brown, Shona, and Kathleen Eisenhardt. "Product Development: Past Research, Present Findings and Future Directions." *Academy of Management Review* 20, no. 2 (1995): 343–378.

Burgelman, Robert A., and L. R. Sayles. *Inside Corporate Innovation*. New York: The Free Press, 1986.

Chakrabarti, A. K., and J. Hauschildt. "The Division of Labor in Innovation Management." *R&D Management* 19, no. 2 (1989): 161–171.

Chandy, Rajesh K., and Gerard J. Tellis. "Organizing for Radical Product Innovation: The Overlooked Role of Willingness to Cannibalize." *Journal of Marketing Research* 35 (November 1998): 474–487.

Chang, Yegmin, and Howard Thomas. "The Impact of Diversification on Risk-Return Performance." *Strategic Management Journal* 19 (1989): 271–284.

Cheng, Yu-Ting, and Andrew H. Van de Ven. "Learning the Innovation Journey: Order Out of Chaos?" *Organization Science* 7, no. 6 (November–December 1996): 593–614.

Christensen, Clayton. *The Innovator's Dilemma.* Boston: Harvard Business School Press, 1997.

Cohen, W. M., and R. C. Levin. "Empirical Studies of Innovation and Market Structure." In *Handbook of Industrial Organization,* edited by R. Schmalensee and R. D. Willig. New York: North-Holland, 1989.

Cooper, Robert G., and Elko J. Kleinschmidt. "An Investigation into the New Product Process: Steps, Deficiencies and Impact." *Journal of Product Innovation Management* 3, no. 2 (1986): 71–85.

Courtney, Hugh, Jane Kirkland, and Patrick Viguerie. "Strategy under Uncertainty." *Harvard Business Review* 75 (November–December 1997): 66–79.

Day, Diana. "Raising Radicals: Different Processes for Championing Innovative Corporate Ventures." *Organization Science* 5, no. 2 (1994): 149–172.

Deci, Edward L. *Intrinsic Motivation.* New York: Plenum Press, 1975.

Dolan, Robert J. "Industrial Market Research: Beta Test Site Management." Case 9-592-010. Boston: Harvard Business School, 1992.

Dougherty, Deborah. "Interpretive Barriers to Successful Product Innovation in Large Firms." *Organization Science* 3, no. 2 (1992): 179–202.

Dougherty, Deborah, and Cynthia Hardy. "Sustained Product Innovation in Large, Mature Organizations: Overcoming Innovation-to-Organization Problems." *Academy of Management Journal* 39, no. 5 (1996): 1120–1153.

Dougherty, Deborah, and T. Heller. "The Illegitimacy of Successful Product Innovations in Established Firms." *Organizational Science* 5, no. 2 (1994): 200–218.

Ettlie, J. E., W. P. Bridges, and R. D. O'Keefe. "Organization Strategy and Structural Differences for Radical Versus Incremental Innovation." *Management Science* 30, no. 6 (1984): 682–695.

Fast, N. D. "The Future of Industrial New Venture Departments." *Industrial Marketing Management* 8 (1979): 264–279.

Fishman, Charles. "The War for Talent." *Fast Company,* August 1998, 104–107.

Foster, Richard N. "Timing Technological Transitions." In *Technology in the Modern Corporation: A Strategic Perspective,* edited by Mel Horwitch. New York: Pergamon Press, 1986.

Galbraith, Craig, Bruce Samuelson, Curt Stiles, and Greg Merrill. "Diversification, Industry Research and Development, and Market

Performance." *Academy of Management Proceedings* (1986): 17–20.

Galbraith, J. R. "Designing the Innovative Organization." *Organizational Dynamics* (Winter 1982): 5–25.

Gomes-Casseres, Benjamin. "Computers: Alliances and Industry Evolution." In *Beyond Free Trade*, edited by David Yoffie. Boston, MA: Harvard Business School Press, 1993.

Guilford, J. P. "Three Faces of Intellect." *The American Psychologist* 14, no. 8 (1959): 469–479.

Hamel, Gary. "Bringing Silicon Valley Inside." *Harvard Business Review* 77 (September–October 1999): 71–84.

Hamel, Gary, and Yves L. Doz. *Alliance Advantage: The Art of Creating Value through Partnering*. Boston: Harvard Business School Press, 1998.

Hamel, Gary, and C. K. Prahalad. *Competing for the Future*. Boston: Harvard Business School Press, 1994.

Hamel, Gary, and C. K. Prahalad. "Corporate Imagination and Expeditionary Marketing." *Harvard Business Review* 69 (July–August 1991): 81–92.

Henderson, Rebecca. "Underinvestment and Incompetence as Responses to Radical Innovation: Evidence from the Photolithographic Alignment Equipment Industry." *Rand Journal of Economics* 24, no. 2 (Summer 1993): 248–270.

Henderson, R. M., and Kim B. Clark. "Architectural Innovation: The Reconfiguration of Existing Product Technologies and the Failure of Established Firms." *Administrative Science Quarterly* 35 (1990): 9–30.

Holahan, Patricia, and Stephen K. Markham. "Factors Affecting Multifunctional Team Effectiveness." In *The PDMA Handbook of New Product Development*, edited by Milton D. Rosenau, Jr. New York: John Wiley, 1996.

Howell, Jane M., and Christopher A. Higgins. "Champions of Change: Identifying, Understanding and Supporting Champions of Technological Innovations." *Organizational Dynamics* (1991): 40–55.

Jelinek, J. J., and C. B. Schoonhoven. *The Innovation Marathon*. Cambridge, U.K.: Basil Blackwell, 1990.

Jolly, Vijay K. *Commercializing New Technologies: Getting from Mind to Market*. Boston: Harvard Business School Press, 1997.

Kanter, Rosabeth Moss. "Swimming in Newstreams: Mastering Innovation Dilemmas." *California Management Review* (Summer 1989): 45–69.

———. *When Giants Learn to Dance*. New York: Simon and Schuster, 1989.

———. "When a Thousand Flowers Bloom: Structural, Collective, and Social Conditions for Innovation in Organizations." In *Research in*

Organizational Behavior, vol. 10, edited by B. Staw and L. Cummings. Greenwich, CT: JAI Press, 1988.

Kanter, Rosabeth Moss, Jeffrey North, Lisa Richardson, Cynthia Ingols, and Joseph Zolner. "Engines of Progress: Designing and Running Entrepreneurial Vehicles in Established Companies: Raytheon's New Product Center, 1969–1989." *Journal of Business Venturing* 6 (1991): 145–163.

Katz, Ralph. "Managing Creative Performance in R&D Teams." In *The Human Side of Managing Technological Innovation: A Collection of Readings*, edited by Ralph Katz. New York: Oxford University Press, 1997.

Katz, Ralph, and Thomas Allen. "Organizational Issues in the Introduction of New Technologies." In *The Management of Productivity and Technology in Manufacturing*, edited by P. R. Kleindorfer. New York: Plenum Press, 1985.

Kazmin, Amy Louise. "Bitter Words over Better Seeds." *Business Week*, 11 January 1999.

Kleinschmidt, E. J., and Robert J. Cooper. "The Impact of Product Innovativeness on Performance." *Journal of Product Innovation Management* 8, no. 4 (1991): 240–251.

Koen, Peter A. "Corporate Entrepreneuring: Securing Funding for 'Initiative from Below' Fuzzy Front End Projects." In *Achieving Excellence in New Product Development and Management*, edited by Chuck Tomkovick. 1998 Proceedings of the Product Development and Management Association.

Koenig, Richard. "Tricky Roll-Out: Rich in New Products: Monsanto Must Only Get Them on Market." *Wall Street Journal*, 1 May 1990, A1.

Leavitt, Harold, and Jean Lipman-Blumen. "Hot Groups." *Harvard Business Review* 73 (July–August 1995): 109–116.

Lee, M., and D. Na. "Determinants of Technical Success in Product Development when Innovation Radicalness Is Considered." *Journal of Product Innovation Management* 11 (1994): 62–68.

Leonard-Barton, Dorothy. *Wellsprings of Knowledge: Building and Sustaining the Sources of Innovation*. Boston: Harvard Business School Press, 1995.

Lorange, Peter, and Johan Roos. *Strategic Alliances: Formation, Implementation and Evolution*. Cambridge, MA: Blackwell Publishers, 1992.

Lynn, Gary S., Joseph G. Morone, and Albert S. Paulson. "Marketing and Discontinuous Innovation: The Probe and Learn Process." *California Management Review* 38, no. 3 (Spring 1996): 8–37.

MacMillan, Ian C., and M. L. McCaffery. "Strategy for Financial Services: Cashing in on Competitive Inertia." *Journal of Business Strategy* (1983): 58–65.

Maidique, Modesto A. "Entrepreneurs, Champions, and Technological Innovation." *Sloan Management Review* (Winter 1980): 59–76.

March, James G. "Exploration and Exploitation in Organizational Learning." *Organization Science* 2, no. 1 (February 1991): 71–87.

McGrath, Rita G., and Ian C. MacMillan. "Discovery Driven Planning." *Harvard Business Review* 73 (July–August 1995): 4–12.

McIntyre, Shelby H. "Market Adaptation as a Process in the Product Life Cycle of Radical Innovations and High Technology Products." *Journal of Product Innovation Management* 5 (1988): 140–149.

McQuarrie, Edward F. *Customer Visits: Building a Better Market Focus.* Newbury Park, CA: Sage Publications, 1993.

Mick, David G., and Susan Fournier. "Paradoxes of Technology: Consumer Cognizance, Emotions, and Coping Strategies." Marketing Sciences Institute, working paper # 98-112, July 1988.

Moore, Geoffrey A. *Crossing the Chasm.* New York: HarperBusiness, 1991.

Montgomery, Cynthia, and Harbir Singh. "Diversification Strategy and Systematic Risk." *Strategic Management Journal* 5 (1984): 181–191.

Morone, Joseph G. *Winning in High-Tech Markets.* Boston: Harvard Business School Press, 1993.

Norling, Parry, and Robert J. Statz. "How Discontinuous Innovation Really Happens." *Research-Technology Management* 41, no. 3 (May 1998): 41–44.

Olson, Eric M., Orville C. Walker, Jr., and Robert W. Ruekert. "Organizing for Effective New Product Development: The Moderating Role of Product Innovativeness." *Journal of Marketing* 59, no. 1 (January 1995): 48–62.

Page, Albert L., and John S. Stovall. "Importance of the Early Stages in the New Product Development Process." In *Bridging the Gap from Concept to Commercialization,* edited by Edward F. McDonough III and Chuck Tomkovick. 1994 Proceedings of the Product Development and Management Association, Boston, MA.

Peters, Thomas. "The Mythology of Innovation, or a Skunkwork's Tale, Part II." *The Stanford Magazine,* Stanford Alumni Association, Palo Alto, 1983.

Pinchot, Gifford III. "Innovation through Intrapreneuring." *Research-Technology Management* 30 (1987): March–April: 14–20.

Prahalad, C. K., and Richard A. Bettis. "The Dominant Logic: A New Linkage between Diversity and Performance." *Strategic Management Journal* 7 (1986): 485–501.

The Project Management Book of Knowledge. Project Management Institute, 1996.

Quinn, James Brian. "Managing Innovation: Controlled Chaos." *Harvard Business Review* 63 (May–June 1985): 73–84.

Roberts, Edward B., and Charles A. Berry. "Entering New Businesses: Selecting Strategies for Success." *Sloan Management Review* (Spring 1985): 3–17.

Roberts, Edward B., and Alan R. Fusfeld. "Critical Functions: Needed Roles in the Innovation Process." In *Career Issues in Human Resource Management*, edited by R. Katz. Englewood Cliffs, NJ: Prentice-Hall, 1982.

Roberts, Edward B., and Alan R. Fusfeld. "Staffing the Innovative Technology-Based Organization." *Sloan Management Review* (Spring 1981): 19–26.

Robertson, Thomas, and S. Hubert Gatignon. "Technology Development Mode: A Transaction Cost Conceptualization." *Strategic Management Journal* 19 (June 1998): 515–531.

Rosenbloom, Richard S., and Michael A. Cusumano. "Technological Pioneering and Competitive Advantage: The Birth of the VCR Industry." *California Management Review* 29, no 4 (1987).

Rotman, David. "The Next Biotech Harvest." *Technology Review* (September–October 1998): 34–41.

Rumelt, Richard. "Diversification Strategy and Profitability." *Strategic Management Journal* 3 (1982): 359–369.

———. "Strategy, Structure and Economic Performance." Ph.D. dissertation Harvard University, 1974.

Schein, Edgar. *Organizational Culture and Leadership: A Dynamic View*. San Francisco: Jossey-Bass, 1985.

Schmidt, Jeffrey B., and Roger J. Calantone. "Are Really New Product Development Projects Harder to Shut Down?" *Journal of Product Innovation Management* 15 (1998): 111–123.

Schrage, Michael. *Serious Play: How the World's Best Companies Simulate to Innovate*. Boston: Harvard Business School Press, 2000.

———. "What's That Bad Odor at Innovation Skunkworks?" *Fortune*, 20 December 1999, 338.

Schroeder, Roger G., Andrew H. Van de Ven, Gary D. Scudder, and Douglas Polley. "The Development of Innovation Ideas." In *Research on the Management of Innovation: The Minnesota Studies*, edited by Andrew H. Van de Ven, Harold Angle, and Marshall Scott Poole. New York: Harper and Row, 1989.

Schumpeter, Joseph A. *Capitalism, Socialism and Democracy*, 3rd. ed. New York: Harper, 1950.

———. *The Theory of Economic Development*. Cambridge, MA: Harvard University Press, 1934.

Slowinski, Gene. "Managing Technology-Based Strategic Alliances between Large and Small Firms." *S.A.M. Advanced Management Journal* (Spring 1996): 42–48.

Slowinski, Gene, G. Oliva, and L. Lowenstein. "Medusa Alliances:

Managing Complex Interorganizational Relationships." *Business Horizons* (July–August 1995): 48–52.

Smith, Clayton G., and Arnold C. Cooper. "Established Companies Diversifying into Young Industries: A Comparison of Firms with Different Levels of Performance." *Strategic Management Journal* 9 (1988): 111–121.

Souder, William E. "Encouraging Entrepreneurship in the Large Corporation." *Research Management* (May 1994): 18–22.

Stevens, Greg A., and James Burley. "3,000 Raw Ideas = 1 Commercial Success." *Research Technology Management* (May–June 1997): 16–27.

Stone, Irving. *The Agony and the Ecstasy: A Novel of Michaelangelo.* New York: Doubleday, 1961.

Stopford, J., and C. W. F. Baden-Fuller. "Creating Corporate Entrepreneurship." *Strategic Management Journal* 15 (1994): 521–536.

Sykes, H. B., and Zenas Block. "Corporate Venturing Obstacles: Sources and Solutions." *Journal of Business Venturing* 4, no. 3 (1989): 159–167.

Sykes, Hollister B., and David Dunham. "Critical Assumption Planning: A Practical Tool for Managing Business Development Risk." *Journal of Business Venturing* 10, no. 6 (November 1995): 413–424.

Tushman, Michael L., and Charles A. O'Reilly III. *Winning through Innovation: A Practical Guide to Leading Organizational Change and Renewal.* Boston: Harvard Business School Press, 1997.

Van de Ven, Andrew H. "Central Problems in the Management of Innovation." *Management Science* 32, no. 5 (1986): 590–607.

Van de Ven, Andrew, and Douglas Polley. "Learning While Innovating." *Organization Science* 3, no. 1 (February 1992): 92–116.

Venkataraman, S., R. G. McGrath, and I. C. MacMillan. "Progress in Research on Corporate Venturing." In *The State of the Art of Entrepreneurship*, edited by Donald L. Sexton and John D. Kasarda. Boston: PWS Kent, 1992.

Venkataraman, S., and Andrew H. Van de Ven. "Hostile Environments, Environmental Jolts, Transaction Set, and New Business." *Journal of Business Venturing* (May 1998): 231–255.

Von Hippel, Eric. "Lead Users: A Source of Novel Product Concepts." *Management Science* 32 (July 1986): 791–805.

———. *The Sources of Innovation.* New York: Oxford University Press, 1988.

Wenger, Etienne C., and William M. Snyder. "Communities of Practice: The Organizational Frontier." *Harvard Business Review* 78 (January–February 2000): 139–145.

Wheelwright, Steven C., and Kim B. Clark. *Revolutionizing Product Development: Quantum Leaps to Speed, Efficiency and Quality.* New York: The Free Press, 1992.

ACKNOWLEDGMENTS

While development of this book has been a three-year effort, the research that it was based on began in 1995. Without the involvement of many people, neither the research effort nor the book would have been started and sustained.

We have had two partners in this project. The Alfred P. Sloan Foundation provided a major grant to support the research effort. With this support, we were able to maintain ongoing, in-depth data gathering and to offer a variety of meetings, workshops, and seminars to provide feedback to our industrial partners. We thank in particular Dr. Hirsh Cohen, vice president of the Sloan Foundation, and Gail Pesyna, program director.

Our second major partner, the Industrial Research Institute (IRI) was instrumental in gaining support and cooperation from our industrial partners. We are indebted to Chuck Larsen, IRI president; Robert E. Burkart, director, professional development services, who helped organize our IRI workshops; and especially Margaret R. Grucza, director, research services, who has worked tirelessly to help our IRI committees be effective and productive. The IRI Research-on-Research Committee established two successive subcommittees to work with our research team from Rensselaer. We thank all the members of the two committees, especially the cochairs, Dr. Miles Drake (director, GEG Technology, Air Products and Chemicals, Inc.) and Dr. Al Schmidt (vice president, Information Technology, Arch Chemicals Corporation), who chaired the first subcommittee; and Dr. Richard Hendricks (vice president, Innovation Processes for Armstrong Corporation) and Dr. Terry

McPherson, (director, Research Effectiveness, Lucent Technologies Corporation), who are the cochairs of the year 2000 subcommittee.

We would like to thank the Center for Innovation Management Studies and its director, Dr. Al Bean, for providing funding for the study of the role of market visioning.

Six anonymous external reviewers recruited by Harvard Business School Press and our senior editor at the Press, Hollis Heimbouch, offered valuable input and challenged us to engage in continuous and sometimes radical improvement of the manuscript. We recruited two additional individuals—Professor Zenas Block and Dr. Nick Colarelli—who contributed tremendous efforts to help us make a big leap forward during the last revision. We'd also like to acknowledge the key role, early on, of Michael Corrado from IBM who was instrumental in bringing our research to the attention of *Business Week*. That article launched our public presence, bringing our research to the attention of a great many practitioners. Finally, we would like to thank Dick Luecke, who had the challenging task of helping us weave all the material and all the voices into one manuscript that is understandable to both practicing radical innovators and academics interested in the subject. We are grateful for all of your efforts and contributions.

This project would not have been possible without the unstinting cooperation and openness of our participating companies. It is impossible to name the more than 100 people who took part in our interviews and at least another 75 who participated in our major workshops and seminars. However, we would like to express our appreciation and gratitude for your help.

Management of radical innovation—at the firm and project levels—is the most challenging kind of management. Throughout this book, we have referred to a cadre of researchers who have explored this field during the past several decades and on whose shoulders we stand. We are indebted to them for helping us—through their writings and, in some cases, through their direct, personal guidance. Their insights have helped prepare us in the design and implementation of the research effort and in the interpretation of the extensive data we have collected.

We also thank the capable staff in the Lally School of Management and Technology, who have helped (and tolerated) us through all the crises and deadlines. Special thanks to Jill Keyes and Liz

Katzman, and our current dean, Joe Ecker, who supported and encouraged us during the past three years.

Dr. Joseph G. Morone, currently president of Bentley College, initiated the project during the time he served as dean of the Lally School. Dr. Morone recruited our two primary partners, the Sloan Foundation and the IRI. His support and guidance were invaluable, especially early in the life of the project. We feel a deep sense of gratitude for his efforts.

Finally we would each like to make our own special dedications:

Richard Leifer: My gratitude for the love and support I received from my wife, Jane, and my two sons, Gabriel and Jeffrey, during the journey of getting this book written.

Chris McDermott: I'd like to acknowledge my family—Peggy, Kelsey, and Matt—for their patience and support through this project.

Gina O'Connor: I dedicate my efforts on this book to my husband, Patrick, and our children, Dan, Christine, and Kenny. Special thanks go to Nick Colarelli, my father, who has been a strong supporter of this work throughout the entire research process. His window into the world of academia and his work helping organizations transition during times of radical innovation have been key resources for me.

Lois Peters: As always I must thank my husband Garrett McCarey and the rest of my family for accepting my idiosyncratic ways of behavior. Their flexibility allows me opportunities that I am grateful for. A special thanks goes to my friend and colleague Herbert Fusfeld, who first opened my mind to the significance of industrial research in creating outcomes of far-reaching social value.

Mark Rice: My thanks and deepest appreciation to Lisa, Lia, and Katie for your tolerance and understanding.

Bob Veryzer: I would like to sincerely thank the many people who have had a positive impact on both this endeavor and my life; my understanding and supportive parents; and my brother for his inspiration. I also wish to thank my coauthors—it has been a wondrous journey!

INDEX

ABOUT THE AUTHORS

RICHARD LEIFER is an Associate Professor of Management at Rensselaer Polytechnic Institute (RPI), where he has worked since 1983. At RPI he teaches and conducts research in organizational behavior, high performance management, and leadership. He received both a bachelor's degree in psychology and a master's degree in engineering science from the University of California at Berkeley and received his Ph.D. in organizational design from the University of Wisconsin. He has published or presented over seventy refereed articles in the areas of organizational design, management of research and development, and managing and designing management information systems. His articles have appeared in numerous journals including *The Academy of Management Journal*, *The Academy of Management Review*, *Administrative Science Quarterly*, *MIS Quarterly*, *IEEE Transactions on Engineering Management*, and *Human Relations*. His current research activities are concerned with organizational correlates of radical innovation, reengineering, and new approaches to designing organizations.

CHRISTOPHER M. McDERMOTT is a Professor at RPI, where he teaches operations/technology management as well as strategy at the master's, Ph.D., and executive levels. He is also the coordinator of RPI's flagship M.B.A. course on New Product Development. Professor McDermott's courses engage corporate clients such as General Motors, Ford, IBM, Hewlett-Packard, and General Electric through RPI's satellite distance education program. His research is based on his ongoing interactions with numerous organizations as both a researcher and consultant. He has a B.S. in Engineering from Duke University and received his Ph.D. in Business from the University of North Carolina. He previously held positions at Westinghouse Electric Company and at Fairchild, where he was an on-site contractor at NASA's Goddard Space Flight Center.

GINA COLARELLI O'CONNOR, Ph.D., is Assistant Professor of Marketing and New Product Development at RPI. She also serves as Research Director of the Radical Innovation Program at the Lally School of Management and Technology at RPI. Prior to joining academia, she worked for Monsanto Chemical Corporation and for McDonnell Douglas Corporation. The majority of her research efforts focus on how firms link advanced technology development to market opportunities. Her doctorate, which she earned from New York University, is in marketing and corporate strategy. She has published a number of papers in this area, and also teaches and consults on the subject.

LOIS S. PETERS is an Associate Professor, the Director of the Ph.D. program, and the Director of the Center for Science and Technology Policy at the Lally School of Management and Technology. She is on the Board of Governors IEEE Engineering Management Society and is a past board member of the International Trade and Finance Association. Dr. Peters has organized and participated in numerous conferences focusing on technology policy and management of innovation and has been invited to speak in Japan, the OECD, EC, and Latin America, among other places. In June 1992, Dr. Peters was a visiting professor at the Max-Planck-Institut fur Gessellschaftsforschung. For more than two decades she has focused on policy implications of research and technology partnering among and between multinational firms, entrepreneurial small firms, and universities. Her current focus is on the impact of pioneering technology on human behavior and how that translates into business opportunities and new management practices. She holds a Ph.D. from New York University in Biology.

MARK P. RICE is the Cofounder and Director of the Severino Center for Technological Entrepreneurship, Director of the Lally Radical Innovation Research Project, and an Associate Professor in the Lally School of Management and Technology. He served as Assistant Dean and then Associate Dean at RPI between 1993 and

1998, and for the previous five years as Director of the Rensselaer Incubator Program. He has been a Director and Chairman of the National Business Incubation Association, which honored him in 1998 with its Founder's Award. With Dr. Jana Matthews, he coauthored *Growing New Ventures, Creating New Jobs: Principles and Practices of Successful Business Incubation*. Dr. Rice received B.S. and M.S. degrees in mechanical engineering, as well as a Ph.D. in management, all from RPI.

ROBERT W. VERYZER is an Associate Professor in the Lally School of Management and Technology. He is also a visiting Research Professor in the School of Industrial Design Engineering at Delft University of Technology, Delft, The Netherlands. His previous industry experience included product management and product planning positions with Fortune 500 firms, as well as design and new product development consulting. He holds an M.B.A. from Michigan State University and a Ph.D. in consumer research and marketing from the University of Florida. Dr. Veryzer's research interests include product design, new product development, and various aspects of consumer behavior. His articles appear in leading professional journals such as the *Journal of Consumer Research*, *Journal of Product Innovation Management* (which granted one of his articles their Best Paper Award), and the *Design Management Journal*. He is a past recipient of the Lally School of Management's Outstanding Faculty Award for teaching.